AUTUMN AND WINTER DAYS

Rowland Purton

AUTUMN AND WINTER DAYS

Basil Blackwell

First published 1983

Published by
Basil Blackwell Publisher
108 Cowley Road
Oxford OX4 1JF

British Library Cataloguing in Publication Data

Purton, Rowland W.
  Autumn and winter days.
  1. Encyclopedias and dictionaries
  I. Title
  032'. 02   AE6

ISBN 0 631 13204 X

Typeset in eleven point Palatino by Oxford Publishing Services
Printed in Great Britain

Contents

Acknowledgements

The author and publisher are grateful to Messrs. Evans Bros. & Co. for permission to reproduce the poems 'Autumn Song' by Margaret Rose (p. 40) and 'In February' by P. A. Ropes (p. 193) both from *The Book of a Thousand Poems*, from which the verse from 'September' by Mary Howitt (p. 2) was also taken. Quotation from *Lark Rise to Candleford* by Flora Thompson is reproduced by permission of the Oxford University Press.

If the use of any other material has unwittingly infringed copyright the author tenders his sincere apologies and, if notified, will gladly rectify any such omissions in future editions.

Thanks are expressed by the author to the many people who have supplied information and offered encouragement in the compilation of these books, not the least being his wife Sylvia, who has spent very many hours in the preparation of the books.

Introduction

These two books, *Autumn and Winter Days* and *Spring and Summer Days*, have been written both for general interest and as resource books for teachers. The books have been so arranged that the former covers the first half of the school year and the latter the second half.

For ease of reference the books have been comprehensively indexed, having a general index and an index of related themes (pp. 229–246), in which many entries have been listed by theme with main and sub-headings which link subjects that may be associated in projects.

As books of days there is much of general interest — births, deaths, events, sayings, quotations, folklore and customs for every day of the year.

Every effort has been made to ensure accuracy but discrepancies regarding some dates appear even in otherwise reliable sources. There is the added confusion of dates, Russian for example, which differ, some being indicated as 'OS' (Old Style), a result of the change in the calendar. Further complications arise, as with the first moon landing, when a few hours' deviation of time records that they landed on one day according to US Eastern Daylight Time but on the following day according to Greenwich Mean Time.

Apart from the calendar dates, monthly themes open each month and a list of movable or variable dates is given at the end, including local customs and shows. A complete list of shows, giving locations, dates and names of local secretaries, is published annually by Agricultural Press Ltd., Information Service, Surrey House, 1 Throwley Way, Sutton, Surrey SM1 4QQ, who will be pleased to send a copy on request (S.A.E. please).

The British Tourist Authority's magazine *In Britain*, available from booksellers, lists forthcoming events. Also available from booksellers, or from the publishers, TEE Publishing, 216 Coventry Road, Hinckley, Leics LE10 ONG (1983–4, £1.10) is the Steam Yearbook, a guide to preserved transport and industrial archaeology with a diary of events.

Local information officers are also only too pleased to give information about events in their immediate neighbourhood. There are many such events and ceremonies which bring the past to the present, adding colour and interest to any study of 'days'.

R. P.

SEPTEMBER

September

In the Roman calendar, September was originally not the ninth month but the seventh and it took its name from the Latin *septem* (seven). Our Anglo–Saxon ancestors had a much more descriptive name for it: it was Gerstmonath, the Barley month, when they were busy gathering the grain harvest. It was also the Halegmonath, the holy month, or month of offerings, no doubt the heathen festival to give thanks for the harvest.

> *There are twelve months throughout the year*
> *From January to December —*
> *And the primest month of all the twelve*
> *Is the merry month of September.*
> *Then apples so red*
> *Hang overhead,*
> *And nuts ripe–brown*
> *Come showering down*
> *In the bountiful days of September.*
>
> Mary Howitt

There are many people who regard September as the best month of the year. The really hot days of summer are past and the onset of winter is yet to come. Blackberries are there to be gathered and other fruits will soon be ripe.

> *By all these lovely tokens*
> *September days are here,*
> *With summer's best of weather*
> *And autumn's best of cheer.*
>
> Helen Hunt Jackson

September sees the change of season, for the autumnal equinox falls about 21–23 September. Gales and high tides are often experienced about the time of the equinox. September Spring tides — the tides which occur at new or full moon — are often the highest of the year and, if they coincide with equinoctial gales, can bring disaster round the coast. These gales can also cause havoc in the orchard if they come before the fruit has been gathered. Hence the old saying . . . the fruit farmer's prayer to Mother Nature:

> *September blow soft*
> *Till the fruit's in the loft.*

Harvest

September is the month of harvest, though much of the harvesting may have been done during August. Combine harvesters are still in many of the fields and palls of smoke rise from the burning stubble as farmers clear the last traces of this year's crop. There is a lot of co-operation between farmers at harvest-time but it is not the festive occasion that it was in the past, when every pair of hands was needed to ensure that the harvest was gathered.

This was the scene in the 1880s:
'In the fields where the harvest had begun all was bustle and activity. At that time the mechanical reaper with long, red revolving arms like windmill sails had already appeared in the locality, but it was looked upon by the men as an auxiliary, a farmer's toy; the scythe still did most of the work and they did not dream it would ever be superseded. So while the red sails revolved in one field and the youth on the driver's seat of the machine called cheerily to his horses, and women followed behind to bind the sheaves, in the next field a band of men would be whetting their scythes and mowing by hand as their fathers had done before them.

With no idea that they were at the end of a long tradition, they still kept up the old country custom of choosing as their leader the tallest and most highly skilled man amongst them, who was then called "King of the Mowers". With a wreath of poppies and green bindweed trails around his wide, rush-plaited hat, he led the band down the swathes as they mowed. . . .

After the mowing and reaping and binding came the carry-ing, the busiest time of all. Every man and boy put his best foot forward then, for when the corn was cut and dried it was imperative to get it stacked before the weather broke. All day and far into the twilight the yellow-and-blue painted farm wagons passed and repassed along the roads between the field and the stackyard. Big carthorses returning with an empty wagon were made to gallop like two-year-olds. Straws hung on the roadside hedges and many a gatepost was knocked down through hasty driving. In the fields men pitchforked the sheaves to the one who was building the load on the wagon, and the air resounded with "Hold tights" and "Wert ups" and "Who-o-as".'

Lark Rise to Candleford, Flora Thompson

Heap high the farmer's wintry hoard!
Heap high the golden corn
John Greenleaf Whittier

The final act of the actual harvesting used to be the ceremonial cutting of the last sheaf in which it was believed that the Corn Spirit had taken refuge. In some places it was considered to be unlucky to cut this and there were times when, with no volunteer, the stalks would be bound together and all the men in a wide circle hurled their sickles at the sheaf, thus making it a shared responsibility.

However, cut it had to be, for the Corn Spirit had to be kept for the following year, perhaps woven as a corn dolly. The last sheaf went by various names such as the Maiden Sheaf. In Cornwall it was The Neck. It was customary there to have bonfire celebrations at which the farmer who owned the field would cut and bind the last sheaf. He would then hold it high and shout,

'I have'n! I have'n! I have'n!'
'What 'ave ee? What 'ave ee? What 'ave ee?'
'A Neck! A Neck! A Neck!'
'Hurrah!'

That last 'Hurrah!' was a great cheer from all assembled and echoed across the countryside.

From various parts of the country come rhymes and sayings, many of them harvest shouts as the work was completed.

Up! Up! Up! a merry harvest home.
We have sowed; we have mowed;
We have carried our last load.

Hip! Hip! Hip! for the harvest home,
Now we've taken the last load home.
I ripped my shirt and I teared my skin
To get my master's harvest in.

In East Anglia, the last cart-load, or Horkey Load, was carried on a wagon decorated with greenery and flowers. The horses wore garlands and coloured ribbons. The men rode on top of the load, shouting and singing.

Harvest home! Harvest home!
The boughs do shake and the bells do ring,

So merrily comes our harvest in,
Our harvest in, our harvest in,
So merrily comes our harvest in.

That evening it was customary to hold a Harvest Supper, or Horkey or Mell Supper, known in some places as Harvest Home. Usually a large barn was cleaned for the occasion and it was decorated with greenery and flowers, perhaps with a place of honour for the Corn Maiden. It was a great feast of home-made food, washed down with plenty of home-brewed beer or cider. It was the farmer's way of saying thank you to all who had helped bring in his harvest. During the evening, the barn re-echoed to the strains of traditional songs, similar in many parts of the country.

Here's a health unto our master, the founder of the feast;
God bless his endeavours and give him increase;
God send him good crops that we may meet another year:
Here's the master's good health, boys: come drink of your beer!

Here's a health to the barley-mow:
Here's a health to the man, who very well can
Both harrow and plough and sow.
When it is well sown,
See it is well mown,
And raked a careful glean
And stacked in the barn
To lie dry, safe from harm,
Till he can thrash it clean.

Toward the end of September, or early in October, thanksgiving services are held in many churches to give thanks for the harvest. The institution of such Harvest Festival services is attributed to Rev. R. S. Hawker, who became vicar of Morwenstow, Cornwall, in 1834. He suggested that people should bring a thankoffering to God, much as people did in Old Testament days. Congregations praise God with the joyful singing of hymns such as

Come, ye thankful people, come,
Raise the song of harvest home.

That is not quite the end of the harvest story, for, toward the end of the month, on 29 September, is Michaelmas (p.34). This

5

is one of the English Quarter Days on which land rents are paid and maybe leases renewed. Farmers have always looked to a good harvest to enable them to pay their rents.

In some parts of the country it has been the custom to send a present to the landlord —perhaps as a token of appreciation, or maybe to keep on the right side of him. Usually, at Michaelmas the gift was a goose, as an old Exmoor verse suggests:

> And when the tenants come to pay their quarter's rent,
> They bring some fowl at Michaelmas, a dish of fish at Lent,
> At Christmas a capon, at Michaelmas a goose,
> And something else at New Year's Eve for fear the lease fly loose.

Michaelmas was always celebrated as a holiday and, in some places with great fairs, some of which are still held, though mainly as fun-fairs. There were also the hiring fairs (p. 42) at which workers would be engaged.

One last word about Michaelmas:

> So many days old the moon on Michaelmas,
> So many floods after.

The period from early September to late October is very important for Jewish people as it contains several of their most important festivals. The dates vary from year to year because they have a lunar calendar. The first of these is Rosh Hashanah, the Jewish New Year. It may be as early as 6 September or as late as 5 October. Ten days later is Yom Kippur, the solemn Day of Atonement. Sukkoth, the Feast of Booths or Tabernacles, one of the harvest festivals, comes a few days later and then Simchath Torah, the day of rejoicing for the Law.

At this same time of the year the Hindu people are holding their great autumn festival of Dashara, with the last day as Durga Puja, the worship of the goddess Durga. It is a time of great rejoicing and merrymaking.

St. Giles, or Aegidius, was a hermit, living in a cave near the mouth of the river Rhone, probably about the 8th Century. Legend tells how he kept a pet deer which, one day, was chased by the king, who shot an arrow at the deer but wounded Giles who was protecting his pet. Because of his injury, St. Giles has come to be regarded as the patron saint of cripples, remembered on this his feast day.

Another who made friends with many animals was Tarzan, not a real person but a fictional character created by the American novelist Edgar Rice Burroughs, who was born on 1 September 1875. Tarzan, the son of an English nobleman, was left in the jungle in infancy and brought up by apes. His adventures eventually filled about 30 books, were translated into over 56 languages and were seen in comic strips, films and television programmes.

Other creatures popular with some people, not alive but as delicacies to be eaten, are oysters. The Oyster Fishing Season at Colchester, Essex, is opened on 1 September (see p. 37).

Some of the postage stamps that have long been sought by philatelists are the triangular Cape of Good Hope stamps, the first of which were issued on 1 September 1853. One of the windfalls of Stanley Gibbons, the stamp dealer, about ten years later, was an offer of thousands of these triangulars by a sailor who had won them in a raffle in Cape Town. These, of course, are not as valuable as the original issue.

In Britain, it was on 1 September 1894 that it first became permissible to use postcards with adhesive stamps.

Also on this day. . . .
Edward Alleyn, born in 1566, became one of the greatest actors in Elizabethan times and founded Dulwich College, London.
Pope Adrian IV, the only English Pope (Nicholas Breakspear), died on 1 September 1159.
Sir Richard Steele, essayist, journalist, dramatist, politician, principal author of *The Tatler* and *The Spectator*, died in 1729.
In 1715 Louis XIV of France, the 'Sun King', died.
In 1854 Engelbert Humperdinck, German composer, was born.
In 1939 German armies invaded Poland.

Disaster in London on 2 September 1666. Fire broke out in a baker's shop in Pudding Lane and quickly spread until it was quite out of control. John Evelyn wrote in his diary:
'The noise and crackling and thunder of the flames, the hurry of the people, the fall of towers, houses and churches was like an awful storm. The air was so hot that at last men were not able to approach the fire, and were forced to stand still and let the flames burn on, which they did for nearly two miles in length and one in breadth. The clouds of smoke were dismal and reached nearly fifty-six miles in length. London was, but is no more!'
Four days later, the fire ended, having destroyed 13,200 homes and made 80,000 people homeless.

Disaster on this day, in 31 BC for Mark Antony, who stood and watched helplessly as his fleet of galleys burned out at the end of the Battle of Actium, Greece. Mark Antony had been penned in by Octavian and his admiral Agrippa but Cleopatra had come, with 200 ships, to her lover's rescue. However, Agrippa surrounded and destroyed most of the combined fleet. Anthony lost not only his ships but any chance of future leadership.

Disaster, too, on 2 September 1898, for the Mahdist movement in the Sudan. In 1885, the Mahdi had captured Omdurman. He and his successor made it the capital of their territories which covered the Sudan and parts of Egypt. On this day, the combined Anglo-Egyptian forces under Major General Sir Herbert Kitchener fought and won the Battle of Omdurman, giving control of the Sudan to Britain.

It was a different kind of battle that John Howard fought. Born on this day in 1726, this British philanthropist and reformer devoted the latter part of his life to the improvement of conditions in prisons and the removal of some of the abuses found in the penal system.

Thomas Telford, Scottish cival engineer, builder of roads, bridges, canals and harbours, died on 2 September 1834.
Professor J.R.R. Tolkien, author of *The Hobbit* and *Lord of the Rings*, (p.159), died this day in 1973.

3 September

On 3 September 1189, Richard I, King of England, known as Coeur-de-Lion, the Lion-hearted, made his way in a splendid procession from the Palace of Westminster to the Abbey for his coronation, setting a pattern that would be followed by many other monarchs. Anointed with oil on head, shoulders and chest, he was then gorgeously adorned and acclaimed. England had a king of whom she could be proud.

Or had she? Certainly she saw little of him, for he was off to fight in the Crusades and cost the country a pretty penny to finance his expeditions and later pay his ransom. One historian refers to him as 'a bad son, a bad husband and a bad king, but a gallant and splendid soldier.' It is as the last that he is chiefly remembered in history.

3 September has many associations with battle and war. Two of the significant battles of the Civil War in England took place on this day, the Battle of Dunbar in 1650 and the Battle of Worcester in 1651. Charles II had been crowned by the Scots, following the execution of his father, and he invaded England with a Scottish army. Oliver Cromwell completely defeated the Scots at Dunbar. At Worcester, Charles's army was defeated. The king escaped and fled across the Channel to France. Strangely, it was on this very date seven years later, 3 September 1658, that the victor, Oliver Cromwell, died of a fever and opened the way for the restoration of the monarchy.

It was on this date, in 1939, that Britain and France declared war on Hitler's Germany following the invasion of Poland.

Two airship happenings on this day: in 1916, the first Zeppelin to be destroyed in an air raid on Britain; in 1925, the *Shenandoah*, a United States airship, broke apart at Caldwell, Ohio.

On 3 September 1878, hundreds of happy Londoners were making the most of the last stage of an outing to the seaside aboard the river steamer *Princess Alice,* suddenly the ship was swept off course into the path of another steamer. The *Princess Alice* was cut in two and sank. Well over 600 were drowned.

Today, in 590 AD, Gregory the Great was consecrated Pope.

On 4 September 1909, the first Boy Scout Rally was held at the Crystal Palace in London, when eleven thousand boys proudly marched past their founder, General Sir Robert Baden-Powell. It was a big occasion in the history of the Boy Scout movement.

But it was to become an important occasion for girls, too, for Baden-Powell noticed a small group of girls dressed in broad-brimmed hats and long skirts, each carrying a stave.

'Who are you supposed to be?' asked Baden–Powell.

'We're Girl Scouts, ' came the reply.

'Nonsense! You can't be. There aren't any.'

'There are — 'cos we're them.'

This brief interlude led to the formation, in the following year, of the Girl Guide Movement.

> *Abide with me, fast falls the eventide,*
> *The darkness deepens, Lord, with me abide*

This famous hymn, that has brought comfort and help to so many people, was written on 4 September 1847 by the Rev. Henry Francis Lyte, knowing that illness was bringing his own life to a close. He died a couple of months later.

The presence and guidance of God was also a great reality for one who died on 4 September 1965. Dr. Albert Schweitzer had devoted himself to the work of God in the hospital at Lambarene in Central Africa. Often referred to as 'the Genius of the Jungle', Schweitzer was a doctor four-times over, of Music, Philosophy, Theology and Medicine, and he used these talents in one of the remotest places, leaving it only occasionally to raise money for his hospital and once, in 1952, to receive the Nobel Prize for Peace.

Life also drew to its close on this day, in 1907, for Edvard Grieg, the Norwegian composer.

On 4 September 1964, the new Forth Road Bridge was opened near the famous Forth Railway Bridge at Queensferry, Scotland.

Nothing happened on this day in 1752. It was the first of the eleven days to be 'lost' for the necessary adjustment when the Gregorian Calendar was introduced into Britain.

Suleiman I was the greatest of the sultans of the Ottoman Empire. He increased his dominions by conquests as far north-east as Hungary and south-west as Algiers. His fleets, under Khayr ad-Din (Barbarossa) commanded the Mediterranean but failed to take Malta. He was a great patron of the arts and a builder of architectural masterpieces. He is often referred to as Suleiman the Magnificent but, to his own people, he was Suleiman the Lawgiver *(Kanuni),* so named because of a system of laws he introduced. He died on 5 September 1566.

Mention of Malta serves as a reminder that the island became a British possession on this day in 1800 (until 1964).

This was the birthday, in 1638, of another who was to become a legendary ruler. Louis XIV of France became known as le Roi-Soleil — 'the Sun King'. Determined to be powerful, he assumed the government of France on the death of Mazarin and claimed his divine right to rule as dictator. He did much for France by developing roads, canals, a police force, a navy and military defences. His wars gave him glory and more territory. His domestic policies brought internal peace to France. But his activities brought France to financial ruin and the power he assumed led later to the French Revolution.

It was, in fact, on this day, in 1792, that the French Republic was declared and, a year later, on 5 September 1793, that the Reign of Terror began.

Jesse James brought his own reign of terror to the United States after the American Civil War. This most famous of all American outlaws was born on 5 September 1847.

A legendary figure of the 20th Century was Sir Douglas Bader, the flying ace who lost both legs in an accident but refused to give up flying. He served with distinction in World War II and was much decorated. Until his death on 5 September 1982, he spent his life in encouraging other disabled people.

On this day, in 1866, *Taiping* and *Ariel* raced up the Channel at the end of the famous China Clipper race (p. 12).

In 1980, the new St. Gotthard Tunnel, the longest road tunnel in the world, was opened on 5 September.

6 September

On 6 September 1666, the Great Fire of London (p. 8) ended and Londoners were faced with the daunting task of rebuilding the city and making new homes for the homeless.

A new home, and a free one, was the thought in the minds of the Pilgrim Fathers as they left Plymouth on 6 September 1620 in the *Mayflower*, beginning an arduous voyage across the Atlantic to North America, where they would be free from the religious persecution which, as Separatists, they had suffered.

This day saw the end of an eventful voyage in 1522, when *Victoria* sailed into harbour in the Bay of Cadiz, captained by Juan del Cano, who had left there three years earlier with Ferdinand Magellan. In those three years, all but 18 of the 265 men who left Cadiz had died, including Magellan himself, killed in the Philippines. Juan del Cano and his few companions had become the first to circumnavigate the world.

Another remarkable voyage ending, at London, on 6 September 1866, was the almost dead heat in the annual tea clipper race from China. *Taiping*, *Ariel* and *Serica* all docked within a couple of hours, having left Foochow, China, together 99 days earlier and sailed some 14,000 miles (22,500 km).

Also from one side of the world to the other . . . .Cricket Test Matches have been played between England and Australia since 1877. The first in England was played on this day in 1880 at the Oval. England won by five wickets.

On 6 September 1970, members of the Palestine Liberation Organisation hijacked two air liners, one Swiss and one American, and forced them to land on a desert airstrip in Jordan. The passengers of these and a British plane hijacked later were held hostage for the release of PLO prisoners. All three airliners were destroyed by fire bombs.

Also on this day. . . .
In 1757 The Marquis de Lafayette, soldier, was born.
In 1766 John Dalton, chemist and physicist, was born.
In 1869 Sir Henry Walford Davies, organist/composer, was born.
In 1901 President Mckinley (USA) was shot. (Died 14 September.)

7 September

Early in the morning of 7 September 1838, Grace Horsley Darling looked from the lighthouse on the Farne Islands, Northumberland, of which her father was the keeper and saw the wreck of the steamer *Forfarshire*, which had struck the rocks during the night. Clinging to the wreck were nine survivors. She helped her father row to the wreck and together they rescued them. Grace was awarded medals for her bravery — a courageous act for a sick young woman who died, aged 26, only four years later.

A courageous act was recorded on 7 September 1972, when Norman Croucher reached the summit of the Eiger, in the Swiss Alps. It was a great achievement for a man who had only artificial legs.

It was a courageous act too, on the part of the Rev. William Mompesson and the villagers of Eyam, Derbyshire, in September 1665. Plague reached the village on this day and the Rector and villagers agreed to isolate the village so that the plague could be contained. Of the 350 villagers, over 250 died.

Courage was needed too by the pilots of the fighter aircraft defending Britain from enemy attack during World War II. It was on this day, in 1940, that the German air force, the Luftwaffe, began the 'Blitz', a concentrated bombing attack on cities in Britain.

'Good Queen Bess' was born on 7 September 1533. Daughter of Henry VIII and Anne Boleyn, she became Queen Elizabeth I in 1558 and reigned until her death in 1603. She is generally considered one of the greatest English monarchs.

Also on this day. . . .
In 1812 Battle of Borodino between Napoleon and Russians.
In 1855 William Friese-Greene, motion-picture pioneer, was born.
In 1860 Grandma Moses, popular American folk painter, was born. She lived to be 101.
In 1892 John Greenleaf Whittier, poet and hymnwriter, died.
In 1910 William Holman-Hunt, Pre-Raphaelite artist, died.

On 7 September 1892, in the first heavyweight boxing title fight with gloves and three-minute rounds, 'Gentleman' Jim Corbett beat John L. Sullivan in 21 rounds.

8 September

Antonín Dvořák was born on 8 September 1841, in the land then known as Bohemia, now Czechoslovakia, in a little village near Prague, where his father was the village innkeeper and butcher. As a child, the only music he heard was very simple music and church music but it was not long before he developed great musical ability. In 1857, he went to the organ school in Prague and, two years later, produced the first of his many compositions. He was later to receive, in 1874, the state prize for composing music.

In 1885, Dvořák bought a country estate near Prague, which remained his home, though he did travel abroad on various visits to England and to the United States, where, from 1892 to 1895, he was director of the New York Conservatoire (School of Music). Holidays were spent at a Czech settlement in Iowa. It was at this stage that he wrote his ninth and probably best-known Symphony, which has acquired the sub-title 'From the New World'. Here is a blend of Czech music with tunes from the States appearing here and there.

After 1895, Dvořák returned to Prague, where he continued composing, and where he died on 1 May 1904, leaving a vast heritage of orchestral and choral pieces, songs, hymns, operas and other kinds of music that have provided hours of enjoyment for many people.

Another great composer is remembered today, for it was on 8 September 1949 that Richard Strauss died. Born in Munich in 1864, he was brought up in a musical atmosphere, for his father was a professional musician. Richard began composing at the age of six, learned to play the piano and the violin, and proved to have great ability as a conductor. His first opera was produced in May 1894. The heroine's part was played by Pauline de Ahna, whom Strauss married during the following month.

Richard Strauss wrote many operas and also orchestral works, large and small, much of it in his home in the Bavarian highlands. He is regarded by many as one of the greater of the German composers.

Also today. . . .
Richard I, Coeur-de-Lion, King of England, was born in 1157.
The first V2 rocket bomb landed in England in 1944.

9 September

This day in 1591 witnessed one of the most celebrated heroic encounters in maritime history. An English fleet had been sent to the Azores to intercept Spanish treasure ships but, on the arrival of 53 Spanish ships, the English fleet withdrew, leaving one ship, the *Revenge*, commanded by Sir Richard Grenville, in port.

When he was able to sail, Grenville, with his crew of 190, was cut off by 15 Spanish galleons. He decided to attempt to break through the enemy line. It took the Spanish force of 15 ships and 5,000 men fifteen hours to capture the *Revenge*. Grenville, mortally wounded, was taken aboard the Spanish flagship, where he died a few days later.

A few years earlier, on 9 September 1583, another of the Elizabethan sea-dogs died at sea. Sir Humphrey Gilbert, on his way home from America, ran into a great storm in which his small ship disappeared beneath the waves.

William the Conqueror died on 9 September 1087. Duke of Normandy, he changed the course of English history by his conquest. Then he invaded France but fell from his horse and died six weeks later from internal injuries sustained.

Chairman Mao also died on 9 September, in 1976. As Chairman of the People's Republic of China, Mao Tse-tung influenced many millions of Chinese, setting out his thoughts and doctrines in his *Little Red Book*.

Today's birthdays. . . .
    In 1585 Cardinal Richelieu, powerful French statesman.
    In 1737 Luigi Galvani, Italian pioneer of electricity.
    In 1754 William Bligh, Captain of HMS *Bounty*.
    In 1828 Count Leo Tolstoy, Russian writer (28 August OS).
    In 1890 'Colonel' Sanders (Kentucky Fried Chicken) (p. 136).
    In 1900 James Hilton, novelist *(Lost Horizon* and others).
    In 1949 John Curry, ice-skating gold medallist.
    In 1963 The first giant panda born in captivity (China).

In the Battle of Flodden, fought in Northumberland on 9 September 1513, King James IV of Scotland was killed, with at least 10,000 of his subjects, by the English army.

10 September

One of the great tourist attractions of Brittany is the shrine of Mont-Saint-Michel. It was founded in AD 709 by St. Aubert of Avranches, who had dreamed three times that Michael the Archangel told him to build the church. Today is the feast day of St. Aubert.

On 10 September 1771, Mungo Park was born near Selkirk, Scotland. He qualified as a doctor and made a voyage to India before being engaged to trace the course of the River Niger. This he did, and returned home to become a country doctor in Peebles. But, in 1805, he accepted an invitation to command a Government expedition to the Niger. He never returned and is thought to have been drowned whilst trying to escape from some hostile tribesmen who attacked the party.

Nowadays we hear a lot about Women's Lib and equal rights for women. This is nothing new. A book entitled *Vindication of the Rights of Women* was written as long ago as 1792 by Mary Wollstonecraft. She died on 10 September 1797.

11 September

We go round the world today to remember the birthdays, on 11 September, of four writers of different kinds of literature. In France, Pierre de Ronsard, writer of patriotic and love poems, was born in 1524. The Scottish poet, James Thomson, whose famous poem *The Seasons* was published in four parts, was born in 1700. Sir James Jeans, born in 1877, was an English scientist and author of important books about astronomy. Across the Atlantic, William Sydney Porter was born in 1862 and became a popular short story writer under the name of O. Henry. His last words were, 'Turn up the lights, I don't want to go home in the dark.'

One who did go home on this day in 1950 was Field-Marshal Jan Christiaan Smuts, whose death was mourned worldwide. A soldier in the Boer War, he worked to unite South Africa, was twice its Prime Minister and helped form the United Nations.

Five boys from Montignac, France, decided, on 12 September 1940, to explore some caves at Lascaux. They discovered on the walls paintings which had been done by stone age people thousands of years before.

One treasure from the past was set up, on 12 September 1878, on the Embankment in London. Cleopatra's Needle, a rose-red granite obelisk first set up in Heliopolis, Egypt, had been brought to England by Sir Erasmus Wilson, an eminent surgeon, at a cost of £10,000. The venture nearly failed as the cylindrical vessel built to carry the obelisk was cast adrift in storms in the Bay of Biscay but it was found later and towed on the final stage of the journey.

The journey of the *Lusitania*, which ended on this day in 1907, was much smoother. She entered New York at the end of a maiden voyage which had taken only 5 days 54 minutes, a new speed record for the transatlantic crossing.

Her port of arrival, New York, is at the mouth of the Hudson River, which takes its name from Henry Hudson, who first discovered it on this day in 1609.

Whilst in America, we recall that this was the birthday, in 1818, of Richard J. Gatling, the inventor of the Gatling gun with 10 parallel barrels capable of firing 1,200 shots per minute.

Off like a shot was 'Jesse' Owens. Born on 12 September 1913, J.C.Owens, the coloured American athlete, was one of the outstanding runners and gold medallists of the 1936 Olympics.

An outstanding runner in a different sphere was Nijinsky, one of the great racehorses of recent times. On 12 September 1970, he won the St. Leger, having previously won the Derby and the Two Thousand Guineas that same year — the first horse in 35 years to win the flat-racing 'triple crown'.

Also on this day. . . .
    In 1819 Gebhard von Blucher, Prussian Field-Marshal, died.
    In 1852 H. H. Asquith, British Liberal prime minister, born.
    In 1888 Maurice Chevalier, French actor and singer, was born.
    In 1908 Winston Churchill was married to Clementine.
    In 1953 John F. Kennedy married Jacqueline Lee Bouvier.
    In 1959 The Russians launched their first rocket that hit the moon.

13 September

Titus, Roman Emperor for about 2 years from AD 79 to 81, helped reconstruct Rome after the fire and completed the Colosseum. Earlier, he had conquered Jerusalem, in 70, causing the death of perhaps a million Jews. Suetonius described him as 'the darling of the human race'. No doubt the Jews thought otherwise, as did his brother, Domitian, who possibly conspired in Titus's death on 13 September 81.

Behind many a successful ruler are good advisers. Queen Elizabeth I was well served in this respect by William Cecil, Lord Burghley. Born on 13 September 1520, he became a lawyer and was later appointed sole secretary to the Queen, whom he advised wisely and astutely for most of her reign.

A great victory of Elizabeth's reign was the defeat of the Spanish Armada, sent by King Philip II of Spain, who died on this day in 1598. He had waged war against various countries.

On the subject of war, this was the day on which the generals of opposing armies both received mortal wounds. At the Battle of Quebec, on 13 September 1759, General James Wolfe died as his British army was victorious. The French general, Montcalm, died of his wounds the following day.

Born today, in 1860, was the American General John J. 'Black Jack' Pershing, American commander-in-chief in World War I. Another American, General Burnside, Union general in the Civil War, whose bushy sidewhiskers started the fashion known later as 'sideburns', died on 13 September 1881.

Troops were called out in London in 1804 to preserve order when William Betty first appeared at Covent Garden. Born this day in 1791 in Shrewsbury, he was an outstanding child actor.

When people refer to a complicated or impractical machine as 'a Heath Robinson contraption', they recall the drawings of fantastic machines by cartoonist and book illustrator, William Heath Robinson, who died on 13 September 1944.

About sunset on 13 September 1806, Charles Fox, the politician who had helped end the British slave trade, came to the end of the road. He said, 'I die happy. . . .'

September 14 is Holy Rood Day commemorating the traditional finding of the cross in the 4th Century by St. Helena on which it was supposed Jesus had been crucified. The day became a holy day or holiday on which, in bygone days, people went nutting in the countryside.

Italy's greatest poet was Dante Alighieri. He was also a writer of prose, a political thinker and a moral philosopher. His ideal lady, whom he knew as a child, was Beatrice Portinari. His spiritual love for Beatrice served as the inspiration for much of his work, the greatest of which was *The Divine Comedy*, probably written over a period of many years. Dante died on 14 September 1321.

One of the romances of the 20th Century ended abruptly on 14 September 1982. It had begun in 1955 when film star Grace Kelly went to Cannes for the film festival. There she met Prince Rainier, ruler of the small principality of Monaco. There, in 1956, they were married and Grace Kelly, the blonde iceberg of the films, became Princess Grace of Monaco. Driving a car on 13 September, she suffered a stroke. The car left the mountain road and plunged down an embankment. Princess Grace died in hospital on the following day.

On 14 September 1812, Napoleon's army swept into Moscow, thinking they had won a great victory. Before long the survivors were struggling back to France, victims of wily Russians and their great ally — winter.

On this day, in 1854, British and French forces landed in the Crimea at the outset of the Crimean War.

The largest rigid airship ever built, the German *Graf Zeppelin II*, made her maiden flight on 14 September 1938. She was 803.8 ft (245 m) long.

Also on this day. . . .
In 1735 Robert Raikes, founder of Sunday Schools, was born.
In 1852 the Duke of Wellington, soldier and statesman, died.
In 1860 the Niagara Falls were first illuminated.
In 1909 Sir Peter Scott, wildlife artist and conservationist, was born.

This day is celebrated as Battle of Britain Day, the day on which people recall how, in the dark days of World War II, the might of the German Air Force was challenged by a much smaller Royal Air Force. Sir Winston Churchill commented:'Never in the field of human conflict has so much been owed by so many to so few'. On 15 September people remember 'the Few' whose brave actions may well have saved Britain from defeat.

Among the aircraft of the German Air Force, the Luftwaffe, some of the most advanced were the Messerschmitt aircraft, designed by Wilhelm Messerschmitt and built in the works he had established in 1923. After the war he continued to build aircraft and also cars. Ironically, Willy Messerschmitt died on Battle of Britain Day, 15 September 1978.

On the subject of warfare, it was on 15 September 1916, during World War I, that tanks were first used.

Many forms of transport have associations with this day.

In 1784, Vincenzo Lunardi made the first balloon flight in Britain, from Moorfields in London to Standon, Hertfordshire, with a brief stop at North Mimms to let out his cat which was suffering from the cold.

On this day, in 1830, the Liverpool and Manchester Railway, one of the earliest passenger railways, was opened.

Railways were also the province of Isambard Kingdom Brunel, who was engineer for the Great Western Railway but also very concerned with shipbuilding, notably the *Great Eastern*, the largest ship of her day. Brunel died on 15 September 1859.

Some of the most famous racing cars of the 1930s were those built by Ettore Bugatti, born in Milan on this day in 1881.

Nowadays in towns and cities much of the traffic is regulated by Traffic Wardens. They were first introduced into London on this day in 1960.

The world's most famous elephant died on 15 September 1885. Jumbo, purchased from London Zoo by Phineas T. Barnum, was struck by a goods train.

Also on this day. . . .

In 1789 James Fennimore Cooper, American author, was born.

In 1864 John Hanning Speke, explorer of African lakes, died.

In 1890 Agatha Christie, author of detective novels, was born.

What is the temperature today? A glance at a thermometer will provide us with the answer. But on what scale is the temperature measured? Centigrade (Celsius) or Fahrenheit? Nowadays temperatures are more frequently given in the former but for many years the Fahrenheit scale was more commonly used. It takes its name from its creator, the German physicist, Gabriel Daniel Fahrenheit, who invented both the alcohol and the mercury thermometers. His original scale ranged from the temperature of a mixture of ice and salt to the normal temperature of the human body. The scale was changed later to one in which water froze at 32° and boiled at 212°. Fahrenheit, who spent most of his life in the Netherlands studying physics, died on 16 September 1736.

Temperatures in Spain frequently chilled at the mere mention of the name of Tomás de Torquemada, grand inquisitor, whose name will always be associated with the cruelty, horror, torture, burnings, fanaticism and bigotry of the Inquisition. A Dominican monk, he was appointed grand inquisitor in 1483 and between then and his death was probably responsible for the burning of about 2,000 people as heretics. There was many a sigh of relief when he died, aged 78, on 16 September 1498.

It was perhaps as well for John Colet that he lived in England and not Spain. His interpretations of the scriptures certainly differed from those of most theologians of his day and charges of heresy were brought against him. However, many, including Erasmus, were influenced by him. He was appointed Dean of St. Paul's, London (1504), founded St. Paul's School (1509), and died on 16 September 1519.

Others who died on this day. . . .
    In 1911 Edward Whymper, mountaineer and artist.
    In 1932 Sir Ronald Ross, physician, researcher of malaria.
    In 1952 Vesta Tilley, comedienne and male impersonator.

Also on 16 September. . . .
    In 1859 David Livingstone discovered Lake Nyasa.
    In 1861 Post Office Savings Banks were introduced to Britain.
    In 1893 Sir Alexander Korda, film producer, was born.
    In 1941 Muhammad Reza Shah Pahlavi became Shah of Iran.

This is Constitution Day in the United States of America. It was on this day, in 1787, that the final draft of the US Constitution was approved at the Philadelphia Convention.

It was on this day, too, nine years earlier, on 17 September 1778, that the first treaty was made between the US government and the North American Indians.

Another treaty was made, many years later, between the United States and other free countries of the Western world: The North Atlantic Treaty Organisation (NATO) was set up to counter the powerful Soviet military presence in Europe. Members included Belgium, Canada, Denmark, France, West Germany, Greece, Iceland, Italy, Luxemburg, the Netherlands, Norway, Portugal, the United Kingdom and the United States. The first meeting of the NATO Council was held on 17 September 1949.

On that same day the first meeting was held of freely elected members of a German parliament since Hitler had assumed power in 1933. Konrad Adenauer was elected Chancellor.

For many years there has been hostility in Palestine between Jews and Arabs. In 1948, the United Nations sent a mediator to try to get agreement. He was Count Folke Bernadotte, a Swedish soldier and diplomat, who had been an official of the Boy Scout movement and had headed the Swedish Red Cross. Shortly after his arrival, he was assassinated in Jerusalem by members of a Jewish extremist group, the Stern gang, on 17 September 1948.

A great adventure began on 17 September 1901 with the birth of Francis Chichester. As a young man he left his native Devon to go to New Zealand but returned and soon took up flying in small Gypsy Moth biplanes. He captured the imagination of many people in later years with his solo voyages, also in a craft named *Gypsy Moth* and particularly his circumnavigation in *Gypsy Moth IV*, in 1966–7, at the age of 65, after which he was knighted.

For Stirling Moss, born this day in 1929, adventure and excitement came at the wheel of racing cars. He was one of the world's top drivers in the 1950s but retired, after injury, in 1962.

Each year on 18 September, or the Saturday nearest to that date, the Dr. Johnson commemoration is held in Lichfield, Staffordshire. The Mayor, Sheriffs and other civic officials, together with members of the Johnson Society, visit the Johnson statue in the town square. A laurel wreath is laid at the foot of the statue; the choir sings hymns; and the Johnson Prayer is recited from the steps of the house where Samuel Johnson was born on 18 September 1709. In the evening a commemoration supper is held by candlelight. The menu consists of Dr. Johnson's favourite foods, steak and kidney pudding with mushrooms or saddle of mutton, followed by apple tart and cream, washed down with ale and hot punch. It was what the Doctor would have wished. He enjoyed good food and talking with his friends.

Samuel Johnson was the son of a poor bookseller. He went to Oxford University but had to leave through lack of money. He was unsuccessful as a teacher and earned very little working for a Birmingham publisher; so he went to London to earn a living as a writer. He wrote for various journals including *The Gentleman's Magazine;* he wrote books and poems; but his most important work was his *Dictionary of the English Language.*

We know a lot about Dr. Johnson because James Boswell wrote a book about him. He was a tall man, who did not take a lot of care over his personal appearance. He was clever and liked a joke but people sometimes found him rude. He was a man with many superstitions, always walking out of a doorway right foot first, never stepping on cracks between paving stones and touching every wooden post he passed to bring good luck.

He also had a guilty conscience over an incident in his early life when he had refused to help his father, Michael, run a bookstall in Uttoxeter market. They quarrelled and father died before the rift had been healed. In penance, Samuel stood bareheaded in the rain for several hours on the spot where the stall once stood. This, too, is commemorated to this day by an annual ceremony in Uttoxeter, when a wreath is hung on a memorial plaque in an old stone kiosk in the market place.

Also on 18 September. . . .
Births: Jean Foucault, scientist, 1819; Greta Garbo, actress, 1905. Deaths: Joseph Locke, engineer, 1860; Dag Hammarskjöld, UN Secretary-General, in a 'plane crash, 1961.

We begin today on a sweet note by thinking of chocolate — bars of chocolate, boxes of chocolate and drinking chocolate — and, of all the names associated with chocolate, no doubt the best known is Cadbury.

Its story began when George Cadbury, who was born on this day in 1839, together with his elder brother Richard, took over the family firm and, by introducing new methods, produced a much higher quality product.

But the Cadburys were concerned not only with their business but the people who made it possible. They moved from Birmingham to a site which they called Bournville. There they built a new kind of town with many amenities, good housing, gardens and also a private social security programme. George Cadbury was an enthusiastic Quaker and supporter of the Liberal Party. In order to express his views to a wider public, he bought the London *Daily News*, which later became the *News Chronicle*.

Invited to England by the *Daily News* was one of the greatest of all modern political cartoonists, David Low, a New Zealander. However, most of his work was with the evening papers *The Star* and the *Evening Standard*. Sir David Low was knighted in 1962 and died on 19 September 1963.

Some of today's news headlines. . . .

In 1356 Edward, the Black Prince, with English troops commanded by Sir John Chandos and Gascon troops under the Captal de Buch, inflicted a catastrophic defeat on the French King John II in the Battle of Poitiers at the end of the first phase of the Hundred Years' War.

In 1881 President Garfield of the USA died having lain unconscious after being shot by an assassin on 2 July only four months after becoming president.

In 1905 the great friend of destitute children, Dr. Thomas Barnardo, died. He founded over 90 homes for such children, the first, in Stepney, in 1870, with financial help from the Earl of Shaftesbury. Barnardo is dead but his work is very much alive.

Born on this day. . . .

In 1802 Lajos Kossuth, Hungarian independence leader.

In 1867 Arthur Rackham, artist, illustrator of fairy tales.

20 September

Today might be regarded as a day of beginnings and endings. It was, for example, a beginning for Salisbury Cathedral, which was consecrated on this day in 1258. It was also a beginning for the Methodist Church of Great Britain and Ireland, which came into being on this day in 1932 following the amalgamation of the Wesleyan, United and Primitive Methodist Churches.

Rahere died on 20 September 1144. That may seem more like an ending than a beginning, but he is remembered especially for his work in founding St. Bartholomew's Hospital, which, to this day, has remained one of the principal hospitals in London.

It was on this day, in 1519, that a very important voyage began. Ferdinand Magellan set sail from Seville with five small ships and 260 men. He headed south-west, rounded Cape Horn and sailed across the Pacific Ocean. Before they sighted land again, they had run short of food and water, eating such delicacies as sawdust, rats and leather! At the Philippine Islands, on 27 April 1521, Magellan was slain in a skirmish. Only one vessel, the *Victoria*, was able to continue and, under the command of Sebastian del Cano, with only 17 other sailors, reached Seville on 7 September 1522 — the first voyage round the world.

Nowadays people prefer to travel the world in comfort. And how better than on a luxury cruise liner such as the *Queen Elizabeth 2* ? She was launched at Clydebank, Scotland, on 20 September 1967.

For Sir Titus Salt today was the beginning and the end. He was born on 20 September 1803 and died on the same date in 1876. He is remembered as one of the far-seeing planners of his day. On his 50th birthday he opened a fine modern mill with good housing for the workers, at Saltaire, near Bradford.

Today marked the end for Jakob Grimm, German folklore collector and writer, who died in 1863, and of the Finnish composer, Jean Sibelius, who died in 1957.

And, in 1959, a few moist eyes turned skyward to watch the last fly-past of *Hurricane* aircraft over London, commemorating the Battle of Britain in 1940 and its gallant 'Few' pilots.

The troubles in the United States in the 19th Century between white settlers and Indians were many and varied, often leading to bloodshed and cruelty on both sides. One of the prominent Indian leaders was Chief Joseph, or In-mut-too-yah-lat, of the Nez Percé tribe in the fertile lands of the North West. Joseph and many of his tribe were Christian and regretted hostile acts but, despite all his efforts, Chief Joseph found himself at war.

Fighting was inevitable but Joseph gained a high reputation for his treatment of women and children, his humane attitude toward prisoners and his buying of provisions instead of stealing them. At last he had to surrender and did so with an eloquent speech:

Hear me, my chiefs, my heart is sick and sad. From where the Sun now stands, I will fight no more forever.

He kept his word, though the authorities failed to keep their promises. Chief Joseph died on 21 September 1904.

Girolamo Savonarola also clashed with those in authority. Born on 21 September 1452, he entered the Dominican order, became a powerful preacher and reformer and, at one time, was leader of Florence, setting up a democratic republic. But enemies in the state and church plotted his downfall until, after excommunication and a trial, he was hanged and burned.

Two great writers are remembered today. Sir Walter Scott, one of the most popular authors of his day, who may be described as the inventor of the historical novel, died on 21 September 1832. His novel *Waverley* was the first of the 'Waverley novels' which were published anonymously. Scott, who may have considered writing novels to be undignified, later admitted to their authorship.

Born on this day in 1866 was H. G. Wells, sociologist, journalist, historian and novelist, creator of characters such as Kipps and Mr. Polly and of books filled with imagination.

And two composers . . . Gustav Holst was born this day in 1874 and Roger Quilter died on 21 September 1953.

In 1745 The Battle of Prestonpans — resounding victory for Jacobites.
In 1756 John McAdam, Scottish roadbuilder, was born.
In 1964 Malta independent after 164 years of British rule.

Once more into the breach, dear friends, once more;
Or close the wall up with our English dead

With these words, according to Shakespeare, Henry V encouraged his men at the battle for the French port of Harfleur, fought on this day in 1415.

It was on or about this day in 1586 that Sir Philip Sidney was mortally wounded during the Battle of Zutphen in the Netherlands. Shot in the leg, he struggled back to the English lines gasping for water but, seeing a wounded soldier in great distress, he handed over the bottle untouched, with the immortal words, 'Your need is greater than mine'.

At Soldier's Field, Chicago, on this day in 1927, there was a fight of a different kind, the most controversial heavyweight fight in the history of boxing. Jack Dempsey had knocked down Gene Tunney in the seventh round, then went to the wrong corner. The referee delayed counting until he had moved, enabling Tunney to get to his feet within the count. Tunney then boxed on to win on points.

Snorri Sturlason got himself into a bit of a corner, too, and paid for so doing with his life. He was an Icelandic historian and poet, composer of sagas of the Norwegian kings. In 1215, Snorri was elected supreme judge of the island but he became involved in intrigues with King Haakon of Norway, who had him murdered on this day in 1241.

President Juan Peron of Argentina was more fortunate. On 22 September 1955, he was deposed in a military coup, but lived to serve a further term as president.

Also on this day. . . .

In 1694 Lord Chesterfield was born. An English statesman and humorous writer, he was also literary patron to others.

In 1776 Nathan Hale, American spy, was executed by the British in New York.

In 1791 Michael Faraday, English chemist, who experimented in many fields but particularly electricity, was born.

In 1880 Dame Christabel Pankhurst, suffragette, was born.

In 1955 the first independent television broadcast in Britain was screened.

It was on this day in 1940 that two new awards were instituted, the George Cross and the George Medal, named after King George VI. Just as the Victoria Cross was the highest award for military service, so the George Cross was to be the highest for those who showed great bravery, forgetting their own personal safety in the course of their duty. Awards have been made for such actions as bomb disposal and for bravery by lifeboatmen, policemen, firemen and others as well as servicemen not in combat.

Born on 23 September 63 BC was Gaius Octavius, also known as Octavian. Adopted by his great-uncle, Julius Caesar, as son and heir, he returned to Rome after the assassination of Caesar. He fought against Mark Antony but the Roman empire was divided into two, with Octavian ruling the west and Antony the east. After a while, Octavian declared war on Antony and Cleopatra who was assisting him. At the naval battle of Actium (p. 8), Octavian soundly defeated Antony, leaving himself, at 33, sole ruler of the Roman empire. Four years later he was awarded the title of Princeps (first citizen) and the name Augustus ('venerable' or 'exalted'). He thus became the first Roman emperor and the man who brought peace after a hundred years of fighting. The month of August was named after him and, after his death, he was worshipped as a god.

Johann Galle, a German astronomer, discovered the planet Neptune on 23 September 1846. Its likely existence had been suggested by the French astronomer Urbain Leverrier, who calculated, a few days beforehand, the point in the heavens at which a new planet might be expected to be seen.

Some of today's people. . . .
In 1625 Jan de Witt was born. He was a Dutch statesman opposed to the Orange party.
In 1930 Ray Charles was born. Blind by the age of seven, he became a leading popular singer, pianist and music publisher.
Sigmund Freud, Austrian founder of psychoanalysis, died in London on 23 September 1939.
This day, in 1779, witnessed the naval battle between the *Serapis* and the *Bonhomme Richard*, off Flamborough Head, Yorkshire.

For staging military band extravaganzas there can be few to excel Patrick Gilmore, who was responsible for a number of spectacular events in America during the 1860s and 1870s, some having over ten thousand performers. One, in 1869, included cannon fire, church bells and 100 firemen beating anvils for the 'Anvil Chorus'.

A cornet player from Ireland, he emigrated to the USA when 19 and led several bands. When the American Civil War broke out, he took his entire band into the Union Army. From 1872, until his death on 24 September 1892, he led the New York 22nd Regiment Band, which was also known as Gilmore's band. He is remembered not only for his flamboyant showmanship but for his innovations including the introduction into hitherto brass bands of reed instruments such as clarinets and for his band arrangements for the works of leading composers of orchestral music.

Another spectacular associated with this day was the appearance of the first airship on its maiden flight on 24 September 1852. It had been designed by Henri Giffard, a French engineer, who had decreed that there was no future in balloons because they could not be steered. In his airship, which was 144 feet (44 metres) long and driven by a light steam engine, he travelled about 17 miles (27 km) using a sail for steering.

A spectacular event of a different kind was achieved by two mountaineers on 24 September 1975. Doug Scott and Dougal Haston were members of an expedition led by Chris Bonnington, who reached the summit of Mount Everest by the South West face, the steepest and highest mountain face in the world. They were the second climbers to achieve this, a Chinese party having done so during the previous year.

Two writers share this day as their birthday. Horace Walpole, son of Sir Robert Walpole, was born in 1717. He was also a collector and, for a while, Member of Parliament.

Sir Alan Herbert, novelist, playwright and poet, author of over 50 books, independent Member of Parliament, was born in 1890.

The British Broadcasting Corporation began television programmes for schools on this day in 1957.

25 September

One of the best-loved entertainers of the mid 20th Century was Coco the Clown, with his red hair which stood on end, large red nose and very baggy clothes. Nicolai Poliakoff was, in fact, born in a theatre in Russia and began earning money by singing and dancing when only five. As a boy he joined a circus and, apart from military service, his whole life was with circuses, in Russia, Germany and then with Bertram Mills's Circus in Britain. After his retirement from the circus, until his death on 25 September 1974, he gave talks on road safety to thousands of children in many parts of Britain.

There was little need for talks on road safety when Nicolas Joseph Cugnot was born on 25 September 1725: there were no cars then. Cugnot was the man who built the first 'car', in 1769. It was a three-wheeled steam carriage, which could travel at about 2½ miles per hour.

It was on this day, too, that the first motor bus ran in Britain — a Daimler bus in Bradford, in 1897.

Another first, on or about this day, was the discovery of the Pacific Ocean, in 1513, by Vasco Nuñez de Balboa, a Spanish explorer. With his sword in his hand, he plunged into the ocean and claimed it for Spain.

It was a long time before news of his discovery reached his homeland on the other side of the Atlantic. There was no radio or telephone then. Transatlantic cable telephones between North America and Britain became operational on this day in 1956.

Some other of today's people. . . .

Johann Strauss 'the elder', the Viennese violinist and conductor, composer of waltzes and other music, died in 1849.

Dmitri Shostakovich, Russian composer of popular symphonies and not so successful operas, was born in 1906.

Samuel Butler, English satirist from Worcestershire, died in 1860. His great work was the popular *Hiaudibras*, a satirical burlesque poem on Puritanism with words such as

> For, those that fly, may fight again,
> Which he can never do that's slain.

Slain on this day in battle was King Harald Hardrada of Norway, whilst helping Tostig against King Harold of England in that 'other' battle of 1066 at Stamford Bridge.

Sir Francis Drake brought his little ship *Golden Hind* into port on 26 September 1580, having sailed round the world, plundering Spanish ships and possessions as he did so. He was only the second captain to circumnavigate the world and he received the accolade of Queen Elizabeth I, being knighted in 1581.

Not so fortunate was the child queen, Margaret of Scotland, who never set foot in her kingdom but died in a shipwreck on Orkney on this day in 1290 whilst on voyage from Norway.

Travelling in those days was very uncomfortable and precarious in open boats. Many years passed before the advent of the luxury liner. One of the most famous, the *Queen Mary*, first of the Cunard 'Queen' liners, was launched at Clydebank on this day in 1934.

Also 'launched' on this day, in 1881, was the world's first public supply of electricity, at Godalming, Surrey, produced at a hydro-electric station on the River Wey, which operated until 1884.

On this day, in 1887, the first gramophone for playing disc type recordings was patented by Emile Berliner in the USA. Previous recordings had been on cylinders.

Some of today's birthdays. . . .

Lord Collingwood was born this day in 1750. A British admiral, he was closely associated with Nelson and was eventually buried alongside him in St. Paul's Cathedral.

Sir Barnes Neville Wallis, inventor, in World War II, of the bouncing bomb, was born in 1887.

One year later, this was the birthday of T. S. Eliot, poet and playwright. Born in America, he became a naturalised British subject in 1927 and writer of many well-known works.

Also born in America, on this day in 1898, was George Gershwin, writer of successful musical comedies, of which 'Porgy and Bess', his negro opera, received wide acclaim.

The Revd. Wilson Carlile died, aged 95, on 26 September 1942. He had declared war on sin and formed the Church Army to help fight the battle. Its work, in helping the distressed, prisoners, down-and-outs and many others, continues to this day.

Béla Bartók, composer and collector of Hungarian and other Balkan folk music, died on 26 September 1945.

So near and yet so far. The Finnish explorer Nils Nordenskjöld, who had become a naturalised Swede, set out to see whether he could sail the north-east passage round the north of Europe, from the Atlantic to the Pacific. On 27 September 1878, when within a few hours sailing of his objective, he dropped anchor — and there he remained for the next ten months for his ship became frozen in the ice. On his return to Sweden he was honoured for his achievement by being created a baron.

This was the day, in 1938, on which the world's largest passenger liner, the Cunard *Queen Elizabeth*, was launched. On the outbreak of war she sailed to America for completion and served as a troopship before employment in her peacetime role on the transatlantic route.

Another achievement on this day was the opening, in 1825, of the first passenger railway, the Stockton-Darlington Railway. The train was pulled by George Stephenson's *Locomotion*, which was capable of pulling 48 tons (48.7 tonnes) at a speed of 15 mph (24 km/h). Soon afterwards, steam was used only for goods wagons, the passenger carriages being drawn by horses.

George Cruikshank, the artist, was born on 27 September 1792. He gained fame as a caricaturist and book illustrator, perhaps best known as an illustrator of the novels of Dickens.
    This was also the birthday, in 1862, of Louis Botha, the Boer leader, who became first prime minister of the Union of South Africa.

William of Wykeham, Bishop of Winchester, died on 27 September 1404. He founded New College, Oxford, and, later, Winchester College, with the famous motto 'Manners Maketh Man'.

This day also marked the end of the road for. . . .
    St. Vincent de Paul, priest and philanthropist, in 1660.
    Edgar Degas, French Impressionist artist, in 1917.
    Adelina Patti, internationally famed opera singer, in 1919.
    Engelbert Humperdinck, German composer, in 1921.
    Sir Henry Wickham, pioneer rubber planter, in 1928.
    Aimee McPherson, American pentecostal evangelist, in 1944.
    Gracie Fields, popular English music hall singer, in 1979.

28 September

Louis Pasteur discovered that many of the big problems of the world have very small beginnings — bacteria or micro-organisms which cause many kinds of disease. His well-known process for the pasteurisation of milk was but one of many discoveries which proved beneficial to mankind. In 1888, he founded the Pasteur Institute in Paris and he worked there until his death on 28 September 1895.

Whilst thinking of medical matters, it was thirty years earlier to the day that Elizabeth Garrett Anderson was accepted on the register as a physician and surgeon — the first woman in Britain to so qualify.

Another first time occasion, on 28 September 1745, was the singing in public of the national anthem by a theatre audience. It was at the Drury Lane Theatre in London and was an expression of loyalty to King George II at the time of the Jacobite rebellion led by Bonnie Prince Charlie.

Yet another first, on this day in 1923, was the publication of the *Radio Times* giving advance information about radio programmes to be transmitted by the BBC.

This day marked the end of the road for these. . . .

Pompey, or Gnaeus Pompeius Magnus, was one of the powerful leaders of Rome, second only in popularity to Julius Caesar. He was a very able general who regained territories in Africa and cleared the Mediterranean of pirates. To strengthen his position, he linked with Julius Caesar and Crassus to form the 'First Triumvirate'. It was short-lived. During Caesar's absence, Pompey took more power but Caesar crossed the Rubicon, and, within two months, was master of Italy. Pompey fled to Egypt but he was murdered, on landing, on 28 September 48 BC.

St. Wenceslaus, whose feast day this is, was also murdered—on 28 September 929. He is the 'Good King Wenceslas' who set himself to promote Christianity and good order in Bohemia. However, he angered a semi-pagan group of the nobility, much of the opposition coming from Wenceslaus's brother Boleslaw. It was while staying on Boleslaw's estate that a quarrel was started and Wenceslaus was killed by his brother's supporters. Wenceslaus is now the patron saint of Czechoslovakia.

Émile Zola, the French novelist, died on 28 September 1902, accidentally suffocated by charcoal fumes.

Michaelmas takes its name from St. Michael — not a saint in the usual sense but an angel, of whom one can read in the Bible, who came to be regarded as the protector of those who tried to conquer evil and helper of Christian armies against the heathen. His name is often linked with that of St. George.

Michaelmas Day, 29 September, is an important day in the year for many people. It is one of the English Quarter Days on which land rents are paid. It is also the most important of these, for it is the day on which many annual contracts are made or renewed. It was also the day, in the past, when servants and labourers might be hired for the ensuing year to work in the house or on the land (see p. 43).

This is also the day on which it has been customary, for many years, to elect mayors, sheriffs, bailiffs and others, who would hold office for the following year. Since 1546, this has been the day for the election of the Lord Mayor of London. In the Guildhall, where the ceremony takes place, the platform is strewn with herbs to offer protection from plague and witch-craft — once considered .very necessary. The candidates are chosen, at a colourful ceremony steeped in history, from Alder-men, who have already served as Sheriff. The Lord Mayor who is elected does not take up office until early in November.

One of the strangest customs of Michaelmas Day was a Lawless Hour at Kidderminster, Worcestershire. On that day a new Bailiff was elected. The former Bailiff retired at 3 o'clock and the new one took office at 4 o'clock — so there was an hour when no one was in charge. It was known as the Lawless Hour or Kellums.

As the town bell sounded at 3 pm the streets suddenly filled with townspeople, who pelted each other with cabbage stalks. During this hour no one could be arrested no matter what damage he did, for all law and order was suspended.

At 4 pm the new Bailiff and Corporation walked in a proces-sion, led by a drum and fife band, to visit the retiring Bailiff. They too were pelted but with apples — and by the most respectable townsfolk! The Lawless Hour ended at 4 pm — and the observance of this strange custom ended in 1845.

Since St. Michael is one of the patron saints of soldiers, it may be appropriate to think of soldiers and others who have fought a good fight.

Way back in history, in 490 BC, the Battle of Marathon was fought between the Greeks and the Persians. News of the Athenian victory on the plain of Marathon was said to have been carried by a Greek soldier who ran from Marathon to Athens, a distance of about 25 miles (40 km) — the original Marathon race.

Gustav Eriksson was a member of a Swedish noble family. He fought in the war against Denmark in 1517—18 and was taken prisoner, returning to Sweden in 1520. He then led a revolt against the Danes, freeing Sweden from the control of Denmark. He was chosen to be King of Sweden and took the name of Gustav Vasa. He died on 29 September 1560.

Robert Clive was born on 29 September 1725. He went to India in 1743 to work for the British East India Company. Those were troubled times with a struggle for power between the British and French. Clive commanded a small British expedition which was so successful that he became famous. His great victory against the Indian ruler Siraj-ud-Dawlah at the Battle of Plassey, in 1757, took Clive to the height of his career. He returned to England in 1760 and was created a Knight of the Bath. He is remembered as 'Clive of India' (see p. 105).

Sir William Orpen, who was an official artist in World War I and painted many war pictures now in the Imperial War Museum, died on 29 September 1931.

Nelson was a fighter, too, but mainly at sea, becoming one of Britain's greatest national heroes (see p. 65). This was his birthday in 1758.

Sir John Cobb's battle was not against people but to be the fastest man on land and sea. In 1947, he set a land speed record of 403.1 mph (648.7 km/h) on Bonneville Salt Flats, Utah. On 29 September 1952, on Loch Ness, he was travelling in his jet engined speedboat at over 249 mph (400 km/h) when the boat hit a ripple and disintegrated, killing Sir John.

30 September

Remembered on this day as St. Jerome, Eusebius Hyeronimus was one of the most learned men in the early Christian Church. About 366 he was baptised, then travelled a great deal, learning Hebrew and Greek. By 389 he had established a monastery at Bethlehem and it was there that he did a great deal of writing. His most important work was a translation of the Bible into Latin, known as the Latin Vulgate.

The contribution of George Whitefield to the Christian Church was of a somewhat different nature. At Oxford he linked up with the Wesleys, who had already laid the foundations for Methodism, and became an enthusiastic evangelist. Whitefield took holy orders in 1736 and thereafter spent most of his life in travelling and preaching in Britain and America. After a split with Wesley, he linked with the Countess of Huntingdon to form an offshoot of Methodism. In America he is remembered for founding an orphanage and some 50 colleges and universities. He died on 30 September 1770.

James Brindley was responsible for constructing a network of some 360 miles (579 km) of canals in Britain. It began when he was hired by the Duke of Bridgewater to build a ten-mile canal to transport coal from his mines in Worsley to the textile manufacturing centre in Manchester. These canals, an improvement in communication, helped hasten the Industrial Revolution. James Brindley, a self-made engineer, died this day in 1772.

Sir Fulke Greville, poet and writer, had the words inscribed on his tomb: 'Servant to Q. Eliz., councellor to King James and friend to Sir Philip Sidney.' He was sent to his tomb on 30 September 1628 by being stabbed by a servant.

Born on this day, in 1832, was Earl Roberts, British field-marshal, who distinguished himself in the Indian Mutiny, Afghan Wars and South African (Boer) War.

Today's firsts. . . .
In 1791 the premiere of Mozart's *Magic Flute*.
In 1929 the first BBC experimental television broadcast.
In 1939 Identity Cards first issued in Britain.

Some September Events and Commemorations

1st   Colchester, Essex: Opening of the Oyster Fishing Season. Oyster fishing is not permitted in months which do not contain a letter R. The season opens with an inspection of the oyster beds by the Mayor, members of the Town Council and the Fishery Board. After the Town Clerk has read the 1256 proclamation that the fishing rights belong to the Corporation of the Borough of Colchester, a toast is drunk and then the Mayor lowers a trawl to bring up the first oysters.

Monday after the Sunday after the 4th   Abbots Bromley, Staffordshire:Horn Dance. This processional dance lasts all day, touring the countryside and covering some 20 miles (32 km). The six dancers carry replicas of reindeer heads and horns carved from wood. Three sets are white and three black, symbolising good and evil. As they dance, they engage in mock battle. They are accompanied by a Fool, a Hobby-horse (also known as Robin Hood), a Man-Woman (Maid Marian), a young bowman and two musicians. Its origins are ancient, probably connected with primitive hunting and fertility rights.

Second Friday   Musselburgh, Lothian: Fishermen's Walk. A local fishermen's harvest festival with bands and dancing. Women and girls, dressed as fisher-wives, process to a field for sports and games.

Usually First Saturday   Richmond, Yorkshire: First Fruits of the Harvest. A Civic function including Beating the Bounds every seventh year. New pennies distributed.

Saturday   nearest   8th   Lichfield,   Staffordshire: Sheriff's Ride. Under the Royal Charter of 1553, the Sheriff is required to tour the city boundaries. He does so on horseback with others, covering 24 miles (38.6 km) with stops for refreshment.

Sunday   after   8th   Wirksworth,   Derbyshire: Clipping (Encircling) the Church on Wakes Sunday.

Early in September   Rochester, Kent: Beating the Bounds of the Admiral's Jurisdiction. The Mayor, Water Bailiff and the Chamberlain of the Oyster Beds process by barge on the Medway.

Saturday nearest 18th   Lichfield, Staffordshire: Dr. Johnson Commemoration (see p. 23).

Sunday after 14th   Avening, Gloucestershire: Pig Face Day. After evensong, Pig Face sandwiches are served in the village hall commemorating the consecration of the church in 1080, attended by Queen Matilda, when wild boar was served.

Sunday nearest 19th Painswick, Gloucestershire: Clipping the Church. Procession round churchyard then joining hands to encircle the church. Buns now given to children instead of the traditional Puppy Dog Pie.

21st or near London: Christ's Hospital (Bluecoat) School march with own band from Newgate to Mansion House.

25th Ashton-under-Lyne, Greater Manchester: Pageant of the Black Knight. Effigy of local tyrant of Middle Ages paraded round town, taken to the park and strung up on Old Cross.

27th Bristol, Avon. Indian Pilgrimage to tomb of Rajah Ram-Mohun Ray, representative of Indian King, who died in 1833.

Michaelmas Malmesbury, Wiltshire: Old Corporation Court. Southampton, Hampshire : Court Leet.

Sometime in month Bridport, Dorset; Poole Harbour, Dorset (every third year): Beating the Bounds.

Southend-on-Sea, Essex. Whitebait Festival.

SOME SEPTEMBER FAIRS

In many places: Michaelmas and Statute Fairs (see pp. 42–3).

Bedford: Michaelmas Fair once noted for sale of hot baked pears from Warden Abbey.

Sheep Fairs: *First Friday* Winslow, Buckinghamshire. *14th* Findon, Sussex. *Second Thursday* Wilton, Wiltshire. *Third Thursday* Dorchester, Dorset. *19th* Northampton. *Sometime* Sleaford, Lincolnshire.

Ram and Horse Fair: *First Wednesday* Worcester.

Horse Fairs: *First weekend* Barnet, Hertfordshire. *17th* Lee Gap, Yorkshire. *Sometime* Truro, Cornwall.

Pony Fairs: *Second Tuesday* Widecombe, Devon. *Sometime* Tavistock, Devon. *End of month* Brough Hill, Cumbria. *Wednesday nearest 21st* Bridgwater, Somerset (ponies and cattle).

During month Frome, Somerset: Cheese Fair.

Helston, Cornwall: Plum Harvest Fair.

Saturday nearest 18th Egremont, Cumbria. Crab Fair. Scrambling for crab apples and gurning competitions.

SOME AGRICULTURAL SHOWS AND EVENTS

Bucks County, Dorchester, Newbury and District, Romsey, Wokingham and District, Dairy Farming Event, International Sheepdog Trials.

OCTOBER

October

October was originally the eighth month of the Roman calendar, hence the name derived from *octo* (eight). The more descriptive Anglo-Saxon names for the month were Wynmonath, the wine-making month, or Winterfylleth, the appearance of the full moon before the onset of winter.

Once October is upon us, there are clear signs of the end of summer and the approaching winter. Days are shortening and the sun has lost its summer strength.

> *October is a piper,*
> *Piping down the dell —*
> *Sad sweet songs of sunshine —*
> *Summer's last farewell.*
> *He pipes till grey November*
> *Comes in the mist and rain,*
> *And then he puts his pipe away*
> *Till Autumn comes again.*
> Margaret Rose.

October is the month of falling leaves, when the countryside is a blaze of reds and golds and browns — autumn in all its beauty, yet a passing phase for soon the winds and the rain will whisk those leaves away to form their winter carpet on the earth.

> *October turned my maple's leaves to gold;*
> *The most are gone now; here and there one lingers;*
> *Soon these will slip from out the twig's weak hold*
> *Like coins between a dying miser's fingers.*
> Thomas Bailey Adrich

October may be the wettest month of the year. It is not unusual to awaken, even on fine days, to damp misty mornings and foggy weather is often experienced. However, it is not uncommon to have a period of fine weather about the middle to the end of the month — sometimes coinciding with the school half-term holiday. It is known as St. Luke's Summer because it falls on or near St. Luke's Day, which is 18 October.

The October winds and rains bring down not only the leaves but many of the acorns and nuts too.

A good October and a good blast
Will blow the hog his acorn and mast.

Among the nuts that come tumbling down are the conkers from the horse-chestnut trees. Lots of children cannot wait for nature to do her work but throw missiles into the trees to knock down the conkers. For many years conkers have been threaded onto strings, having been hardened in various ways, then aimed with dexterity to smash another's conker.

Hobbley hobbley onker,
My first conker,
Hobbley hobbley ho,
My first go.

For contests, of course, conkers should be untreated. One annual contest is held on the Wednesday nearest to 20 October at the New Inn, Goodleigh, near Barnstaple, Devon. Often over one hundred contestants play with their locally collected conkers.

But how many conkers can a conker conquer? The record, set at the BBC Conker Conquest in 1954, was over 5,000 but it has been questioned as to whether it was a true conker from the horse chestnut. Anyway, most conker contestants will happily settle for a champion conker that falls far short of being a '5,000er'.

It is not only hogs and boys that appreciate the autumn fruits. Squirrels and other animals are busy collecting some for their winter food. Other animals are preparing for hibernation. Many of the birds are enjoying a feast of berries, so fulfilling the function of nature by carrying within them the seeds to be dropped elsewhere. The last of the swallows and martins may be seen gathering on the telegraph wires before their long flight south.

The beginning of October sees the end of the Harvest Festivals (p. 5). Two colourful London ones, on the first Sunday, are the one at St. Martin-in-the-Fields, attended by the Pearly Kings and Queens, and the Billingsgate Harvest of the Sea.

Fairs

Many fairs are held early in October, some of them known as Michaelmas fairs, which may seem strange when Michaelmas Day is 29 September. The reason for this dates from the year 1752, when the calendar was changed because the old one was inaccurate and, over a long period, had gradually run ahead of the seasons. To correct the error, eleven days were lost and the calendar jumped from 3 September to 15 September (p. 10). October 10 was, therefore, Old Michaelmas Day and some of the fairs remained about that time.

In years gone by, there were two main kinds of fair — charter fairs and statute or hiring fairs. The great business fairs of the Middle Ages were charter fairs. They were held by people who had been granted a charter by the King giving permission for the fair. Perhaps the greatest of the fairs was St. Bartholomew's Fair, held at Smithfield, London, from 1133 to 1855. It gained a bad reputation for bringing out all the worst aspects of human nature and respectable people breathed a sigh of relief when it came to an end.

Some of the great provincial charter fairs were: Sturbridge, near Cambridge; St.Ives, then Huntingdonshire; the Bishop's or St. Giles Fair, Winchester. There were many other smaller charter fairs, the charters being granted in many instances to religious establishments.

Mediaeval fairs were primarily for business and people would travel far, even from the continent, to buy and sell at the fair. There was plenty of entertainment, too, and gradually this took over until the fairs became the fun fairs that we know today.

There were strict laws regarding the conduct of fairs. It was customary for the normal laws of the town to be suspended for the duration of the fair and for special Pie Powder courts to be set up. The name is a corruption of the French *pieds poudreux* — the 'dusty footed' — and the idea was to deal with all offences as swiftly as possible whilst the dust of the fair was still on the feet of the offenders. It was, and still is in some places, the custom to hoist a wooden hand or glove to indicate that the fair had begun.

Most of the Michaelmas fairs were hiring fairs. They began to take shape in 14th Century after the Black Death had killed so many people that there was a great shortage of labourers and servants. Various laws were passed, known as Statutes of

Labourers, by which Justices of the Peace could fix wages. This was done at special sessions, many of them held at Michaelmas, which was the end of the farming year, but some at Whitsuntide or on dates that were locally convenient.

Local farmers, employers and labourers often attended these sessions in large numbers to learn what the agreed wages would be. Many agreements were made there and then for a year. As there were many people present, the food sellers also came. So did the pedlars and the entertainers. Gradually these meetings developed into fairs, some of them quite large, often known as statute (or 'stattit') fairs, but also as hiring or mop fairs — a name still retained by fairs in some towns today, though they are now no more than fun fairs.

Until the beginning of the present century, it was customary for people to enter into agreements of employment at the hiring fair and for a section of the fairground to be set apart for this purpose. Those who were seeking employment wore or carried a token of their trade, a kind of visual aid by which they could easily be recognised by employers looking for servants or labourers. So a shepherd might carry a crook or wear a piece of wool, a milkmaid might wear a tuft of cowhair or carry a pail and a housemaid would wear an apron or carry a sponge. Those who were engaged were given a coin as a token. At one time it was a penny, known as the 'hiring penny' or 'fasten-penny', later one shilling. The recipient would then remove or lay down the token of his or her trade and go off to enjoy the fun of the fair.

Afterwards there were some who regretted the agreement. An employer may not have found his employee satisfactory, nor a servant a master to her liking. So, in many places, a Runaway Fair was held a week later, which provided each with opportunity for finding someone else and a second chance for those who had not found employment the previous week.

It is not possible here to list all the fairs that originated as hiring fairs but the Michaelmas fairs, mostly held about 10 October, are found mainly in the counties of Bedfordshire, Berkshire, Buckinghamshire, Cambridgeshire, Hertfordshire, Oxfordshire, Warwickshire, Wiltshire and Worcestershire.

At this same time of the year there are many specialised fairs, mainly for the sale of animals. Some, particularly the horse fairs, have been held earlier in the year during August and early September (see *Spring and Summer Days* p. 194). Most of the October fairs are for the sale of sheep, some of the fairs being very large. Between 10,000 and 17,000 sheep may be sold at the Great Fair at Findon, Sussex, on 14 September, whilst the September fair at Wilton, Wiltshire, is said to be the largest sheep fair in the south-west of England. Some other sheep fairs are at Alresford in Hampshire, Northampton, Leicester, Winslow in Buckinghamshire, Dorchester, Bridgewater and Glastonbury.

A reminder of the once very extensive business in geese at Michaelmas is found in the Goose fairs at Nottingham and Tavistock, where thousands once changed hands but now not a goose is to be seen. Both are held early in October.

The fair that was possibly the oldest in England was Weyhill Fair, Hampshire, on Old Michaelmas Day, 10 October. It was held on a hill top where the old Tin Road from Cornwall, the Gold Road from Wales (and Ireland) and six other drove roads met. It is probable that this was an old meeting place long before the fair was held in the 11th Century. Sheep and horses, hops and cheeses were among the goods sold there. Many are the tales of interesting happenings at Weyhill Fair which sadly faded out in recent years.

Another fair with an interesting custom is the Pack Monday Fair at Sherborne, Dorset, held on the Monday after 10 October. Teddy Roe's Band used to march through the streets soon after midnight making an unearthly noise with dustbin lids, trays, trumpets and anything else to hand. Unfortunately it had to be stopped from 1964 owing to hooliganism.

Fairs have often brought out the worst of human nature and ever change in character according to the times.

Four lions stand guard at the base of Nelson's Column in Trafalgar Square, London. They are, perhaps, the best-known animals in London. They have been looked at, photographed and even climbed upon by people from every part of the world. They are not real lions, of course; they are the sculptures designed by Sir Edwin Landseer, a very popular artist and sculptor of last century. He was born in London in 1802, began drawing at the age of six and had a picture exhibited in the Royal Academy when only thirteen. He loved animals, especially deer and dogs and these he painted. His picture of a stag, *Monarch of the Glen*, is one of his most famous. He also painted portraits, amongst them Queen Victoria and Prince Albert. Sir Edwin died on 1 October 1873.

From lions to camels! Though the man who rode one of the camels can truly be said to have fought like a lion. He was T. E. Lawrence, better known as Lawrence of Arabia, who dressed as an Arab, led the Arabs in battle against the Turks during World War I, blew up trains and bridges and caused so much trouble for the Turks that they offered a reward of £20,000 for his capture. On 1 October 1918, he led the Arabs into Damascus to occupy it.

Today is the birthday of another Lawrence — James Lawrence, born 1 October 1781, but remembered more for his death than his birth. He was an officer in the United States Navy in command of the *Chesapeake*, which was attacked at Boston by the British frigate *Shannon*. Mortally wounded, he encouraged his men with the cry, 'Don't give up the ship', which became a popular battle cry.

Into battle long ago went King Henry III, son of King John, born on 1 October 1207. He did battle with his barons led by Simon de Montfort, and was defeated by them at Lewes in 1264 but a victory at Evesham, in 1265, gave Henry back his power.

Also on the march was the German army which entered Czechoslovakia on 1 October 1938, a prelude to World War II.

Paul Dukas, the French composer of *The Sorcerer's Apprentice* and other music, was born this day in 1865.

How much does it cost to send a postcard today? Postcards could be sent in Britain for one halfpenny from 1 October 1870.

2 October

Mohandas Karamchand Gandhi was born on 2 October 1869. He studied law in London, then returned to India but gave up his practice to go to South Africa, where he spent twenty-one years fighting discrimination there against Indians. Returning to India, he entered upon a campaign of passive civil disobedience in an attempt to gain independence for India, spending several periods in prison and sometimes 'fasting unto death'. He also championed the cause of the 'untouchables', whom he called instead 'sons of god'. Soon after Indian independence, Mahatma ('Great Soul') Gandhi was assassinated by a Hindu fanatic.

Also born on 2 October were two soldiers who were to be on opposite sides during World War I.

Paul von Hindenburg was born this day in 1847. Success against the Russians in 1914 helped lead to his appointment, in 1916, as Chief of General Staff of the German armies on the Western Front. Opposing him, in 1918, was the French Generalissimo of the Allied Armies, Ferdinand Foch. Born on 2 October 1851, he, too, had made a reputation for himself in earlier battles as a great strategist. Both were honoured by their respective countries: Hindenburg was elected president of Germany and Foch became a Marshal of France.

First today. . . .

The first British submarine was launched at Barrow in 1901.

The first Rugby football match at Twickenham was in 1909.

The first television picture was transmitted, from one room to another, by John Logie Baird on 2 October 1925.

First to build a mechanical 'car' — a steam carriage — was Nicholas Joseph Cugnot (p. 30), who died this day in 1804.

First in many races was Olympic gold medallist, Paavo Nurmi, the 'Phantom Finn', who died on 2 October 1973.

The first meeting of the Baptist Missionary Society was held this day in 1792, inspired by cobbler Will Carey, who became one of its first missionaries.

And the man who tried to be first . . . Scottish businessman, Sir Thomas Lipton, philanthropist and founder of the Lipton grocery empire, endeavoured four times to win the America's Cup with his yacht *Shamrock I* but failed to do so.

3 October

Therese of Lisieux was just an ordinary nun who died when only twenty-four, just two years after she had been persuaded to write her life story. Published later as *The Story of a Soul*, this became a best seller and was translated into many languages. Pilgrims began going to her tomb where it is said that miracles were performed. In 1925, twenty-eight years after her death, she was canonised and today is kept as the feast day of St. Therese of Lisieux.

William Morris, who died on this day in 1896, liked beautiful things. One of his first loves was architecture, particularly in the Gothic style. From that he turned to painting, then to various crafts and to house decoration and furnishing. He is remembered, too, as a poet and translator, also for setting up the Kelmscott Press to print beautiful editions of his own and other books.

The world of music was made the poorer twice on 3 October. In 1953 Sir Arnold Bax died. He had been knighted in 1937 and was Master of the King's Music from 1942. His compositions were many and varied, some reflecting his love of Celtic stories and music.

Sir Malcolm Sargent, who died on this day in 1967, was one of Britain's most popular conductors, remembered especially for his promenade concerts, his personality and his humour. He once said, 'I spend up to six hours a day waving my arms about and if everyone else did the same they would stay much healthier.'

Elias Howe, of Massachusetts was the man who invented and patented the sewing machine. After an unsuccessful journey to England to introduce his invention, he returned to find his patent infringed. After a seven-year legal battle, his rights were upheld and he died a very rich man on 3 October 1867.

In Massachusetts this day also marked the death, in 1656, of Myles Standish, military leader of the Pilgrim Fathers.

From a man of war to a man of peace, from wealth to poverty, sums up the life of Francis of Assisi, founder of the Franciscan friars, friend of all creatures and one of the most popular of the saints. He died on 3 October 1226 and is remembered as St. Francis each year on 4 October.

4 October

The Space Age began on 4 October 1957 with the launch of the Russian *Sputnik I*, the first artificial earth satellite. It weighed about 180 lbs (81.6 kg) and took 95 minutes to orbit the earth.

It was not long before satellites were being put into orbit to serve a number of purposes and spacecraft were sent to explore further afield. Another to be launched on 4 October was the Russian *Lunik III* (or *Luna III*) in 1959. Three days later, it took photographs of the far side of the moon.

An achievement of a different kind, which must have seemed just as momentous in its day, was the production of a Bible that had been translated into English. The first printing of this first English Bible was completed on this day in 1535. It was the work of Miles Coverdale and dedicated to King Henry VIII, in whose reign the protestant reformation had come to England.

A Christian campaigner of much later years was Catherine Booth, wife of Salvation Army founder William Booth. She was a fine preacher and a great supporter of her husband in his work. The 'mother of the Salvation Army' died on 4 October 1890 and over 36,000 people attended her funeral service at Olympia.

Sir William A. Smith, in Glasgow, wanted to start a Christian organisation for boys. On 4 October 1883, at the Free College Church Mission, three officers and twenty-eight boys formed the first company of a movement that was to spread throughout the world — the Boys' Brigade.

Perhaps the greatest of the Dutch painters, Rembrandt van Rijn, the son of a miller, was apprenticed to an artist in his home town of Leyden. He moved to Amsterdam, where success in art made him rich and enabled him to live in a fine house filled with things of beauty. Toward the end of his life his fortunes changed and he died in poverty on 4 October 1669.

The art of 'Buster' Keaton was that of the clown in the days of the silent film and at that he excelled, providing fun and laughter for many. This was his birthday, in 1895.

This was the last day, in 1821, for John Rennie, the Scottish civil engineer who became famous as a bridge builder but also for his work on canals, docks, harbours and fenland drainage.

5 October

About 2 am on 5 October 1930 the pride of British airships, the *R101*, crashed into a hillside at Beauvais, France, burst into flames and became a tangled wreck of twisted metal. Forty-six of the 54 people on board lost their lives. The end of the great silver dirigible, which had left Cardington, Bedfordshire, on the previous evening bound for Egypt and India, also marked the end of British airship building. Later disasters to airships of other nations virtually brought to an end the use, for a time at any rate, of airships as a reliable or safe means of transport.

Also in France. . . . this day in 1600 saw the wedding of Henry of Navarre (King Henry IV) to Marie de Medici. From them came the Bourbon line of kings.

But, in France, the monarchy gave way to the republic and kings were replaced by presidents. It was on 5 October 1958, that the Fifth Republic came into being after its constitution had been approved by a referendum. The first president of the Fifth Republic was Charles de Gaulle.

Some years ago the highlight of a visit to Paris would have been a night out to see the cancan being danced. A famous cancan tune was one of many composed by Jacques Offenbach the German-Jewish composer who went to live in Paris, conducted the orchestra in the Théâtre-Français and composed a large number of lively operettas. He died on 5 October 1880.

William Scoresby was born near Whitby, Yorkshire, on 5 October 1789. As a boy he went to sea with his father, a whaling captain, and this gave him a taste for the Arctic. He made several voyages to the whaling grounds off Greenland and recorded his observations, publishing them in *The Arctic Regions*, the first scientific account of this area. He also surveyed 400 miles of the east coast of Greenland. In 1825 he was ordained, his seafaring days behind him.

Charles, 1st Marquis Cornwallis, served in the army and accepted a command in the American War of Independence. After initial successes, he was forced to surrender at Yorktown. Later, as Governor-General of India, he distinguished himself against Tippoo Sahib. He also served well as Lord-Lieutenant of Ireland. He died this day in 1805.

6 October

The greater part of what I can do I have myself acquired
by incredible labour in spite of astonishing difficulty.

The pathway to success is often a hard one and Jenny Lind, who was born on 6 October 1820, knew, when she expressed herself thus, how much effort was needed to make the 'Swedish Nightingale' the admiration of many for her fine singing.

The energies of William Tyndale were directed towards a translation of the Bible into English so that all who could might read it in their own language. Driven from England, he had his Bibles printed in Germany and smuggled into England. At last he was seized by the authorities at Antwerp, condemned for heresy and burned at the stake on 6 October 1536.

George Westinghouse, who was born on 6 October 1846, was an American inventor and manufacturer, concerned mainly with electricity supply and railways. He was chiefly responsible for the adoption of alternating current for electric power transmission in the USA. On the railways he improved signalling but is chiefly remembered for the invention that bears his name, the Westinghouse air brake. He set up companies to manufacture his inventions.

An American industrialist and inventor of later years died on 6 October 1951. W. K. Kellogg invented cornflakes and other breakfast cereals. He was a philanthropist who used his wealth for social improvement, child welfare, schools and a bird sanctuary.

John Willis Griffiths, who was born on 6 October 1809, became a US naval architect and created the *Rainbow* (1845), the first of the great clipper ships for the China tea trade.

The ships of Thor Heyerdahl, who was born this day in 1914, were unusual. *Kon-tiki*, made of balsa wood, and *Ra II* made of papyrus, were used to prove his theories of migration.

Also on 6 October. . . .
In 1892 Alfred, Lord Tennyson, Poet Laureate, died.
In 1895 the first Promenade Concert was held.
In 1973 war broke out between Israel and Arab states.
In 1981 President Anwar Sadat of Egypt was assassinated.

It is an ill wind that blows nobody any good. On 7 October 1753, William Davies, walking home to Twyford, Hampshire, became lost in the fog and was heading straight for the local chalk-pit. Just then he heard the bells ringing in the church, realised his danger and turned to safety. In thankfulness, he made money available so that the bellringers of Twyford could enjoy a feast on this day — as they still do — provided that the bells are rung morning and evening on 7 October.

Athletics history was made on 7 October 1982, when, for the first time, there was a dead heat in a major athletics event. In the Commonwealth Games at Brisbane, Australia, Allan Wells of Scotland and Mike McFarlane of England crossed the finishing line together at the end of the 200-metre final. The race was electronically timed at 20.43 seconds but in the photofinish it was impossible to find a winner. Both runners, therefore, were awarded a gold medal.

It was on this day in 1947 that a pilotless US 'plane was flown from England to Newfoundland by remote control.
A step forward in the space programme also took place on 7 October 1959, when the Russian *Lunik III* took photographs of the far side of the moon.

This day marked the end of the road for Archbishop William Laud, the most unpopular statesman of his time, who was found guilty of treason and beheaded on 7 October 1573.
Marie Lloyd, a popular English music hall artiste, died this day in 1922. In 1918, Sir Hubert Parry, English composer, died and, in 1894, Oliver Wendell Holmes, US physician, poet and humorist, who left many pithy sayings such as

*The world's great men have not commonly been great scholars,
nor its great scholars great men.*

Was Henry Alford one of the exceptions? Born this day in 1810, he became hymn writer, scholar, Bible translator, preacher, lecturer, author, musician, painter and Dean of Canterbury Cathedral.

The naval battle of Lepanto was fought this day in 1571.

Cola di Rienzi was a popular revolutionary leader in 14th Century Rome. The son of an inn-keeper, he plotted a revolution, summoned the people to the Captoline Hill, announced edicts against the nobles, assumed the powers of a dictator and later gave himself the ancient Roman title of tribune. The steps he then took to improve Rome and hopefully to unite Italy were many and varied. Naturally the nobles were angry, Papal authority was set against him and, after seven months, he was forced to flee to Naples.

But he returned seven years later with the authority of a new Pope to crush the nobles and with a new title of senator. He made a triumphal return but such was his conduct that he was soon rejected by the people of Rome. In a riot, on 8 October 1354, he was stoned, then seized and murdered.

The reforms sought by Archbishop Richard Whately, Anglican Archbishop of Dublin, were of a social nature. He opposed the transportation of prisoners to Australia, and he wanted improvements in agriculture, to help the Irish poor.

Today's people in art, literature and music. . . .

Fra Filippo Lippi died on or about 8 October 1469. He was a Carmelite monk and one of the most important Florentine early-Renaissance artists. He is remembered for some fine frescoes, particularly on the choir walls of Prato cathedral and for his series of *Nativities*.

Sir Alfred Munnings, President of the Royal Academy 1944–49, was born in 1878. He became well known for his paintings of horses and his outspoken criticism of modern art.

Sir Henry Fielding, English novelist and playwright, died this day in 1754. Having studied literature, he wrote plays and became author manager of a London theatre. In 1740 he was called to the bar but writing remained his main interest. His novel *Tom Jones, a Foundling* (1749) is rated very highly in English literature. As a Westminster justice of the peace, he endeavoured to suppress the ruffianism of his day.

Kathleen Ferrier, contralto, was one of the finest and best-loved singers of her day. Music was especially written for her by Britten and Bliss. She died of cancer, aged 41, in 1953.

9 October

In Norway, 9 October is celebrated as Leif Ericson Day, commemorating that Norse explorer, generally believed to be the first European to reach the shores of North America, possibly on this day in the year 1000. According to the Icelandic sagas, he had been sent by King Olaf to urge Christianity on the settlers in Greenland. He sailed off course and found a fertile land where grapes grew — possibly the present Nova Scotia province of Canada. He called it Vinland.

On the night of 9–10 October 1799, the frigate *Lutine* was wrecked in a storm off the Netherlands. She sank with over £1,000,000 in gold bullion and pay for British troops in the Netherlands. In 1859, the ship's bell was salvaged and hung in The Room at Lloyd's in London, where shipping insurances are transacted. Traditionally the Lutine Bell is rung whenever it is necessary to announce that a ship is lost or overdue. It has tolled the knell of many a fine ship.

The knell was sounded on 9 October for. . . .
King Alexander I of Jugoslavia in 1934. He had struggled to create a united country from small states and people of different ethnic groups — Serbs, Croats and Slovenes — but he was assassinated by a Croatian separatist agent at Marseilles, whilst on a state visit to France.
'Che' Guevara in 1967. In the 1950s he joined the revolutionary forces of Fidel Castro in Cuba and became the hero of socialist revolutionary movements. From Cuba he went to help revolutionaries in Bolivia, and there he was captured and executed.

So from death to life . . . and life with a capital L as offered by American evangelist, Aimee Semple McPherson, born on this day in 1890. A controversial Pentecostal evangelist, her followers in the International Church of the Foursquare Gospel numbered tens of thousands of those who found joy in her style of worship.

On 9 October in France. . . . The feast day of St. Denis, patron saint of France. La Sorbonne, the University of Paris, takes its name from a theological college founded by Robert de Sorbon, born this day in 1201. Camille Saint-Saëns, born this day in 1835, was a composer, pianist, organist, poet and playwright.

10 October

Headlines for 10 October are concerned with some of the remoter parts of the world. One of the loneliest of these is the island of Tristan da Cunha in the South Atlantic Ocean some 2,000 miles from Cape Town. In 1817 it had been taken over as a British military post and a few from that occupation remained. A weather station and a fish canning factory took others to the island, the population of which numbered about 280 on 10 October 1961, when disaster struck. An island volcano, silent for thousands of years, suddenly erupted, covering the island with lava and making it uninhabitable. The islanders were taken off in haste and transported to Britain.

Fridtjof Nansen, born this day in 1861, became an Arctic explorer, drifting in the Arctic ice in his ship *Fram* and later carrying out other scientific explorations in the polar regions. He is remembered also for his political work, particularly with prisoners of war, for which he received a Nobel Prize for Peace in 1922.

For blind people in the past perhaps more than today the world could seem a little remote. One who tried to help them was Dr. William Moon, inventor, in 1845, of the Moon Alphabet. Dr. Moon died on 10 October 1894.

A few other of today's people. . . .
Antoine Watteau, French artist, was born this day in 1684.
Henry Cavendish, physicist and chemist, born in 1731.
Giuseppe Verdi, Italian opera composer, was born in 1813.
Lord Nuffield, car maker and philanthropist, born 1877.
Sir John Betjeman was appointed Poet Laureate in 1972.

Some firsts in London on 10 October. . . .
In 1881 the Savoy theatre became the first theatre in England to be lit by electricity, powered by steam-driven generators.
In 1889 the first London motor omnibus ran between Kennington and Victoria.
In 1955 the first colour television test transmissions in Britain were made from the Alexandra Palace, Wood Green.

Some Michaelmas fairs are held today (see p. 42).

11 October

On 19 July 1545, King Henry VIII watched with pride as his fine warship *Mary Rose*, flagship of the Tudor fleet, sailed from Portsmouth to do battle with the French. A mile off shore, possibly as a result of overloading, she sank, taking over 700 men with her to become entombed in the silt of the Solent for 437 years. On 11 October 1982, she again saw the light of day and was hoisted onto a barge for the return journey to Portsmouth.

The recovery was a triumph for Alexander McKee, a historian who had begun thinking about the *Mary Rose* 40 years before and searching for her some 20 years later. His amateur divers located the wreck and began to bring up many different artifacts — over 10,000 in all.

The salvage of the *Mary Rose* cost £4 million, administered by the Mary Rose Trust, of which Prince Charles became president. In a drydock in Portsmouth harbour, near Nelson's flagship HMS *Victory*, work began to restore the *Mary Rose* as a fascinating museum of Tudor naval history.

This day, in 1797, saw the British naval triumph over the Dutch in the Battle of Camperdown.

Disaster for King John on this day in 1216, when his valuable baggage was lost in the Wash. It has never been found.

Today's birthdays. . . . In 1821, Sir George Williams, who formed a club in 1844 for 'the improvement of the spiritual condition of young men in the drapery and other trades'. It developed into the Young Men's Christian Association (YMCA).

Eleanor Roosevelt, wife of US president Franklin D. Roosevelt, was born on 11 October 1884. She was a great humanitarian, traveller, lecturer, writer and, after her husband's death, delegate to the United Nations. It was written of her: 'No woman has ever so comforted the distressed or so distressed the comfortable.' (Claire Booth Luce).

Huldrych Zwingli, Swiss Protestant reformer, was killed in battle on this day in 1531 whilst serving as chaplain. Two Frenchmen who died on 11 October were naturalist Jean Henri Fabre in 1823 and Jean Cocteau, artist, poet and writer, in 1963. Samuel Wesley, composer, son of hymnwriter Charles Wesley, died on this day in 1837.

12 October

On 12 October 1492, Christopher Columbus stepped ashore from the *Santa Maria* onto an island which he named San Salvador. It is now called Watling Island, one of the Bahamas. Columbus thought he had reached the Spice Islands, the Indies, of the Far East. Instead he had introduced Europe to a whole New World — the Americas.

Three centuries later, probably on this day in 1792, in New York, Americans began to celebrate Columbus Day each year on 12 October, doing so until 1971, when the Monday Holiday Law moved the celebration to the second Monday in October.

In America this day saw the death, in 1870, of General Robert E. Lee, commander of the Confederate army during the American Civil War.

Ten years earlier, in 1860, it witnessed the birth of Elmer Sperry, inventor and industrialist. He made lamps and dynamos, electric cars and locomotives, mining machinery, cutting machines and, most important of all, the gyroscopic compass. He took out more than 400 patents and founded eight companies to manufacture his inventions.

Robert Stephenson, only son of railway pioneer George Stephenson, became a railway engineer and built many important bridges. He died on 12 October 1859.

Ralph Vaughan Williams, English composer, was born on this day in 1872.

Piero della Francesca, only recently recognised as one of the important Italian Renaissance artists, died on the same day that Columbus set foot on American soil, 12 October 1492.

And so to the ladies. . . .

In the world of entertainment, Helena Modjeska, Polish-US Shakespearean actress, was born in 1844. Sonja Henie, ice skater and film star, died in 1969.

Elizabeth Fry, Quaker philanthropist and promoter of prison reform, died in 1845. Madame Rachel, who sought to improve the lot of women, died in prison this day in 1880. Edith Cavell, nurse, shot this day in 1915 by a German firing squad, remarked at the end, *'Patriotism is not enough, I must have no hatred or bitterness towards anyone.'*

Today is the birthday of Margaret Thatcher, who has the distinction of being the first woman to be Prime Minister of Britain. Other countries had been led by a woman but in Britain it had not seemed likely until Margaret Thatcher was elected as leader of the Conservative Party in 1975 to follow Edward Heath.

Born in 1925 to a grocer in Grantham, Lincolnshire, she studied law whilst seeking election to Parliament, which was achieved in 1959. She became a front-bencher two years later and Secretary of State for Education and Science from 1970 to 1974. It was not long before many people had gained a healthy respect for this determined woman, with her sharp mind and tongue, unbending in the face of opposition. In 1976, the Russians referred to her as the 'Iron Lady'. Soon afterwards she was facing up to the challenges, as Prime Minister, of steering through Parliament policies which were unpopular, even with some of her colleagues, yet doing so with a determination that ensured she would leave her mark on British politics as a true leader.

What a long way women have come in Parliament during the present century! It was, in fact, on this day in 1905 that plans were made at a meeting in Manchester to campaign for votes for women. The campaigners were called 'Suffragettes' and were ably led by Mrs. Emmeline Pankhurst, causing many civil disturbances until women were given the right to vote.

13 October 1862, was the birthday of Mary Kingsley. In days when women travellers were few, she journeyed widely in tropical West Africa. She died of fever in South Africa whilst nursing prisoners in a hospital during the Boer War.

On this day in 1917, three children in Fatima, Portugal, had a vision of the Blessed Virgin Mary. Many people today go there to visit the shrine of Our Lady of the Rosary of Fatima.

Few people travel especially to see the shrine of St. Edward the Confessor but many see it, for it is in Westminster Abbey, London, on the site of the abbey he founded. Today is his feast day.

Also in Westminster Abbey are the ashes of Sir Henry Irving, the first actor to be knighted. He died on 13 October 1905.

War and peace make the headlines today, beginning with one of the best-known dates in history, 1066, when the armies of the invading Duke William of Normandy faced the defensive armies of Harold. In the Battle of Hastings, fought on this day, Harold was slain and William became 'the Conqueror', later King William I of England, first of the Norman kings.

One of the great naval disasters of World War II occurred this day in 1939, when the battleship *Royal Oak* was torpedoed whilst in Scapa Flow, Orkney, with a loss of 810 lives.

Dwight D. Eisenhower, born in the USA on 14 October 1890, led his country's forces in war as World War II supreme commander, and his country in peace as president 1952–60.

William Penn, Quaker, born this day in 1644, was a man of peace who founded Pennsylvania and made peace with the Indians.

Also in America, Martin Luther King endeavoured to gain civil rights by peaceful means. On this day, in 1964, he was awarded a Nobel prize for peace.

Eamon De Valera, born on 14 October 1882, was a front-line fighter for Irish independence from Great Britain, and later served Eire as prime minister then president.

Today in the air, the airship *R101* had its first trials in 1929. In 1947 the supersonic bang was first heard as a Bell XS-1 rocket plane broke the sound barrier at 670 mph (1,078 km/h).

In the world of entertainment on this day. . . .
In 1940 Cliff Richard, popular singer, was born.
In 1942 Dame Marie Tempest, actress, died.
In 1976 Dame Edith Evans, English actress, died.
In 1977 'Bing' Crosby, American popular singer, died.

Josh Billings, real name Henry Wheeler Shaw, who died on 14 October 1885, entertained many people with his almanacks and other collections of witty sayings. The one below could well be used as a guide to human achievement.

Consider the postage stamp; its usefulness consists in the ability to stick to one thing until it gets there.

15 October

Abu-ul-fath-jalal-ud-din Muhammad Akbar was born on 15 October 1542 in Sind (now in Pakistan). Akbar means 'the great' and it was an appropriate name for the one who was to become the greatest of the Mogul Emperors. At thirteen he became governor of the Punjab and at eighteen succeeded his father as emperor. Soon all the states of northern India were within his empire, which he ruled wisely and justly, encouraging trade, justice and good order. Though a Muslim he married a Hindu princess and he allowed Christian priests to teach him, for he wanted people of all religions to live in peace in his empire.

Long before, on 15 October 70 BC, Publius Vergilius Maro was born. He became known as Virgil, the greatest Roman poet, remembered especially for his *Aeneid*, a 12-volume epic based on the legendary founding of Rome by the Trojan Aeneas.

Some other of today's birthdays. . . .
In 1858 John L. Sullivan, one of the most popular heavyweight champions of the bare-knuckle era of boxing. His last fight under the old bare-knuckle (London Prize Ring) rules was a 75-round knockout.
In 1881 P. G. Wodehouse, novelist, short-story writer and playwright, creator of well-known characters such as Jeeves and Bertie Wooster.
In 1905 C. P. (later Baron) Snow, British novelist, physicist and government administrator.

An abrupt end on 15 October. . . .
In 1917 for Mata Hari, Dutch-born seductive female spy of World War I. Accused of spying for the Germans, she was shot by a French firing squad.
In 1945 for Pierre Laval, French statesman who led the Vichy government in France, collaborating with the Germans in World War II. He was tried for treason and executed.
In 1946 Hermann Goering, German Nazi leader. He was found guilty of war crimes at the Nürnberg trials and sentenced to be hanged, but he committed suicide by taking poison.

The Gregorian Calendar was adopted in Catholic countries in 1582.
Ether was first publicly demonstrated as an anaesthetic in 1846.

Be of good comfort, Master Ridley, and play the man. We shall this day light such a candle by God's grace, in England, as I trust shall never be put out.

So spoke Bishop Hugh Latimer to Bishop Nicholas Ridley as they were about to be burned at the stake in front of Balliol College, Oxford, on 16 October 1555. Those were days of religious persecution and intolerance. Because of their part in the protestant changes in England during the reigns of Henry VIII and Edward VI, they were examined during Mary's Roman Catholic reign, found guilty of heresy and burned.

*John Brown's body lies a mouldering in his grave
But his soul goes marching on.*

He, too, helped to fan a flame that was to sweep through America. On 16 October 1859, John Brown, with a band of 21, captured the armoury at Harper's Ferry as part of a plan to establish a stronghold for freed slaves. John Brown was captured with others and executed but he came to be regarded as a martyr in the anti-slavery cause and this raid helped the election of Abraham Lincoln as president of the USA.

A fire of a different sort broke out on this day in 1834 and the House of Commons was burned down. The blaze was started by the burning of old tally sticks.

And a light was started near Plymouth on 16 October 1759, with the official opening of John Smeaton's new Eddystone Lighthouse.

Born today. . . .
In 1758 Noah Webster, American dictionary compiler.
In 1803 Robert Stephenson, railway bridge engineer.
In 1854 Oscar Wilde, Irish poet and dramatist.
In 1900 Edward Ardizzone, illustrator and author of many children's books.

On this day, in 1793, Queen Marie Antoinette went to the guillotine; and John Hunter, Scottish surgeon, died. He was one of the earliest to investigate the human body and carried out many experiments in anatomy, physiology and pathology.

17 October

What things in life are of the greatest value? And how do we assess their value? For the collector, rarity or uniqueness is often the deciding factor. Philatelists know that they will have to pay a lot of money to buy a rare stamp for their collection. For many years the most valuable stamp in the world was one from British Guyana but, at an auction in Hamburg, on 17 October 1978, a Swedish 1855 3-shilling stamp, until then considered the second most valuable, was sold for a record one million Deutschmarks, the equivalent of about £270,000.

And the value of a drink of water? Most people recall how Sir Philip Sidney offered his water to a soldier wounded at Zutphen with the words 'Your need is greater than mine' (p. 27). Sir Philip, who died on 17 October 1586, is probably remembered more for this chivalrous act than for his great achievements as politician, soldier and one of the finest prose and poetry writers of his time.

What price a king? On 17 October 1346, King David of Scotland was captured by the English at the Battle of Neville's Cross. He was imprisoned for eleven years, then released for an agreed ransom of 100,000 marks. It proved more than the Scots could find, however, and most remained unpaid.

The value of an invention may be seen in various ways. Sir Henry Bessemer patented the Bessemer converter for manufacturing steel cheaply on 17 October 1855. It made Sir Henry a very rich man: its value to the world is incalculable.

Al Capone, Chicago gangster, made his wealth from bootlegging and vice but it was of little use when he was sentenced to eleven years in gaol on 17 October 1931 — on a charge of income tax evasion. And Chicago valued his absence from the city!

At St. Audrey's Fair, Ely, on this day long ago, cheap lace — St. Audrey's lace, or 'Tawdry' lace — was sold. But how many young ladies valued that bought by a special young man!

And on 17 October, how might we value these?
. . . the music of Frédéric Chopin, who died this day in 1849.
. . . the plays of Arthur Miller, US playwright, born in 1915.
. . . Calder Hall Atomic Power Station, opened in 1956.

61

St. Luke, patron saint of physicians and painters, writer of the third gospel and of the Acts of the Apostles, is thought to have been a doctor. Luke, the evangelist, accompanied St. Paul on one of his missionary journeys.

Another missionary journey began on 18 October 1932, when former parlourmaid Gladys Aylward left London for Tientsin, China, to begin an adventure which has become a modern-day legend. She began with an inn for mule-drivers but she was soon involved in many ways — as government foot inspector, quelling a gaol riot, but also helping the poor, giving advice and, in an unobtrusive manner, teaching about her Christian faith.

War between China and Japan changed her way of life and led to her involvement in the greatest adventure of all when she led a large band of orphans through hundreds of miles of war-torn partly enemy-occupied territory to safety — a journey that many would have considered quite impossible.

Thomas Alva Edison also did what might have been considered impossible. The American genius took out over 1,000 patents for his inventions (p. 207). He died on 18 October 1931.

The work of Giovanni Antonio Canal, born in Venice on 18 October 1697, was unexpectedly different. As the artist Canaletto, he went out of doors and painted from nature — the Venetian scenes that were to make his reputation.

Some other of today's people. . . .
Richard 'Beau' Nash, leader of fashion (p. 201) born 1674.
Lord Palmerston, British prime minister, died 1865.
Pierre Trudeau, Canadian prime minister, born 1919.
Charles Gounod, French composer, died 1893.

Many women have been grateful to Elizabeth Arden, founder of the cosmetics company of that name. She died on this day in 1966. No doubt her treatment seems preferable to the old-time anointing recommended to young women for St. Luke's Day. If they wanted an insight to future love, they were to anoint themselves with a mixture of marigolds, marjoram, thyme, wormwood, honey and vinegar, then repeat three times in bed:

St. Luke, St. Luke, be kind to me,
In dreams let me my true love see.

19 October

The largest gold nugget ever to be found was discovered on 19 October 1872. The Holtermann Nugget weighed 7,560 ounces (472.5 lbs: 214.32 kg).

Another discovery was announced on this day in 1807. Sir Humphry Davy had discovered how to isolate sodium. Davy, a Cornishman, was one of England's greatest scientists. Besides sodium, he discovered other chemical elements, experimented with gases, invented the Davy safety lamp for miners, researched in agricultural chemistry and other fields of science and delivered many popular lectures.

On this day in 1937 the world lost one of its greatest scientists by the death of Lord Rutherford, a brilliant physicist who laid the foundations for the development of nuclear physics and influenced the work of many other scientists. He was the winner of the Nobel Prize for Chemistry in 1908 and a Member of the Royal Society. His ashes were placed in Westminster Abbey near the remains of other great scientists.

Another physicist to die on this day, in 1875, was Sir Charles Wheatstone (p. 203), who invented the Wheatstone bridge, for accurately measuring electrical resistance, and other devices.

Auguste Lumiére, who was born in France on 19 October 1862, was also a scientist who, with his brother, Louis, put his mind to various aspects of the development of photography. The brothers worked on the means of developing films, improvements in colour photography and means of projection. They also made films and presented the first newsreel.

Jonathan Swift, author of *Gulliver's Travels*, was an Irish poet, writer, satirist and churchman. He became Dean of St. Patrick's Cathedral, Dublin, and was regarded as Dublin's foremost citizen until his death on 19 October 1745.

This day, in 1536, saw the taking of York by Robert Aske in the rebellion in the north of England known as the Pilgrimage of Grace. The pilgrimage achieved nothing. Aske and upwards of 200 of the rebels were executed in the following year.

'If you are seeking his monument, look about you'

These words, engraved in Latin, are to be found on a plain tomb in the crypt of St. Paul's Cathedral. It is the tomb of Sir Christopher Wren and his greatest memorial is indeed the great cathedral which he designed and in which he is buried.

Christopher Wren was born in Wiltshire on 20 October 1632. He was very clever as a scientist, mathematician and astronomer, but it is as a designer of buildings that he is most remembered. Besides St. Paul's Cathedral, he was responsible for rebuilding fifty-one churches in London after the Great Fire. He also designed the Monument, Temple Bar and other buildings in London and Oxford, as well as the Royal Observatory and Maritime Museum at Greenwich.

In Bamburgh, Northumberland, is a memorial of a different kind — a museum of relics connected with Grace Darling, who died when only 27 on 20 October 1842. She became famous four years earlier after helping her father, the keeper of the Longstone lighthouse on the Farne Islands, to rescue nine survivors from the steamer *Forfarshire*, wrecked on a neighbouring island.

Sarah Ann Glover died on 20 October 1867. Who was she? She may not be known to many by name but her contribution to the world of music is continually before people. She invented the Tonic Sol-fa system of notation. So, next time you sing Doh-ray-me, remember Sarah Ann.

Some 20 October birthdays. . . .
Lord Palmerston, statesman, in 1784.
Thomas Hughes, author *(Tom Brown's Schooldays)*,in 1822.
John Burns, statesman, in 1858.

Thomas Linacre, founder of the Royal College of Physicians, died on this day in 1524.
Sir Richard Burton, traveller and writer, translator into English of *The Arabian Nights*, died on 20 October 1890.

Some important battles fought on 20 October. . . Salamis in 480 BC, Ulm in 1805, Navarino in 1827 and Aachen in 1944.

England expects that every man will do his duty.

With this signal, the British men-of-war, led by Lord Nelson on HMS *Victory*, headed for and shattered the French fleet commanded by Admiral de Villeneuve off Cape Trafalgar, near the entrance to the Mediterranean Sea in 1805. In the Battle of Trafalgar the French lost nearly a third of their ships and the British none but, in the closing stages of the battle, the British lost their great Admiral, Nelson, mortally wounded by a sniper's bullet. The Battle of Trafalgar marked the end of Napoleon's hopes to gain the mastery of the seas. It also marked the end of an era, for the 'wooden walls', the great wooden warships, were giving way to those built of iron and steel.

Alfred Nobel, the Swedish philanthropist, was born on 21 October 1833. He studied chemistry and engineering before turning to the development and manufacture of explosives. Thought of as a 'mad scientist', he developed dynamite and other new explosives. His vast fortune was mainly left to establish the Nobel Prizes for peace, literature, physics, chemistry and medicine.

He prayeth well, who loveth well
Both man and bird and beast,
He prayeth best, who loveth best
All things both great and small;
For the dear God who loveth us,
He made and loveth all.

Samuel Taylor Coleridge, who wrote this, was born on 21 October 1772 and became one of the leading English Romantic poets.

Five years later, on this day in 1777, Samuel Foote died. He was an actor and playwright, who delighted many with his wit and mimicry, often at the expense of his friends. He once wrote, 'If we do not take liberties with our friends, with whom can we take liberties?'

There were only tragic faces in Aberfan, South Wales, on 21 October 1966. A coal tip suddenly moved and engulfed the village school, killing 144 including 116 children.

A number of people gazed skyward on 22 October 1797, in Paris, curious to see what was happening. They saw André Garverin float down from a balloon and make the first ever successful parachute jump. As he swung to and fro, he was violently sick — over some of his spectators.

Dr. Hawley Crippen must also have been feeling pretty sick on this day in 1910. Having poisoned and dismembered his wife, he fled with his mistress, Ethel Le Neve, to America but he was apprehended on board and returned to Britain, where he was convicted of murder on 22 October 1910. It was the first time radio had been used for this purpose.

No one was convicted of the murder of Admiral Sir Cloudesley Shovell, who was killed on 22 October 1707. His ship, the *Association*, with three other ships, was wrecked off the Cornish coast on this day and over 2,000 officers and men were drowned. The admiral reached shore alive but was killed for his emerald ring.

A mystery in New York on this day in 1936. What happened to Frederick Lloyd? He was a successful businessman, almost a millionaire and happily married. He stepped into a taxi and was never seen again.

Still in New York, it was on 22 October 1883, that the Metropolitan Opera House opened, on 39th Street. Many famous singers gave performances there until it was replaced in 1966.

This was the birthday, in 1845, of the celebrated French actress Sarah Bernhardt. She played to audiences in many lands and opened her own theatre in Paris.

In the world of music, this was the birthday, in 1811, of Franz Liszt, the greatest piano virtuoso of his day and renowned as a composer. Ludwig Spohr, violinist, composer and conductor, died on 22 October 1859; and Pablo Casals, cellist and conductor, on this day in 1973.

Three others who died . . . Jean Grolier, French patron of writers and printers, in 1565; Thomas Sheraton, English furniture designer, in 1806; and Arnold Toynbee, historian, in 1976.

23 October

Marcus Junius Brutus is remembered mainly as the conspirator in Rome who pulled his dagger and assassinated Julius Caesar in the Senate in March 44 BC. Afterwards he left Rome to raise an army in Macedonia to fight against Mark Antony. Then he fought against Octavian (who later became the Emperor Augustus) and was successful, but in a later battle his army was soundly defeated by Antony and Octavian on 23 October 42 BC. Realising that his republican cause was lost, Brutus took his own life.

On 23 October 1642, 11,000 Royalist supporters lined up against 13,000 Parliamentarians in the first battle of the English Civil War, but the result of the Battle of Edgehill was inconclusive.

Another battle to begin on this day was the second Battle of El Alamein in 1942. It was one of the important battles of World War II. General Bernard Montgomery, the new commander of the Eighth Army, the 'Desert Rats', began an offensive which not only prevented the Germans from reaching Egypt but began to force them back into Tunisia.

William Gilbert Grace did his battling on the cricket fields. The formidable bearded doctor became a legendary figure in English cricket — an outstanding batsman and bowler who drew large crowds to enjoy his psychological tactics as well as his entertaining cricket. He died on this day in 1915.

Edson Arantes do Nascimento was born in Brazil on 23 October 1940. The football pitch became his battleground and he gained international fame under the name of Pelé. He played in the Brazil World Cup-winning teams of 1958, 1962 and 1970 and became the only player to score more than 1,000 goals in first-class football.

Gary Gabelich became the fastest man on earth on this day in 1970, when his rocket-powered *Blue Flame* reached 631.36 mph (1,016 km/h) on the Bonneville Salt Flats, Utah, USA.

Robert Bridges, Poet Laureate 1913–30, was born in 1844. He had previously been a physician in London hospitals.

It was on this day, in 1945, that the United Nations Organisation was established by charter, its main aim being to maintain international peace and security but also develop friendly relationships and to encourage international co-operation to solve the many problems facing the world. Various agencies were later established within the United Nations framework.

We recall that peace came to Europe on this day in 1648, with the signing of the Treaty of Westphalia, bringing to an end the Thirty Years War between the French and the Holy Roman Empire. The term Peace of Westphalia also includes the ending of the Eighty Years War between the Spanish and the Dutch earlier in the year.

It is, perhaps, appropriate that today's people are drawn from many lands.

Tycho Brahe was a Danish astronomer who built an observatory, Uraniborg. His findings were proof of the theories of Copernicus about the solar system. Brahe died this day in 1601.

Antonie van Leeuwenhoek, the Dutch scientist, set his sights much nearer. He was an amateur scientist who built an effective microscope and was the first man to see and study bacteria. In 1680, he was made a Fellow of the British Royal Society. This was his birthday in 1632.

This was also the birthday of Dame Sybil Thorndike, one of the most versatile of English actresses. Born in Lincolnshire in 1882, she later joined the Old Vic Company in London and played many roles, classical and modern, tragic and comic.

Christian Dior, the French dress designer, who led the fashion world in the years following World War II, died in Italy on 24 October 1957.

Franz Lehár, Austrian composer of *The Merry Widow* and other operettas, died on 24 October 1948.

When Norway was occupied by the Germans during World War II, Vidkun Quisling, who had urged Hitler to invade, set himself up as head of the government. When Norway was liberated in 1945, Quisling was tried, found guilty of treason and executed on 24 October of that year.

The finest Gothic cathedral, Notre Dame, in Chartres, France, with magnificent rose windows and fine statues, was consecrated on 24 October 1260.

The twenty-fifth of October,
Cursed be the cobbler
Who goes to bed sober!

This old Herefordshire saying is a reminder that St. Crispin, whose feast day this is, is the patron saint of shoemakers and cobblers and that such people should celebrate appropriately.

This day gave cause for celebration of a different kind long ago, for it was on St. Crispin's Day that the Battle of Agincourt was fought during the Hundred Years' War between England and France. The English longbowmen wrought havoc with the French and won a decisive victory.

How different on this day in 1854! There was not much to celebrate concerning the military blunder in which six hundred men of the Light Brigade were sent to their destruction by Russian guns at Balaclava.

Cannon to right of them,
Cannon to left of them,
Cannon in front of them
Volleyed and thundered.
Into the jaws of Death,
Into the mouth of Hell
Rode the Six Hundred.

This was the birthday, in 1825, of Johann Strauss the Younger, in Vienna. He was the composer of operettas and waltzes including the *Blue Danube*. It was the birthday, too, in 1838, of the French composer of the opera *Carmen* and other music, Georges Bizet. Also born this day, in 1881, was one of the most influential artists of this century, the creator of Cubism, Pablo Picasso. Thomas B. Macaulay, politician and historian, was born on this day, too, in 1800. Richard Byrd, pioneer aviator and polar explorer, was born on 25 October 1888.

Geoffrey Chaucer, the great English poet, who gave us the *Canterbury Tales*, died on 25 October 1400.

The worst ever outbreak of foot-and-mouth disease in Britain began on 25 October 1967. 429,632 animals had to be slaughtered.

Widecombe Fair was first held on this day in 1350.

26 October

Some people seem to have more than their share of burdens, yet succeed in spite of this. Charles P. Steinmetz was badly deformed and could only work whilst supporting himself on a stool whilst half standing, but he fought against his physical difficulties whilst experimenting with electricity until he became a wizard in electrical matters, rivalling Edison in the number of inventions and discoveries. He died on 26 October 1923.

This day also saw the death, in 1764, of William Hogarth, who is remembered especially for his art which made fun of some of the social happenings of his day and for his series of paintings which drew moral stories.

Also on this day. . . .
The Football Association was formed in 1863.
Mohammed Reza Shah Pahlavi, (Iran), was born in 1919.
The new chamber of the House of Commons opened in 1950.
Igor Sikorsky, aeroplane and helicopter engineer, died in 1972.

27 October

A few of today's birthdays. . . .
Desiderius Erasmus was the name adopted by Gerrit Gerritszoon, the great Dutch humanist and scholar of the Middle Ages, born on 27 or 28 October 1466.
Captain James Cook, who surveyed Canadian waters, explored the Pacific, circumnavigated New Zealand and claimed the east of Australia for Britain, was born in 1728.
Nicolo Paganini, one of the world's most famous and talented violinists, was born in Genoa in 1782.
Isaac Singer was born in 1811. He gave the world a greatly improved sewing machine and also promoted the instalment credit plan which was to change the face of business.
In 1854 Sir William A. Smith, founder of the Boys' Brigade.
In 1858 Theodore Roosevelt, 26th president of the USA.
In 1914 Dylan Thomas, Welsh poet and writer.

The Arbroath lifeboat was lost in a full gale this day in 1953.

This was the birthday, in 901, of Alfred the Great, generally accepted as one of the greatest kings in Anglo-Saxon England. King of the West Saxons, his kingdom, Wessex, covered the south-west of England. He fought successfully against the Danish invaders and eventually became overlord of the whole of England. He is remembered for his writings, for his invention of the candle-clock and for legislation and reforms aimed at the improvement of the lot of his people.

Over a thousand years later, another was born who was to affect the lives of many people. He was Jonas Salk, born on 28 October 1914 of Polish-Jewish immigrants living in New York, who became interested in medical research, working for a time on an influenza vaccine and later discovering, in 1953, a vaccine to prevent poliomyelitis, which previously had claimed the lives of many people or crippled them for life. He then channelled his energies into cancer research.

One of the surprises of this day was the election, in 1958, of Cardinal Angelo Giuseppe Roncalli as Pope. To most people he was one of the outsiders, yet, at the age of 77, he was elected and took the title of Pope John XXIII. He had previously held a number of high offices in the Roman Catholic Church as secretary, military chaplain, bishop in Bulgaria, Papal Nuncio to France and Patriarch of Venice, all of which gave him valuable experience and useful contacts. His 4½ years as Pope saw the beginning of various changes in the Roman Catholic Church and a move toward closer co-operation with other Christian denominations. 'That they all may be one', was the prayer frequently on his lips.

John Smeaton brought a little light into the world — for sailors. He was an engineer of waterwheels and windmills, of canals and harbours, but he is especially remembered for his Eddystone lighthouse, the third on those rocks. He died on 28 October 1792.

In 1886 the Statue of Liberty in New York harbour was dedicated.

In Britain, on 28 October 1965, the death penalty for murder was abolished by Act of Parliament.

Give me my scallop-shell of quiet,
My staff of faith to walk upon,
My scrip of joy, immortal diet,
My bottle of salvation.
My gown of glory, hope's true gage,
And thus I'll take my pilgrimage.

Sir Walter Raleigh, whose words these are, had a very varied life as adventurer, navigator, courtier and writer, sometimes in and sometimes out of favour at court. At one time a firm favourite of Queen Elizabeth I, he was later imprisoned in the Tower of London. Then he set out on an expedition to seek the gold of Eldorado. In 1603, he was again arrested, tried and committed to the Tower. Again, in 1617, he sailed for South America but, at the end of a disastrous expedition, he was arrested because Spain wished it, and again committed to the Tower, from which he took the last stage of his pilgrimage to be beheaded in Whitehall on 29 October 1618.

Life's pilgrimage also ended today, in 1911, for Joseph Pulitzer, the American newspaper magnate. Born of Magyar-Jewish and Austro-German parents in Hungary, he emigrated to America and served a while in the army. Then, from being a penniless reporter he began to acquire newspapers, using his wealth to endow the Columbia University School of Journalism and to establish the Pulitzer prizes for various aspects of journalism.

The big news in America on 29 October 1929 was the collapse of the New York stock market. After a slump in stock prices and some panic selling by the Wall Street brokers, thousands of investors lost all their savings and some ended life's pilgrimage by committing suicide rather than face financial ruin. This day is seen by many as the beginning of the great depression of the '30s.

On 29 October 1945, the Atomic Energy Research Establishment was set up at Harwell.

In 1956, Israeli forces invaded the Sinai peninsular at the outset of the Five Day War.

James Boswell, the biographer of Dr. Samuel Johnson, died on this day in 1740.

Visitors to London are often fascinated by the old-time scarlet and gold uniforms of the Yeomen of the Guard, seen, perhaps, in ceremonial processions, at the state opening of Parliament or on duty at the Tower of London — reminders of a bygone age.

Founded on this day in 1485, the Yeomen of the Guard were the personal bodyguard of King Henry VII and, for a couple of hundred years, this was their function, protecting the king in battle. The 20th Century demands a different kind of protection for the sovereign and the duties of the Yeomen of the Guard are of a ceremonial nature, the company consisting of veteran soldiers, proud to wear their colourful 15th-Century uniforms.

Another body recalled today is the International Red Cross, founded as a result of the inspiration of Jean Henri Dunant, the Swiss philanthropist, who died on 30 October 1910.

Edmund Cartwright received his inspiration during a visit to Sir Richard Arkwright's mills in 1784. During the next few years, he developed a power loom, which aided the development of the textile industry during the Industrial Revolution. He also took out patents for wool-combing machines and other inventions. He died on 30 October 1823.

A century and a half later, Sir Barnes Neville Wallis was putting his mind to other developments and inventions. He it was who designed, in the 1920s, the airship *R100* and, during World War II, invented the bouncing bomb. In post-war years, he invented the first swing-wing aircraft. He died this day in 1979.

Angelica Kauffman was born in Switzerland on 30 October 1741. As a child she showed great musical and artistic talent. She painted a number of portraits but is especially remembered for decorative wall paintings in residences designed by Robert Adam and in other public buildings.

Ten years later, Richard Brinsley Sheridan was born in Ireland. From boyhood he lived in England, where he became a showman, playwright, theatre manager and Member of Parliament.

The Battle of Salado, Spain, fought this day in 1340, halted the advance of the Moors into Europe. Thereafter they were slowly driven back to Africa.

Many are the customs and beliefs associated with this day — and particularly the evening — most of them because this was the 'day before'. To the ancient Celts it was the day before winter officially began, and with it the New Year. So this was New Year's Eve when the great fires, the teanleas, tandles or tindles were lit on the hilltops. In later years it became the day before the Christian festival of All Hallows, or All Saints' Day.

Hallowe'en, which naturally adopted some of the old traditions, became the day for driving out evil — and equally for guarding against evil, for it was believed that witches and other undesirables made the most of this evening, since they would be unable to do so on the following holy day.

> For on Hallowmas Eve the Nighthag shall ride,
> And all her nine-fold sweeping on by her side.
> *Waverley*, Sir Walter Scott

Various methods were used to drive away the evil forces. These included the lighting of fires and the making of fearsome turnip-lanterns or 'punkies'. Today they are made more to scare friends than to scare witches! They are part of the fun of this day which may include traditional games such as duck-apple or snap-apple (bob-apple).

Apples play an important role at Hallowe'en in various forms of divination — or prediction. If a girl cut an apple whilst standing before a mirror, it was believed she would see the face of her future husband in the mirror. Another was that she should peel an apple, keeping the peel in one piece, then wave this three times round her head. When dropped to the ground, it would fall into the shape of her future husband's initial. An apple placed under the pillow would induce dreams of a future husband.

Nuts were also used in many parts of the country for similar predictions. Often they were placed on or near the fire and their behaviour as they became hot or burned would indicate all sorts of interesting things about the future. There were many other forms of prediction, too, which could only be performed on this night, using eggs, metals, candles and other suitable objects.

Apples and nuts, however, were by far the most common and were also believed to have anti-witching powers.

One who did not believe in supernatural powers and was always happy to expose mediums and mind readers as fakes, was Harry Houdini, the conjurer who was famous for his great escapes. 'The Great Houdini' could escape from handcuffs and shackles with ease. He performed spectacular escape acts, as from a submerged box that was locked and roped after he had been shackled inside. 'Nothing on earth can hold Houdini a prisoner', claimed the posters advertising his acts, and they appeared to be right.

Various people suggested that he had supernatural powers or the ability to dematerialise and pass through walls but he claimed that everything was carefully planned. Yet he did believe in omens, and he had a strange premonition of his death, which occurred, appropriately enough, on 31 October 1926.

Sir Joseph Swan was born on this day in 1828. Some of his inventions must almost have made him seem like a magician in his day. He invented an electric lamp nearly 20 years before Edison but was unable to find how to make it a practical proposition. He was also a pioneer in photography, inventing dry photographic plates, a new method of printing photographs and bromide paper. He also produced the first artificial fibres for use in the textile industry.

Two great Dutch artists have associations with today. Jan Vermeer was born in 1632 and Meindert Hobbema was baptised in 1638. Vermeer achieved fame with townscapes and portraits renowned for precise detail and the use of natural light. Hobbema painted peaceful landscapes, of which his *The Avenue, Middelharnis,* now in the National Gallery, London, is one of the most popular of Dutch landscape paintings.

Other great and determined people born on 31 October. . . . John Evelyn, author and diarist, in 1620; Chiang Kai-shek, Chinese soldier and ruler, in 1886; Sir Hubert Wilkins, polar explorer in 1888; and John Keats, poet, in 1795, who wrote

I would sooner fail than not be among the greatest.

It was on this day, in 1517, that Martin Luther nailed his 95 Theses to the cathedral door at Wittenburg.

Other October Events and Commemorations

(see also pp. 41–4)

7th Twyford, Hampshire: Bellringers' Feast commemorating the saving, by hearing the church bells, of William Davies from falling down a chalkpit on 7 October 1753, when he was on his way home in the fog. He bequeathed money for an annual feast provided that the bells were rung morning and evening on that day.

10th (unless it is a Sunday) Tewkesbury, Gloucestershire: Barton Fair and Ram Roasting has been held since the 11th Century.

About 20th Colchester, Essex: Oyster Feast. Held annually for hundreds of years. Associated with St. Denys's Fair.

21st Portsmouth, Hampshire, and Trafalgar Square, London: Trafalgar Day Ceremonies commemorating the battle in 1805.

About 23rd Bristol, Avon: Redcliffe Pipe Walk. The vicar and parishioners of St. Mary Redcliffe walk the course of a conduit from Rugewell to the church, commemorating permission given in the 12th Century for water to be taken from this well.

Last Thursday Hinton St. George, Somerset: Punkie Night. Children parade with their hollowed-out mangel-wurzels, singing and asking for money or candles.

Hallowe'en Newcastle-upon-Tyne: Dookie Apple Night.

Sometime in month In various places: Court Leets to appoint local officers or make arrangements for future events.

SOME OCTOBER FAIRS

In various places: Fun fairs, formerly hiring fairs (p. 43).

First Thursday Nottingham Goose Fair (3 days).

6th Petersfield, Hampshire: Horse Fair (formerly known as Taro Fair).

Second Wednesday Tavistock, Devon: Goose Fair.

Second Thursday Wilton, Wiltshire: Sheep Fair.

Second Thursday Leicester: Sheep Fair; *Friday* Cattle Fair.

Week in which 11th falls Hull, Humberside: Corporation Fair.

Last Thursday Bampton, Devon: Pony Fair. Sale of Exmoor ponies.

Sometime in month Chichester, Sussex: Sloe Fair.
Yarm, Yorkshire: Cheese Fair.

SOME OTHER EVENTS

Royal Jersey Autumn Show.
Horse of the Year Show, Wembley.

NOVEMBER

November

November takes its name from the Latin *novem* because it was once the ninth month of the year. To the Anglo-Saxons it may have been known as *Blodmonath* (Blood month) because it was during this month that many of the animals had to be slaughtered owing to the lack of winter fodder. Alternatively it was the *Windmonath*, the windy month.

November is usually considered a rather dreary month, with fog and rain, indeed with very little to be said in its favour, as summarised in these words of Thomas Hood.

No sun, no moon,
No morn, no noon,
No dawn, no dusk, no proper time of day;
No sky, no earthly view,
No distance looking blue.

No road, no street, no t'other side the way;
No end to any row,
No indications where the crescents go,
No top to any steeple,
No recognition of familiar people,
No courtesies for showing them,
No knowing them,
No travelling at all, no locomotion,
No inkling of the way, no notion,
No go by land or ocean,
No mail, no post,
No news from any foreign coast,
No park, no ring, no afternoon gentility,
No company, no nobility,

No warmth, no cheerfulness, no healthful ease,
No comfortable feel in any member,
No shade, no shine, no butterflies, no bees,
No fruits, no flowers, no leaves, no trees:
November!

November's sky is chill and drear,
November's leaf is red and sear.
Marmion, Sir Walter Scott

Amid the greyness, November may have its brighter periods. A warm spell around Martinmas (p. 93) is usually referred to as St. Martin's summer. Very early in the month people are beginning to look for signs that may foretell the winter's weather. One old country saying sums it up:

Ice in November to bear a duck,
Nothing after but slush and muck.

An old rhyme from Buckinghamshire suggests that if ponds freeze at Hollantide, an old name for Hallowe'en, it will be warm at Christmas and vice versa.

If ducks do slide at Hollantide
At Christmas they will swim;
If ducks do swim at Hollantide
At Christmas they will slide.

And All Saints' Day, 1 November, is said to bring with it the second summer. But how long will it last?

All Saints' Summer lasts three hours, three days or three weeks.

However long the second summer may last, there is normally an official ending to any season. For the ancient Celts this was Samhain — 'the end of summer' — coinciding with the present 1 November. It was the most important of their festivals, for it marked the beginning of the new year. The eve of Samhain was regarded as a time for magic and some of the ancient customs and traditions of that day inevitably developed into those of the Hallowe'en of later years (p. 74–5).

In the world of nature, winter is fast approaching. Many of the animals which hibernate have already done so: others will not be long. Certain kinds of bird begin to flock together and huge flocks of starlings may be seen. Some of the birds which winter on our shores have already arrived from the Arctic lands. In this month many people begin to give more thought to feeding the wild birds looking for winter food. Deciduous trees have mainly completed the shedding of their leaves before the end of the month, leaving their branches stark and bare but providing a blanket for small plants in the ground beneath.

Remembrance

November may be regarded as the month of remembrance. It begins with two days in the calendar of the Christian Church in which people of the past are remembered.

1 November is All Saints' Day, or All Hallows. This is the day on which the Church commemorates all the saints who have not been allocated a feast day of their own. The Eastern Church keeps the Sunday after Whitsun for this observance but the Western Church changed the date to 1 November when Pope Gregory III on that date dedicated the Basilica of St. Peter in Rome to 'All the Saints'. So, on this day, special prayers of thanksgiving are offered for holy men and women, whose lives have enriched the world.

2 November is All Souls' Day, when prayers are offered for the souls of all faithful people who have died. It used to be the custom for church bells to toll all day. It was also believed that the souls of the dead might like a meal on that day and so special 'soul cakes' were baked. They were usually spiced, flat biscuit-like cakes. The poor would sometimes go 'a-souling' on the evening of All Hallows to beg for 'soul cakes' . . . or money! (p. 82).

5 November marks remembrance of a different kind as people commemorate the Gunpowder Plot on or about this day (p. 86).

The main remembrance is that of Remembrance Sunday, when people remember those who died in the two World Wars. Originally on Armistice Day, 11 November, the commemoration was moved to the nearest Sunday to that date after World War II (p. 92).

On the Saturday evening a Festival of Remembrance is held in the Royal Albert Hall, London. The procession of flags of the Royal British Legion and the military music are part of a moving ceremony attended by war veterans and relatives of those who died.

In the grounds of Westminster Abbey are the plots of ground in which small wooden crosses with poppies are 'planted' according to service or regiment, in memory of individuals. Nearby, in Whitehall, on Sunday morning, the main Service of Remembrance is held at the Cenotaph, attended by the Queen and national leaders, who lay wreaths there. Such services are held at War Memorials in many towns and villages.

No problems today! All the witches, wizards, warlocks, goblins and evil spirits were put in their place last night amid the noisy or scary celebrations of Hallowe'en. They would not dare, in any case, to appear on a day so holy as All Hallows, or All Saints' Day. So today we can sit back and think of all the saints who have given much to mankind (p. 80).

We think of others, too, who may not be regarded as saints but who have given something of value. Alexander Cruden was a Scottish author who became a London bookseller. In 1737, he published his *Complete Concordance to the Holy Scriptures*, an index of every word in the Bible, giving the setting in which it appears with the name of the book, number of chapter and verse. It has been of great value to Bible scholars, preachers and others. Millions of copies have been sold and are still being sold over two hundred years after Cruden's death on 1 November 1770.

Who cannot recognise a Lowry ? His paintings, so distinctive in style, are to be seen in homes, schools and public buildings far from Salford, where he spent his life painting industrial scenes in dull colours with 'matchstalk men and matchstalk cats and dogs'. They are simple pictures yet full of life and with a character which clearly distinguishes them.

L. S. Lowry was born in Manchester on 1 November 1887. Regarded as a little odd or eccentric, it was not until late in life that he became widely known and accepted as one of the great artists of the 20th Century. Industrial Lancashire became 'Lowryland'.

Also born on this day was an artist with an eye for accuracy and beauty. Benvenuto Cellini was born in Florence in 1500 and was greatly influenced by Michelangelo. He was a sculptor and a goldsmith, producing large sculptures as well as fine gold work such as the famous salt-cellar made for Francis I of France.

A man with an eye for detail in a different sense was John Lindley, a British botanist who introduced a good system for classifying plants. He died on 1 November 1865.

It was on this day in 1922 that radio receiving licences were first introduced in Britain. They cost ten shillings.

In a sense, today began yesterday. In the Christian Calendar, 2 November is designated as All Souls' Day (p. 80). At one time church bells were rung on the evening of All Saints' Day, for people believed that this would help the souls of those who were in purgatory and who would be remembered on All Souls' Day. People would also have been busy making flat spiced 'soul cakes', needed for those who called on 2 November.

At one time the soul cakes might be sent to the relatives of folk who died but gradually it became customary for people to go 'souling' — that is begging for cakes for the souls of the dead.

Again times changed. By last century soul cakes were no longer sought but ale, beer or money. The main soulers then were children, singing verses such as

> *Soul! Soul! for a soul cake,*
> *I pray, good missis, a soul cake!*
> *An apple, a pear, a plum or a cherry —*
> *Any good thing to make us merry.*

They were usually rewarded with sweets or money.

In Cheshire the soulers were sometimes accompanied by the Hodening Horse — a man covered in a white sheet and having a horse's head with fiercely snapping jaws. Also in Cheshire, it was once common to have a mummers' play called a Soul Caking Play, which also featured the Hodening Horse or the Wild Horse.

I know that my Redeemer liveth. These words from Handel's *Messiah* are on the gravestone of Jenny Lind, who died on 2 November 1887, and are an affirmation of the faith of one whose fine soprano voice was at its best when singing the great religious oratorios. Late in life she wrote to a friend:

> *My unceasing prayer is that what I gave to my fellows may continue to live on through eternity and that the Giver of the gift and not the creature to whom He lent it may be acknowledged.*

Born in Sweden, Jenny Lind once went on tour in the US, where she was billed by Phineas Barnum as 'the Swedish Nightingale' — the name by which she is remembered.

This day also saw the death, in 1950, of George Bernard Shaw, recognised as one of the great British playwrights. Born in Dublin, he moved to London at the age of twenty and first made his reputation as a journalist before writing successful works such as *Man and Superman, Major Barbara* and *Saint Joan*. In 1925, he was awarded the Nobel Prize for Literature.

Shaw used his plays as a means of drawing attention to desirable social reforms. He had deep feelings for the needs of others. In *The Devil's Disciple* he says

The worst sin towards our fellow creatures is not to hate them, but to be indifferent to them; that's the essence of inhumanity.

Perhaps this inhumanity of indifference is exemplified by the callous remark attributed to Marie-Antoinette who, when told of the starving poor, commented: 'If they have no bread, let them eat cake!' In fact, that remark was probably made before but it added fuel to the unpopularity of Marie-Antoinette.

Born in Vienna on 2 November 1755, she married Louis XVI of France but she was far from popular. Her arrogant attitude, extravagant expenditure and unwise associations all contributed to the overthrow of the monarchy. Queen Marie-Antoinette went to the guillotine some months after her husband.

This was also the birthday, in 1766, of Joseph Radetzky, who became an Austrian national hero because of his very successful military career spanning over half a century. He led his last campaign in 1848 at the age of 82 and later became governor of Lombardy-Venetia for seven years. Field-Marshal Radetzky was affectionately known as 'Father Radetzky'.

Daniel Boone was also born on or about this day, in 1734. He was an American frontiersman who opened new trails, notably the Cumberland Gap, fought against Indians, founded settlements and became a legendary hero.

A new 'trail' was opened in Britain on 2 November 1959. It was the first section of Britain's first motorway, the M1.

A way was paved for a Jewish national home in Palestine with the Balfour Declaration on 2 November 1917.

Nowadays most people find it convenient to carry their lunch or food for a picnic in the form of sandwiches. But why a 'sandwich'? It had its origin in 1762, when the Earl of Sandwich spent 24 hours gambling and had his food brought to him between slices of bread — the first sandwiches.

This was the birthday, in 1718, of John Montagu, 4th Earl of Sandwich, who travelled abroad before taking his seat in the House of Lords and holding several important offices. Accused by some of corruption, he was nevertheless a very able administrator. Nor was it only the sandwich that was named after him. The Sandwich Islands, in the Pacific, were so named by Captain Cook in honour of the one who was greatly interested in naval matters and exploration.

Karl Baedeker, who was born on 3 November 1801, was also interested in travelling and in helping those who travelled. Why pay guides when they could read for themselves about the places they were visiting? Karl Baedeker was the founder of the publishing house which began producing the famous series of Baedeker guide books, later published in French and in English as well as in German. His business was continued by his sons Ernst, Karl and Fritz.

Robert Raikes was also a founder — with a new idea. It began when he watched poor uneducated children at play and thought they would benefit from Sunday schools on their one day off from the factory. He experimented himself for three years, then used the *Gloucester Journal,* of which he was editor, as a means of launching an appeal for others to form Sunday schools. That was on 3 November 1783. He soon had people writing to him from many parts of the country seeking his advice.

Henri Matisse, regarded by many as the leading French painter of the 20th Century, died on 3 November 1954.

This was the day in 1957 when the Russians launched their second satellite, *Sputnik II,* which had a dog on board, the first living creature to go into orbit round the earth.

In 1975, on 3 November, the Queen inaugurated the first flow of North Sea oil at Dyce, Aberdeenshire.

Tutankhamun, king of Egypt, reigned from 1361 to 1352 BC. He died unexpectedly when about 18 years of age and was laid to rest in magnificent style. His body was laid inside a coffin of pure gold. That, in turn, was laid in one of gold on a wooden frame and that inside a similar one. The coffins were placed within four shrines, each of wood with gold coverings, the outer of which filled the burial chamber. In nearby rooms were all that the king might need on his journey and in his future life — furniture, clothes, a chariot, weapons and numerous other artifacts, with statues of guards and servants and everyday things such as grains of corn. The tomb, in Egypt's Valley of the Kings, was sealed and later covered with rubble when the tomb of Ramses VI was cut immediately above it. Whilst other tombs were pillaged and their treasures stolen, Tutankhamun remained undisturbed until 1923.

Howard Carter first went to Egypt at the age of 17 and began investigating archaeological sites. As Inspector-general of Egypt's Antiquities Department, he had discovered other tombs. Then, on 4 November 1922, he found the first sign of what proved to be Tutankhamun's tomb. After the tomb had been opened in 1923, Carter supervised the removal of the vast treasure, most of which was housed in the Cairo Museum.

Most people count their wealth not in gold but in notes and coins. An aid to shopkeepers was introduced on 4 November 1879, when James J. Ritty of Dayton, Ohio, USA, patented the first cash register.

This was the last day in 1847 for Felix Mendelssohn, composer of romantic music and, in 1924, of Gabriel Fauré, French composer who greatly influenced French music.

Admiral John Benbow also died, on this day in 1702, of wounds received against the French, remaining on deck though his leg had been shattered by gunfire.

This was the birthday, in 1858, of Frank Benson, actor-manager, who was knighted, in 1916, in Drury Lane Theatre. It was also the birthday, in 1879, of Will Rogers, film actor and humorist.

For humour and pranks, this is traditionally Mischief Night in Derbyshire and Yorkshire.

Remember, remember the fifth of November,
Gunpowder, treason and plot:
I see no reason why gunpowder treason
Should ever be forgot.

Today the last of the guys will be seen on the streets; the season of asking 'a penny for the guy' will come to an end; and such guys as there are will end up on tonight's bonfires. November the Fifth is not celebrated now as it was in former years. There are fewer, and generally less carefully prepared guys, whilst the bonfire and firework parties may be held on another more convenient day.

The guy is a reminder of Guy Fawkes, the conspirator who was found in the cellars of the Houses of Parliament ready to light the fuses that would explode barrels of gunpowder, hopefully killing King James I. It was a plot by some Roman Catholics to get rid of a protestant king but information was leaked and the plot failed. Afterwards, Parliament decreed that bonfires should be lit annually on 5 November in thankfulness for their deliverance in 1605.

Some of the most spectacular celebrations are those held in Lewes, Sussex. In fact, bonfires were held at Lewes for half a century before this, commemorating seventeen protestant martyrs who were put to death in 1557. Consequently there is not just an effigy of Guy Fawkes to be burned but one of the Pope as well — Pope Paul IV, who was believed, locally, to be behind the Gunpowder Plot.

There are six Bonfire Societies in Lewes which process from the Town Hall to the War Memorial, where wreaths are laid and a short service held, before continuing by torchlight to the bonfire site outside the town. Each society has a theme for the occasion. The 'Zulus' wear colourful costumes and plumed head-dresses. There are historical characters, Vikings, youth bands and others who all add colour and sound to a spectacular occasion.

Another noteworthy Bonfire Night celebration is at Bridgwater, Somerset, with a carnival and special Bridgwater squibs to liven the occasion. It is said that the origin of the festivities goes back to the rejoicings that took place in Bridgwater as soon as the people heard of the capture of those involved in the Gunpowder Plot.

People may have rejoiced in 1605 that King James I had been spared but equal pleasure was felt in 1688 that Parliament had decided they no longer wanted James II to be King. The crown was offered instead to Prince William of Orange and his wife Mary, the daughter of James II, who were to reign jointly. It was on 5 November 1688 that William landed in Torbay, Devon.

On 5 November 1872, the sailing brig *Mary Celeste* sailed from New York. Her captain, Benjamin Briggs, had with him his wife, his child and seven seamen. The next time the *Mary Celeste* was sighted was on 5 December. But where were the captain and crew? The *Mary Celeste* showed signs of having been hastily abandoned. The last entry in the ship's log was made on 25 November. What had happened? Several theories were put forward but nobody knows why she was deserted. The *Mary Celeste* remains one of the greatest mysteries of the sea.

Maurice Utrillo, the French painter, died on 5 November 1955. He was an alcoholic at the age of 17 and was introduced to painting by his mother in a bid to keep his mind off the drink. He is especially remembered for his Montmartre street scenes and his extensive use of white paint. He painted on site, from postcards and from his own imagination.

Born on this day in 1935 was one of Britain's most successful flat-racing jockeys, Lester Piggott, the winner of the Derby on no less than six occasions and of other classic flat races in Britain and overseas. He rode his first race at the age of twelve and became British champion jockey several times.

Tonight two ancient customs will be observed. Cakes made from oatmeal, butter and treacle may be baked for eating at bonfire celebrations. In Yorkshire they are called parkins: in Lancashire and Derbyshire they are tharcakes or harcakes — a memory of an ancient Norse festival at this time.

At Shebbear, North Devon, people will gather in the square with ropes and crowbars to turn the Devil's Boulder, a green stone said to have been dropped there by the Devil. There is a superstition that, if the stone is not turned, the village will experience bad luck.

'Marches will be the music of the world as long as men like to keep in step.' So declared John Philip Sousa, who wrote more than a hundred of them and saw how people enjoyed them all round the world. Born in Washington DC on 6 November 1854, he was the son of a trombonist in the US Marine Band. So John Philip had military music in his blood.

At the age of 13 he thought of joining a circus but father apprenticed him instead to the Marine Band. He left to try various theatre and musical outlets but returned at the age of 25 to become the youngest leader ever of the Marine Band. The march he wrote for it, *Semper Fidelis,* is still played by the Marine Corps on all special occasions, whilst his *Washington Post,* widely acclaimed throughout America, was taken up by dance bands, introducing the military two-step craze.

In 1892, Sousa created his own band which toured the world. People loved the music and they were captivated by the conductor, whose actions were dramatic, ending in a climax with 'the Sousa swing'. In his lifetime he received various honours. Perhaps one he would have treasured was the decision in 1954, one hundred years after his birth, to make his march, *The Stars and Stripes Forever,* a national march to be used on government occasions.

Adolphe Sax was born on this day in 1814. He was a Belgian musician who invented, in the 1840s, some new instruments such as the saxhorn and saxophone. Saxophones in keys F and C were for orchestras and used by some composers such as Bizet and Debussy. Saxophones in E and B were for bands and are now most commonly used in jazz.

The world of music became the poorer on this day in 1893 with the death, through cholera, of Peter Tchaikovsky, the Russian composer who gave the world some of its finest music — symphonies, concertos, opera, ballet, marches, dances and other music too, which has stirred the emotions and given pleasure to millions.

Also on 6 November. . . .
In 1860 Abraham Lincoln was elected President of the USA.
In 1884 Henry Fawcett, economist and statesman, died.
In 1892 Sir John Alcock, airman, was born.
In 1956 construction began on the Kariba High Dam.

7 November

Londoners can look back with thankfulness to 7 November 1982, the day on which the gates of the River Thames flood barrier were first raised. For years London had been in danger of flooding from high tides. The new barrier, which took eight years to complete at a cost of £450 million, can be raised in any time of flood danger but otherwise rests below the surface to allow shipping to pass unimpeded.

Another great project to be completed on 7 November was the Canadian Pacific Railway, the last spike being driven in on this day in 1885. The railway was important in linking together the provinces which formed Canada.

Three years later, on 7 November 1888, John Carbut of Philadelphia announced the invention of the first celluloid camera film.

Born on this day in 1867 in Poland, Marya Sklodovska was to make a discovery that would benefit very many people. In France, Marie, as she was then known, worked alongside her scientist husband Pierre Curie. Together they discovered how to extract radium from pitchblende and then gave their discovery freely to the world for the relief of suffering.

Another scientist was born on this day, in 1888. He was Sir Chandrasekhara Venkata Raman, an Indian physicist, who became a Nobel prize winner for his discoveries regarding the diffusion of light.

The diffusion of light could well describe the life's work of Dr. Billy Graham, born this day in 1918. The American evangelist and his team of crusaders have led many campaigns to spread the Christian gospel worldwide.

A leading churchman in another sphere, Cardinal Heenan, Roman Catholic Archbishop of Westminster, died in 1975.

King Christian II didn't live up to his name! On 7 November 1520, he invited 82 leading citizens of Stockholm to a banquet. They were seized and later executed by this tyrant.

The October Revolution in Russia began on this day in 1917. And if it seems odd that an October Revolution should begin in November it is because the Old Style Russian Calendar was then in use there and this day was 25 October.

8 November

This is the day on which the Lord Mayor of London is installed, six weeks after his election. The colourful procession, ceremony and pageantry are steeped in hundreds of years of history.

Some of today's birthdays. . . .
In 1656 Edmund Halley, astronomer and mathematician, the discoverer of Halley's Comet.
In 1883 Sir Arnold Bax, composer of romantic music, who was appointed Master of the King's Music in 1941.
In 1900 Margaret Mitchell, whose one book, *Gone with the Wind*, sold over 8,000,000 copies in 40 countries.
In 1922 Dr. Christiaan Barnard, South African surgeon of heart-transplant fame.

Some of today's deaths. . . .
In 1674 John Milton, English poet *(Paradise Lost)*.
In 1828 Thomas Bewick, wood engraver and printmaker.
In 1890 César Franck, organist and composer.
In 1978 Gene Tunney, US heavyweight boxing champion.

Also on this day. . . .
In 1895 William Röntgen discovered X-rays at Wurzburg.
In 1942 British and American forces landed in North Africa.

9 November

Two former prime ministers of Britain died on 9 November — Ramsay MacDonald, the first Labour prime minister, in 1937, and Neville Chamberlain in 1940.
   Across the Channel, this day saw the passing, in 1970, of one of the most influential Frenchmen of the 20th Century. Charles de Gaulle, a prominent soldier, became leader of the Free French forces during World War II. Later, as a statesman, he was the architect of the Fifth Republic and twice president.

Sir Giles Gilbert Scott, architect of Liverpool Cathedral and other large public buildings, was born on this day in 1880.
   In 1953, Dylan Thomas, Welsh poet, died.

To Oliver Goldsmith, poet, naturalist and historian, who left hardly any style of writing untouched, and touched nothing that he did not adorn.

This tribute to Goldsmith by Samuel Johnson reflects his admiration for the works of the Irish playwright, novelist and poet, who was born on 10 November 1728. He was a very warm-hearted, generous man but had many obvious faults which led Johnson also to write: 'No man was more foolish when he had not a pen in his hand, or more wise when he had.'

This was the birthday of several others noted for their creative skills.

William Hogarth, the English painter and engraver, who is especially remembered for his caricatures and morality paintings, was born in 1697.

Sir Jacob Epstein, one of the leading sculptors of the 20th Century, was born in 1880. Some of his symbolic sculptures caused great controversy but he became recognised as a fine modeller of bronze portrait heads. He was also commissioned to create the aluminium 'Christ in Majesty' for Llandaff Cathedral and 'St. Michael and the Devil', in bronze, for the new Coventry Cathedral.

Martin Luther, born in 1483, was one of the leaders of the Protestant Reformation — a deep thinker on religious matters, hymn writer and Bible translator.

It was his deep religious conviction that took David Livingstone to Africa, where he spent his life as missionary, explorer and opponent of slavery. His aim: 'I determined never to stop until I had come to the end and achieved my purpose.' This was the day, in 1871, of his famous meeting with H. M. Stanley.

Richard Chancellor, who opened up trade with Russia in the 16th Century, died this day in 1556 in a shipwreck in Aberdour Bay, Scotland.

The first motor cycle was ridden on 10 November 1885. Paul Daimler rode the machine built by his father, Gottlieb Daimler.

When there is wind on Martinmas eve
There it will be for the rest of winter.

Today is the feast day of St. Martin of Tours, a soldier who became a convert to Christianity and asked to be discharged from the army. 'I am Christ's soldier; I am not allowed to fight,' he said. He was accused of cowardice but, to prove this was not so, he offered to stand unarmed between the opposing lines. He was given his discharge, later becoming a missionary and bishop.

Much of St. Martin's work was done in the region of Tours, where he was respected as a man with great spiritual power, though he did have to face some opposition to his work.

It is, perhaps, appropriate that 11 November is a day on which soldiers are remembered, for this was the day,in 1918, when the armistice was signed at the end of the first World War. Fighting had raged for four years, much of it in the trenches of western Europe, notably in Flanders, but also in eastern Europe,the Middle East, at sea and in the air, with dreadful loss of life — many millions being killed and millions more wounded, many of them permanently disabled.

It was agreed that Armistice Day would be observed as a day of remembrance and that two minutes' silence would be observed each year at the eleventh hour of the eleventh day of the eleventh month. This continued until after World War II, when it was decided to keep silence instead on the nearest Sunday and to remember, at the same time, all those who had lost their lives during the second great war, fought in most parts of the world and claiming the lives of possibly as many as forty-five million.

After World War I, memorials were set up in towns and villages to record the names of those who died. The national memorial, the Cenotaph, was erected in Whitehall, London, and this was unveiled on 11 November 1920. On the same day, the Unknown Warrior was buried in Westminster Abbey.

Ned Kelly waged his own war — against the police. He was an Australian outlaw, or bushranger, who came from a lawless family. With his brother and two others, he committed daring robberies. Banks were raided and three policemen killed. After two years they were trapped at Glenrowan, Victoria, all wearing iron body armour. Three were killed; Ned with serious gun wounds was taken prisoner, found guilty of murder and hanged on 11 November 1880, so bringing his private war to an end.

Guns of a different kind are fired each year on 11 November. These are the Fenny Poppers, fired at Fenny Stratford in Buckinghamshire on the birthday of Dr. Browne Willis, who built the church there and dedicated it in the name of St. Martin, whose feast day falls on that same day.

Dr. Willis also presented to the church six miniature cannon, which look rather like thick mugs, made from gunmetal and weighing about twenty pounds each. He directed that each year on his birthday they should be taken from the belfry, filled with gunpowder and fired at four-hourly intervals from 8 am to 8 pm. After the final salvo has been fired, a sermon is preached and this is followed by a feast paid for with money that has been endowed for this purpose.

It may be that today is fine and warm for this time of year. There is often a brief spell of good weather about now, which is known as St. Martin's Summer.

Thoughts of winter, however, cannot be far away. It was on this day in the past that farmers traditionally considered which animals could be kept through the winter. Before means had been found to store animal fodder, large numbers of animals had to be slaughtered and the meat salted.

Past days were not easy for country folk and we sometimes tend to forget this when we think of *Merrie England*. This is a light opera, composed early this century by Sir Edward German, who died on 11 November 1936. After studying at the Royal Academy of Music, he became musical director of the Globe Theatre. He composed other light operas, incidental music for some of Shakespeare's plays, symphonies, other orchestral works and a Coronation March for King George V.

Another musician, who died on this day in 1945, was Jerome Kern. His musical shows included *Show Boat*, with its famous song 'Old Man River', a reminder of hard times in the USA.

Born on 11 November 1821 was the Russian novelist Feodor Dostoievsky, writer of *The Brothers Karamazov, Crime and Punishment* and other books. He died in 1881.

King Canute died on 12 November 1035. He was the son of Sweyn, the Danish king who conquered half of England. Canute succeeded him and began by devastating much of the east coast and south of the country. After the assassination of Edmund Ironside, Canute was accepted as king of the other half too. He began to change. From being barbarous and cruel he became humane and wise. English customs were restored: Danes and English were given equal rights.

The best-known story told of Canute is of the way he rebuked his flatterers, who said he was such a great king that even the sea would obey him. Sitting on his throne before the rising tide, he commanded the sea not to wet his feet but it did — sure proof that the power of kings was limited.

Man may not be able to rule the sea but there are many who have sought control of the sea routes. The pages of history are filled with stories of naval battles. Sir John Hawkins, who died on this day in 1595, was one of the English 'sea-dogs' of the Elizabethan era, who fought against the Spaniards. Born at Plymouth, he made various voyages and expeditions before being appointed a Vice-Admiral to fight the Armada, for which he received his knighthood. But it has to be admitted that Hawkins was a pirate and some of his business was not pleasant. He took the first negro slaves to the West Indies and it was there, later, that he died.

From the West Indies came various commodities, including rum, which was very popular with sailors, drunk neat until Admiral Edward Vernon decreed, in 1740, that it should be mixed with water. It was then known as 'grog' (from *Grogram* — the nickname of Vernon after the material from which his cloak was made). This day, in 1684, was Vernon's birthday.

Two breath-taking moments. The flying trapeze act was first performed on 12 November 1859, by Jules Leotard at the Circus Napoleon in Paris. And for skill and precision, who could better Nadia Comeneci? Born on this day in 1961, she thrilled the world by gaining the first ever perfect score of 10 points — and a further six scores of 10 — for gymnastics in the 1976 Montreal Olympics.

13 November

Back in the Middle Ages, when the known world was much smaller than it is today, there were those who set their sights much further afield than most. One of these was Prince Henry of Portugal, usually referred to as Henry the Navigator. Having established an observatory and school of navigation at Sagres, he sent seamen into unknown waters. He died on 13 November 1460, but he had paved the way for the discovery of a route round South Africa to India and beyond.

This day, in 1804, saw the passing of Captain Samuel Wallis who discovered Tahiti in the Pacific in 1767. It was on another Pacific island, Samoa, that Robert Louis Stevenson died. Born in Edinburgh on 13 November 1850, he first studied engineering, then law but found writing to be his true vocation. *Treasure Island* is perhaps the best known of his books but he is remembered also for his poems and prayers. It was to help his battle against tuberculosis that he settled on Samoa.

A great Scotsman of earlier years was King Malcolm III, known as Canmore (Gaelic *Ceann-mor* —'Great Chief'). The son of Duncan, who was slain by Macbeth, he waged warfare against the English in the borderlands but was slain at Alnwick on 13 November 1093.

Percival Lowell, the American astronomer who established the observatory at Flagstaff, Arizona, died on this day in 1916. He made a study of the planets and Mars in particular. A closer view of Mars was obtained on 13 November 1971, when the US *Mariner IX* went into orbit round the planet.

Vittorio de Sica was interested in stars of a different kind — film stars. He helped get the Italian film industry back on its feet after World War II, acting and directing almost to the end of his life, at the age of 73, on 13 November 1974.

Charles Worth, born in Lincolnshire on 13 November 1825, went to Paris in 1846 and opened a salon for his dress-designing, which became the centre of fashion. A more recent dress designer, Elsa Schiaparelli, died on this day in 1973.

Two others who died on this day. . . . George Sale, who translated the New Testament into Arabic and the Qur'an into English, died in 1736: Gioacchino Rossini, Italian composer, died in 1868.

14 November

'Old Parr' died on this day in 1635 and was later buried in Westminster Abbey. It might be felt that he had earned this honour by living, according to tradition, to the age of about 152. He was twice married and, in his 152nd year, induced to leave his Shropshire home to be introduced to King Charles I, but in London he died.

November 14 appears to be a bad day for the very old. On this day in 1978 Medzhid Agayev died in Azerbaijan, USSR. He was aged 143.

On the other hand, 14 November has been very beneficial. . . .

It was the birthday, in 1795, of Robert Fulton, the American inventor who invented machines and developed steamboats.

In 1863, Leo Baekeland was born in Ghent, Belgium. He became a chemist and emigrated to America in 1889. There he invented photographic printing paper that could be used with artificial light and discovered the first synthetic resin Bakelite, so introducing plastics to the world.

Sir Frederick Banting was born in Canada on 14 November 1891. He and Professor J. J. R. Macleod discovered insulin and they received jointly a Nobel Prize.

Claude Monet was born in Paris on 14 November 1840. In 1874 he exhibited a painting entitled 'Impression' — which gave the name to the Impressionist movement in art.

Jawaharlal Nehru, who was to become the first prime minister of independent India in 1947, was born on 14 November 1889.

Charles, Prince of Wales, was born on this day in 1948 and it was on his 25th birthday, in 1973, that his sister, Princess Anne, married Captain Mark Phillips.

A few interesting 14 November happenings. . . .

In 1896 the Light Locomotives Act came into force. Motorists no longer had to drive behind a man carrying a red flag and were allowed to travel at speeds up to 14 mph.

In 1832 the first streetcar, or tram, made its appearance in New York. Pulled by two horses, it carried 30 passengers.

The BBC began regular daily broadcasting in 1922.

Following an underwater volcanic eruption, a new island appeared off the coast of Iceland in 1963. It was named Surtsey.

Coventry Cathedral was destroyed by enemy bombing in 1940. A new symbolic cathedral was built beside the ruins.

15 November

Albertus Magnus — Albert the Great — was one of the greatest scholars of his time, in an age when scholarship was considered of far less importance than the more violent pursuits. After studying at Padua, Albert joined the Dominican order, then taught in schools at Hildesheim, Ratisbon and Cologne, lectured in Paris, became Bishop of Ratisbon and finally retired to his convent in Cologne.

Albert steeped himself in Jewish, Arabic and Western literature and his learning was so wide that he became 'Doctor Universalis'. He died at Cologne on 15 November 1280. He was canonised in 1931 and this became the feast day of St. Albert.

In Westminster Abbey there is a statue of a man of whom Macaulay wrote:

He was the first Englishman of his time, and he had made England the first country in the world.

William Pitt, First Earl of Chatham, often referred to as 'Pitt the Elder', was a statesman who spent himself in the service of his country and was renowned for his oratory and strength of character. This was his birthday in 1708.

This was the birthday, in 1891, of one of the outstanding German military leaders of World War II. Field-Marshal Erwin Rommel, nicknamed the 'Desert Fox', had great success at first in North Africa. In 1944, he was accused of plotting against Hitler and, rather than stand trial, committed suicide.

On 15 November 1837, Sir Isaac Pitman published a book entitled *Stenographic Sound Hand*. It was an introduction to the world of the first phonetic shorthand system.

This was the birthday, in 1776, of Per Ling who, with his son, introduced the Swedish system of physical education which laid stress on postural positions and became widely used.

Other of today's people. . . . Johannes Kepler, German astronomer, died in 1630; William Cowper, English poet, born in 1731; Sir William Herschel, astronomer, born in 1738; Christoph Gluck, composer, died in 1787; George Romney, English painter, died in 1802; William Murdock, Scottish engineer and inventor, died in 1839; Harald Sverdrup, meteorologist and oceanographer, born 1888.

The lives of four rulers are recalled today, none of which had a happy ending.

Tiberius Caesar, stepson of Augustus, was born on 16 November 42 BC. He ruled quite well for the first part of his reign and was able to strengthen the state during this time. His last ten years were spent in Capri, leaving the government to others, and there he engaged in cruelty and self-indulgence. His family life was far from happy and marred by many tragedies: the latter part of his life was full of gloom, superstition and maybe insanity.

The Saxon king Edmund II was the son of Ethelred the Unready. He was chosen king in April 1016 in London at the same time as Canute was being chosen in Southampton. Surnamed 'Ironside' because of his fighting spirit and ability, he fought Canute and a compromise was reached whereby each ruled over half of England. A few weeks later, on 16 November 1016, Edmund died somewhat mysteriously and Canute became king of all England.

King Henry III of England, son of John, was a cultured, charitable man with many good qualities but rather an ineffective ruler. His reign was troubled with revolt by the barons under Simon de Montfort, rebelling against high taxation. He was forced to agree to major reforms known as the Provisions of Oxford. For the last few years he was weak and senile, his son Edward ruling for him. Henry died on 16 November 1272.

Ataw Wallpa Inka (Atahuallpa) gained the Inca Empire by fighting his half-brother and savagely removing all opposition. However, his reign saw the arrival of Spanish conquistador Pizarro, who kidnapped Atahuallpa on 16 November 1532 and later strangled him on a trumped up charge of treason.

Jack Sheppard was hanged on 16 November 1724 at Tyburn. The most amiable of highwaymen, he escaped twice from Newgate but put his head back in the noose through his bravado.

Clark Gable, leading Hollywood film actor for a quarter of a century and star of over 70 films, died on 16 November 1960.

Arthur Askey, cheerful little comic of stage, screen and television ('Hello, playmates!'), died on 16 November 1982.

The Suez Canal was formally opened at Port Said in 1869.

Considered by some to be one of the greatest British generals, Bernard Law Montgomery was born in a London vicarage on 17 November 1887. He was a very determined young man whom nothing seemed able to stop — even a rifle bullet through his chest during World War I. He was also a very compassionate man, caring greatly for the well-being of his men.

He showed his exceptional military ability at its best after he was appointed to command the Eighth Army in the North African desert in 1942. He found a dispirited army which he transformed by his leadership until 'Monty' and the 'Desert Rats' were going from victory to victory. Recalled to England after the invasion of Sicily and Italy, he led the allied forces in the Normandy landings, accepted the surrender of the German armies and was appointed Chief of the Imperial General Staff, the highest post in the British army.

Field-Marshal Viscount Montgomery of Alamein, a familiar figure with seven rows of medal ribbons, was greatly loved and respected by those who worked with him.

Long before, a greatly loved queen died on 17 November 1093. Margaret of Scotland was a Hungarian princess who married Malcolm Canmore. Learned and pious, she did much to civilise Scotland and to draw the old Celtic Church into the general pattern of Christendom. She was canonised as St. Margaret.

A less popular queen to die on this day was Mary I, Queen of England. Her death, in 1558, marked the end of a five-year reign of persecution, for which she earned the name of 'Bloody Mary', though it is uncertain how far she was personally responsible. She died broken-hearted at the heartlessness of her husband, Philip of Spain, and sorrow at the loss of Calais.

Reference to Calais is a reminder of the story of the Burghers of that town in an earlier era. They are the subject of one of the most famous sculptures of the French Auguste Rodin, who died on 17 November 1917.

This day also saw the death, in 1858, of Robert Owen, social reformer and part owner of the cotton mills at New Lanark.

The world's first Cycle Road Race was held this day in 1869 between Paris and Rouen and won by James Moore of England.

Nowadays we take books for granted. There are so many of them and on any subject we may desire. It is difficult to appreciate the day when all books were written by hand and we can imagine the great excitement when printed books became available. It was William Caxton who introduced printed books to England, firstly those printed on the continent. Then he set up a press at Westminster on which the first book to be printed in England was produced. It was an English translation of *Dictes and Sayenges of the Phylosophers* and it appeared on 18 November 1477. Thereafter Caxton never looked back but printed just about all the English literature that was available, some being especially commissioned by royal and noble patrons.

This was the birthday in 1789 of another pioneer, three centuries later. Louis Daguerre, a French physicist and painter, invented the daguerreotype — the first practical method of producing a photograph. He worked then with Joseph Niepce, who had been trying a different process, and continued experimenting after the death of Niepce. Many daguerreotypes were made, especially portraits.

Living at the same time was the Scottish portrait painter and printmaker, Sir David Wilkie, born on 18 November 1785.

Mickey Mouse also made his first appearance on 18 November, in 1928, in a film called *Steamboat Willie* at the Colony Theatre on Broadway. He was the creation of Walt Disney, whose animated cartoon films became very popular. Mickey Mouse does not seem to have aged: he is as popular as ever.

Still popular, too, are the Savoy comic operas of Gilbert and Sullivan, written over a century ago. This was the birthday, in 1836, of Sir W. S. Gilbert, who wrote the words.

Also born this day in 1860 was the pianist Ignacy Paderewski, who entertained many with his playing but is also remembered as a great patriot who gave much of his time and his money to help his native country, Poland.

Nowadays we frequently hear of opinion polls being conducted especially at the time of an election or to test public opinion on important issues. Sometimes they are referred to as Gallup polls, the name being that of the American journalist George Gallup, born on 18 November 1901, who conducted the first such poll in 1932.

19 November

On 19 November 1863, President Abraham Lincoln dedicated the national cemetery on the site of the Civil War battlefield at Gettysburg, Pennsylvania. The final words of his speech have been widely acclaimed and frequently quoted.

That this nation, under God, shall have a new birth of freedom; and that government of the people, by the people, and for the people, shall not perish from the earth.

There wasn't much freedom in France in the 17th and 18th Centuries. Nor was there any government by the people. The king could do exactly as he pleased and if he wished to imprison someone there was nothing to prevent him from so doing. It was on 19 November 1703 that a mysterious prisoner died in the notorious Bastille in Paris. Who was he? No one knew. In fact in the five years he had spent in the dungeons no one had seen his face, for it was covered by a black velvet mask. When he arrived at the Bastille, he had already spent 29 years in solitary confinement.

It was not until many years later that documents came to light indicating that the prisoner was Eustache Dauger, a rogue who was probably masked because of his likeness to King Louis XIV. Whether he had used that likeness to pretend he was the king, no one knows. Many years later, Alexandre Dumas wrote a book about this prisoner, *The Man in the Iron Mask*. At least the prisoner in the Bastille was spared that: the velvet mask must have been bad enough.

Born on 19 November 1917, and daughter of independent India's first Prime Minister Jawaharlal Nehru, Mrs. Indira Ghandi has also been Prime Minister of India for more than one term of office.

Also on 19 November. . . .
Bertel Thorvaldsen, Danish sculptor, was born in 1770.
Ferdinand de Lesseps, Suez Canal engineer, born 1805.
Franz Schubert, Austrian composer, died in 1828.
James Garfield, US statesman and president, born 1831.
Sir William Siemens, engineer and inventor, died in 1883.
Sir Basil Spence, architect (Coventry Cathedral), died in 1976.
The German army was surrounded at Stalingrad in 1942.

If I omit to practise one day, I notice it; if two days, my friends notice it; if three days, the public notices it.

Anton Rubinstein was a Russian composer and one of the greatest pianists of the 19th Century. After touring Europe, he settled in St. Petersburg, where his first opera was produced. He also wrote other music oratorios, concertos, songs and piano pieces but he is especially remembered for the brilliance and sensitivity of his piano playing. He died on 20 November 1894.

'Practice makes perfect' could also have been the motto of the world-famous Brazilian footballer Pelé, regarded as one of the finest players in the world. He was only 17 when he helped Brazil win the World Cup in 1958; and he was in the winning teams of 1962 and 1970. He reached a landmark in his career on 20 November 1969, when he scored his one thousandth goal, the highest number scored by any footballer.

Life ended on 20 November for these. . . .
Edmund, King of East Anglia, was captured by the Danes whilst trying to defend his kingdom in 870. Refusing to share his kingdom with pagans, he was consequently tied to a tree and slain with arrows. His body was later buried in the abbey, now known as Bury St. Edmunds, and he is remembered on this day, his feast day, as St. Edmund.
Roger Payne, who died this day in 1797, had the reputation of being the most artistic book-binder in London.
Henry Francis Lyte, Scottish composer of greatly-loved hymns such as *Abide with me,* died this day in 1847.
Sir John Fowler, co-designer of the Forth Bridge, died in 1898.
Count Leo Tolstoy, Russian author, died in 1910.
General Franco, dictator of Spain 1936–75, died in office.

Naval occasions. . . . Admiral Sir Edward Hawke's victory over the French at Quiberon Bay, on 20 November 1759, put an end to any French plans to invade Britain. Admiral Jellicoe, who died this day in 1935, had made the German navy ineffective after his victory at Jutland during World War I.

In 1947 Princess Elizabeth married Philip, Duke of Edinburgh.

The beautifully decorated paper and cloth balloon, designed by the Montgolfier brothers, rose into the air from a garden in Paris, its hot air created by a fire slung beneath the balloon. On board were Louis XIV's historian, Jean de Rozier, and the Marquis d'Arlandes, who had volunteered to fly and so became the first men in the world to make a free flight: previous balloons had remained tethered to the ground. On this day, 21 November 1783, they flew at a height of about 3,000 ft (914 m) and travelled some 9,000 yards (8,230 m) during which time they were kept busy dampening the balloon to prevent its catching fire.

On this day, in 1843, an invention was patented that would greatly affect future forms of transport. Vulcanised rubber made possible the use of tyres for road vehicles.

And for ease of future transport, the construction of the new Forth Road Bridge began on 21 November 1958. When completed, this fine suspension bridge eliminated the slow ferry journey between North and South Queensferry.

This agglomeration which was called and still calls itself the Holy Roman Empire was neither holy, nor Roman, nor an empire in any way.

The French writer Voltaire (François Marie Arouet), who was born on 21 November 1694, did not mind what he said and his lampooning of those in authority led to his imprisonment in the Bastille and subsequent exile from France. He is remembered as one of the greatest French writers but also as a crusader against all forms of tyranny, cruelty and bigotry.

Also born on 21 November, in 1863, was the Cornish novelist, poet and anthologist, Sir Arthur Quiller-Couch, whose humorous novels were written under the pseudonym 'Q'.

Some who died on 21 November. . . .

In 1579 Sir Thomas Gresham, founder of Royal Exchange, London.

In 1695 Henry Purcell, English composer and organist, aged 36.

In 1835 James Hogg, Scottish poet,the 'Ettrick Shepherd'.

In 1970 Sir Chandrasekhara Venkata Raman, physicist.

The mystery of the Piltdown skull (found 1911) ended on this day in 1953 when it was proven to be a hoax.

St. Cecilia is one of the Christian martyrs of the 3rd Century of whom little is known. She has, however, been famous since the 16th Century as the patron saint of musicians. It was written of her that at her wedding feast, 'as the organs were playing, Cecilia sung to the Lord . . .'. Who better to be chosen as the patron saint of the Rome Academy of Music when it was founded in 1584?

Alexander Pope (1688–1744) wrote an *Ode for Music on St. Cecilia's day* and John Dryden (1631–1700) a *Song for St. Cecilia's Day*:

> *From harmony, from heavenly harmony*
> *This universal frame began:*
> *From harmony to harmony*
> *Through all the compass of the notes it ran. . . .*

And from the same poem:

> *What passion cannot music raise and quell!*

Harmony! Passion! Musicians have a reputation for being temperamental or unpredictable. Sir Arthur Sullivan died on St. Cecilia's Day in 1900. He is particularly remembered for his work with Sir W. S. Gilbert, producing the Savoy operas — *The Mikado, The Pirates of Penzance* and others. Gilbert wrote the words and Sullivan the music, sometimes working in harmony and sometimes quarrelling, until they finally fell out over a carpet.

Sullivan is remembered for other great music too, such as *The Lost Cord* and the tune for *Onward, Christian Soldiers*. He was the first Principal of the National Training College which became the Royal College of Music.

In later years, a young student of the Royal College of Music was to become one of Britain's leading musicians. He was Benjamin Britten, born at Lowestoft on St. Cecilia's Day, 1913. While at college he began writing music and he never looked back. Much of his work has been of a religious nature, *Noyes Fludde* being but one such work. For children he also wrote *The Young Person's Guide to the Orchestra*. He wrote the opera *Peter Grimes* and many other kinds of music. He is remembered, too, as one of the founders of the Aldeburgh Festival to which, each year, people travel from many places to enjoy the music.

Cecil Sharp was also born on St. Cecilia's Day, in 1859. He played a very important role in the collection of folk music and dancing. He travelled to many parts of the country, recording all the information he could find so that old dances and songs would never be forgotten.

22 November is also a day to remember travellers of a more adventurous kind — the intrepid explorers who journeyed uncharted seas to open up the world as we know it. On this day, in 1497, Vasco da Gama, the Portuguese voyager, rounded the Cape of Good Hope to prove that it was possible to sail round Africa and Europe to India.

On 22 November 1594, Sir Martin Frobisher died of wounds received whilst fighting the Spaniards at Brest, France. This was not his first encounter with the Spaniards: he commanded the largest ship in the battle against the Spanish Armada and had sailed with Drake to the West Indies.

But Frobisher is remembered, too, as one of the courageous men who sailed the North Atlantic to see whether there was a North-west Passage north of Canada to link the Atlantic and Pacific oceans. He rediscovered Greenland and Labrador.

Robert Clive found his adventure in India. It was largely through his efforts that India became a part of the British Empire. He won several great victories and was regarded as a national hero. Later he became a Member of Parliament but poor health worried him and he took his own life on 22 November 1774.

Perhaps you prefer your adventure of a quieter nature or ready made for you.

A planned holiday with Thomas Cook's? Thomas Cook, the travel-agent, was born on 22 November 1808.

The thrill of a Ferris Wheel at the fairground? Its American inventor, in 1892, George Ferris, died on this day in 1896.

In an armchair with a good book? C. S. Lewis, author of religious and children's books, died on 22 November 1963.

President de Gaulle (France) was born on this day in 1890. President John F. Kennedy (USA) was assassinated in 1963.

Today is St. Clement's Day. He was one of the earliest Popes, put to death by being tied to an anchor and dropped into the sea. Because anchors were made by blacksmiths he became their patron saint. In former days when there were more blacksmiths than there are today, 'Old Clem' became the subject of noisy celebrations.

Much more musical than those of the blacksmith's hammers, were the notes struck by Thomas Tallis, organist of the Chapel Royal in the time of Queen Elizabeth I. He wrote a lot of choral and instrumental music before death ended his work on this day in 1585. Today is the birthday of a musician of much later years — Manuel de Falla, the Spanish composer who was born in 1876.

Nowadays many like their music taped. What would life be like without cassettes? A special birthday thought today for Valdemar Poulsen, born in 1869, who invented the tape recorder.

A couple of 'firsts' today. . . . It was on this day in 1852 that the first pillar boxes in Britain were set up — in St. Helier, Jersey. It was also on this day, in 1858, that the General Medical Council met for the first time.

Dr. Crippen has the distinction of being another 'first'. Having committed murder he took ship to Canada but became the first man arrested as a result of a radio message. Brought back to England, he was tried, found guilty and executed on 23 November 1910. Also executed on this day was Perkin Warbeck, in 1499. He was an imposter who said he was one of the Princes actually murdered in the Tower, then claimed to be King Richard IV of England. He was hanged at Tyburn.

Justice must not only be done but be seen to be done. Today, in Laxton, Nottinghamshire, where much of the land is shared on the old open field system, the jurors of the Court Leet tour the fields to see that none of the ancient laws has been broken. Offenders are fined . . . and the fines spent on beer!

'God is not on the side of force, but of truth and justice.' So said Alexander Nevsky, a Russian hero, canonised by the Russian Orthodox Church, whose feast day this is.

24 November

Charles Darwin set the cat among the pigeons on 24 November 1859, when he published *On the Origin of Species*. His theory of evolution was controversial, to say the least, and was condemned by many, who saw it as undermining the fundamental beliefs in creation as recorded in the Book of Genesis. The controversy raised in this, and in a subsequent book *The Descent of Man* was to continue for a long time.

A controversial philosopher of earlier years was Baruch (or Benedict) Spinoza, born in Amsterdam of Jewish parents on 24 November 1632. He was a deeply religious man, who concluded that everything and every person that exists is a part of God — a view that upset many of his contemporaries, both Jewish and Christian.

John Knox, who died on this day in 1572, was one of the most powerful Scots of his day, liked by some and hated by others according to their beliefs in those days of the Reformation. Knox, a follower of Calvinism, promoted Presbyterianism in Scotland and denounced Roman Catholicism. His strong personality and his forthright preaching had a lasting effect.

Forthright and determined in a different age and sphere was Lilian Baylis, who turned London's Royal Victoria Hall into the 'Old Vic' theatre, a centre for Shakespeare and opera. Later she bought and rebuilt the Sadler's Wells Theatre, where she formed opera and ballet companies. She died on 24 November 1937 but her 'Old Vic' became the temporary home of the National Theatre Company, whilst her Sadler's Wells companies became the English National Opera and the Royal Ballet respectively.

On the subject of opera, one recalls Lilli Lehman, the German soprano, who was born on 24 November 1848. She was admired for her dramatic personality, her fine voice and her versatility. She had a repertoire of 170 operatic roles and 600 lieder. From 1905 she helped organise the Salzburg festivals.

Also on 24 November. . . .
In 1642 Abel Tasman discovered Van Diemen's Land (Tasmania).
In 1815 Grace Darling, shipwreck rescue heroine, was born.
In 1864 Henri de Toulouse-Lautrec, Montmartre artist, was born.

Today we remember St. Catherine, the 4th Century martyr, whose death on a spiked wheel inspired the firework of that name. This day in the past was a day of merrymaking and one on which young women would use various means of divination to seek information about possible future husbands.

This might also be said to be a day of beginning in lots of different spheres.

It was the day, in 1735, on which the heaviest bell in the world was cast. The Tsar Kolokol weighs 196 tonnes. It has stood cracked and unrung on a platform in the Kremlin since 1836.

It was the day, in 1823, on which the first seaside pier was opened. The Chain Pier at Brighton was eventually destroyed completely by gales on 4 December 1892.

On 25 November 1952, the curtains were raised for the first performance of Agatha Christie's 'whodunit' play *The Mousetrap* which was to become the longest running play, still performed over 30 years later.

At 8 am on 25 November 1872, Captain Briggs made the last entry in the log book of the *Mary Celeste*. That may seem like an end rather than a beginning but it began a mystery. Why was the *Mary Celeste* found later sailing the Atlantic with no trace of her crew? The mystery has remained.

More beginnings. . . .

Carl Benz was born on 25 November 1844. The German motor engineer first built a two-stroke engine in 1879 then cars. His first, in 1885, was one of the earliest petrol driven cars.

Angelo Roncalli was born on this day in 1881. His surprise election as Pope John XXIII, in 1958, marked the beginning of new relationships between the Roman Catholic Church and other Christian denominations.

Andrew Carnegie was born on 25 November 1835. In his lifetime he built up a great steel empire in America worth over one hundred million pounds, most of which he gave away.

Isaac Watts was never a rich man in terms of wealth, but when he died, on 25 November 1748, he left behind a vast treasury of hymns which, to this day, are counted amongst the finest and are found in many hymn books.

26 November

The first National Thanksgiving Day was held in the USA on this day in 1789. Commemorating the first Thanksgiving Day, in 1863, it was kept as a national holiday on this day until 1963, when it was set on the last Thursday in November (after 1941, the fourth Thursday).

America owes its discovery to Christopher Columbus who, himself, was indebted to King Ferdinand and Queen Isabella of Spain, who paid for his expedition in 1492. Queen Isabella, whose marriage to King Ferdinand had united the kingdoms of Aragon, Castille and Leon, died on 26 November 1504.

A later voyager to America was John Harvard. Born this day in 1607, he became a clergyman and then emigrated, in 1637, to the Massachusetts Bay Colony. He died only a year later, leaving a sum of money and his collection of 400 books toward the foundation of the university which was given his name.

William George Armstrong was born at Newcastle-upon-Tyne on 26 November 1810. He became interested in engineering and began to invent and improve hydraulic machinery. The company which he set up produced cranes, engines, generators and bridges. Later it built guns and ships. Armstrong was created a baron in 1887 and, ten years later, amalgamated his firm with that of Joseph Whitworth to form Armstrong-Whitworth.

A great engineering feat was completed in 1966 in France. The Rance Barrage, opened on this day near St. Malo, harnesses the sea water flowing in and out of the estuary to produce electricity.

This day, in 1836, marked the death of John McAdam, the Scottish civil engineer who invented the method of road-making, now widely used and known as 'macadam'.

Also on this day. . . .
William Cowper, poet and hymnwriter, was born in 1731.
Coventry Patmore, poet, died in 1896.

It was on this night, in 1703, that the Great Storm swept across southern England, destroying buildings and tearing up trees by the roots. Also destroyed was the first Eddystone lighthouse together with its builder, Henry Winstanley, the English architect and engraver.

Remember, when life's path is steep, to keep an even mind.

Words of wisdom from the *Odes* of Horace, the Roman poet and satirist, whose poems have provided more remembered phrases than the rest of Latin literature together. Educated in Rome and Athens, Horace had an adventurous life, serving in the republican army under Brutus, and having his property in Italy confiscated. He became a civil servant and began writing poetry, later becoming Poet Laureate. He died on 27 November 8 BC, leaving much to future generations and ensuring the truth of the words, also from his *Odes*:

I have completed a monument more lasting than brass.

The same could also be said of a number of other people who are associated with this day.

Athanasius Kircher died on 27 November 1680. He was a German scholar and has been credited with the invention of the magic lantern.

Anders Celsius, the Swedish astronomer, was born at Uppsala on 27 November 1701. He became professor of astronomy there in 1730 and an observatory was erected there for him ten years later. In 1742 he devised the centigrade thermometer, generally referred to today by his name, Celsius.

Andrew Meikle, the Scottish engineer who invented the first successful threshing machine, died on this day in 1811.

In 1901 this day saw the death of Clement Studebaker. With his brother, Henry, he opened a blacksmith and wagon shop. Soon the well-known name Studebaker appeared on many kinds of road vehicle with world-wide sales.

On this day, in 1518, Daniel Bomberg completed his preparation of the Rabbinical Bible.

On 27 November 1095, whilst in Clermont, France, Pope Urban II urged Christians to take up arms against the Muslims who were occupying the Holy Land, so initiating the First Crusade.

Miss M. Allen and Miss E. Harburn assumed the duties of police women at Grantham, Lincolnshire, on 27 November 1914, the first policewomen in England.

How many children have not encountered Noddy, the Famous Five or the Secret Seven during their early years? They are characters from the very popular children's books of Enid Blyton, who wrote more then 400 books before she died on 28 November 1968. The popularity of the books is evident from the sales; over eleven million Noddy books have already been sold; the total sales of her books are over fifty million; and they have been translated into at least 165 languages.

Children like a good story too. How many have enjoyed hearing or reading about Rip van Winkle? It is one of the short stories retold and popularised by Washington Irving, who also died on this day, in 1859. Irving has been described as 'the inventor of the short story'. He was the first American writer to be acclaimed outside America: he has been described as 'the first American man of letters' and 'the father of American literature'.

William Blake, who was born on 28 November 1757, was a book illustrator and engraver who became a brilliant, if unusual, poet and painter. He claimed to have had visions from early in his life and his works express his deep thoughts about life.

> *Bring me my bow of burning gold!*
> *Bring me my arrows of desire!*
> *Bring me my spear! O clouds unfold!*
> *Bring me my chariot of fire!*
> *I will not cease from mental fight,*
> *Nor shall my sword sleep in my hand,*
> *Till we have built Jerusalem*
> *In England's green and pleasant land.*

Many people who might not have been able to do so are able to enjoy life, thanks to Jonas Salk, who was born on this day in 1914. As a research scientist, he introduced a vaccine which has prevented many people from getting poliomyelitis.

The Sanger brothers, John and George, became circus proprietors in 1853 and made their circus the largest in England in the 19th Century with circuses in several cities. Each took the title 'Lord'. 'Lord' George Sanger was shot dead by a former employee on 28 November 1911.

One achievement in aviation history was the development of the supersonic aircraft *Concorde*, which first flew in 1969. It carries up to 128 passengers, cruises at 1,450 mph (2,333 km/h) and was the first supersonic aircraft used on passenger services. *Concorde* was developed jointly by Britain (BAC) and France (Aerospatiale) under an agreement reached on 29 November 1962.

The technology that enabled *Concorde* to be built makes earlier inventions appear insignificant, yet the present has been built on the past and one imagines a great deal of interest being aroused by the steam engine that was first used on 29 November 1814 to print *The Times* newspaper. The initial production of 1,200 copies per hour was later increased to 4,000.

Another innovation, on this day in 1897, was the first motor cycle race in Great Britain, held at Richmond, Surrey.

Louisa May Alcott, who was born on 29 November 1832, did not have an easy life. Anxious to help her family, she worked at sewing, at teaching and in domestic service before taking up writing. As a nurse in the American Civil War she contracted typhoid, from which she never fully recovered. She wrote short stories for a magazine and was then asked to write a story book for girls. She did — an autobiographical book entitled *Little Women*, which became an outstanding success and which she followed with others based upon her own experiences.

Also born on this day, in 1898, was another writer of popular books for children, C. S. Lewis. His *Chronicles of Narnia* are classics of fantasy. He wrote for adults too, his 40 or so books including science fiction novels and books on religion, notably *The Screwtape Letters*, in which an elderly devil instructs his junior in the arts of temptation.

In conclusion, some who died on 29 November. . . .

Prince Rupert, Royalist commander in the Civil War, in 1682.

Giocomo Puccini, great Italian composer of opera, in 1924.

Cardinal Thomas Wolsey in 1530. He was a statesman to whom Henry VIII entrusted many affairs of state until Wolsey fell from favour and faced a charge of treason. He died this day in 1530 after writing: *Had I but served God as diligently as I have served the King, he would not have given me over in my gray hairs.*

Scots will need no reminder that today is St. Andrew's Day, on which they commemorate their patron saint, one of the original disciples of Jesus Christ and a leader in the early Christian Church.

In Scotland, on St. Andrew's Day 1872, the first soccer international match was played at Partick, Glasgow, between England and Scotland. There was no score.

Some of today's birthdays. . . .
In 1554 Sir Philip Sidney, English soldier and poet, remembered for his chivalrous words at the Battle of Zutphen (p. 27).
In 1667 Dean Jonathan Swift (p. 63), author of *Gulliver's Travels* and other writings.
In 1835 Samuel Langhorne Clemens, better known as Mark Twain, author of *Tom Sawyer* and *Huckleberry Finn*.
In 1858 Sir Jagadis Chandra Bose, Indian physicist and botanist, who studied electric waves and growth of plants.
In 1874 Sir Winston Churchill, politician, war-time leader, prime minister and author.

Two who died. . . .
In 1900 Oscar Wilde, Irish dramatist, poet and humorist, author of *The Importance of Being Ernest.*
In 1957 Beniamino Gigli, Italian operatic tenor.

On 30 November 1928, the American aviator and antarctic explorer, Richard Byrd, flew over the South Pole.
On this day, in 1936, the Crystal Palace was destroyed by fire, only one tower remaining.

Tonight, according to ancient tradition, is one of the best nights on which to catch a glimpse of a future spouse. Two girls sit together alone from midnight to 1 o'clock. During this time they pluck from their heads as many hairs as the years of their ages and lay them on a sheet. As the clock strikes one, they should turn each hair separately and say:

> *I offer this my sacrifice*
> *To him most precious in my eyes.*
> *I charge thee now, come forth to me,*
> *That I this minute may thee see.*

Other November Events and Commemorations

(*see also p. 80*)

About 2nd (All Souls' Day)   Comberbach, Cheshire: Mummers' Play performed by Soulcakers.

5th   In various places: Guy Fawkes celebrations (p. 86).
Shebbear, Devon: Turning the Devil's Boulder (p. 86).
Ottery St. Mary, Devon: Burning Tar Barrels.

Second Saturday   London: Lord Mayor's Show. The mile-long procession travels through the City to the Law Courts to take the oath before the Lord Chief Justice, then through as many wards of the City of London as can be arranged. In the evening there is a sumptuous banquet.

30th   Eton, Buckinghamshire: Wall Game at Eton College. It is a form of Rugby Football with its own rules, played between Collegers, who are resident in College, and Oppidans, who board in the town.

Some time in month   Portland and Wareham, Dorset: Court Leets.

Ashburton, Devon: Court Leet and Ale Tasting. Officers are appointed, including the Portreeve, Ale Tasters, Bread Weighers, Pig Drivers and Surveyors of Markets. The Ale Tasters are then entitled to visit all ale houses in town and test, by tasting, the quality of the ale.

SOME NOVEMBER FAIRS

Martinmas (11th)   Some former hiring fairs (p. 43) were held at Martinmas instead of Michaelmas and the fairs are now held on or about this date.

18th Truro, Cornwall: Glove Fair.

OTHER EVENTS
Birmingham Fatstock Show.

DECEMBER

December

December was originally the tenth month of the Roman calendar and takes its name from the Latin *decem* (ten). The Anglo-Saxons had two names for it. It was the *Wintermonath* or Winter month. It was also the last month of the Anglo-Saxon year and was linked with the first month under the general title of *Giuli*, or 'Yule'. After their conversion to Christianity, Wintermonath was sometimes called *Halighmonath*, the Holy month.

December is usually a dull, wet month, not usually the coldest in the year but one in which most of nature seems to be asleep. The Roman poet Martia referred to December as the hoary month because of the snows which fell and as the smoky month, the smoke coming from the many bonfires lit for warmth. It is the month in the northern hemisphere in which days are at their shortest until the Winter solstice. Small wonder that Shakespeare refers to it as 'dark December'. It is the time of year when people, unable to hibernate as many animals have done, enjoy the cosiness of their homes.

> *While I have a home, and can do as I will,*
> *December may rage over ocean and hill,*
> *And batter my door — as he does once a year —*
> *I laugh at his storming and drink his good cheer.*

The words of this old English song serve as a reminder of the festivities which also take place at this time of year (pp. 117-20) with their revelry, drinking, eating, family gatherings and ancient customs.

And, in these days of sophisticated decorations of paper, plastic and foil, people still step out into the cold to gather, or to buy, the living symbols of the world of nature, the evergreens of various kinds that were gathered in abundance in former days, the most popular being the holly with its bright red berries.

But all nature is not asleep. In the mild December some snowdrops may bloom and there are signs of new life on other plants and trees. Many birds are active in their search for food and thankful for kind human friends.

December festivals

Most of the December festivals and today's 'Merry Christmas' have their origins in the distant past. Midwinter came toward the end of December and it was then that people of old used to light their fires and make sacrifices that would encourage the gods to give back the warmth and light.

In northern Europe the midwinter festival was Yule or Jol. It was celebrated with bonfires and the burning of the Yule log which lasted for three days as people feasted, drank, sang and recalled the ancient legends. As the wild wind blew, their eyes turned skyward to see whether Odin was on his travels. Mistletoe was cut and greenery was taken into the houses. The Yule log survived until recently in Britain and it was considered to be lucky if this could be kept burning for the 12 days of Christmas.

In Sweden, 13 December is Little Yule, or St. Lucia's Day, when girls will don their wreaths of seven candles, then take their Lucia buns, ginger snaps and coffee to the family.

The Roman festival of Saturnalia began on 17 December and included the 'Birthday of the Invincible Sun' on 25 December. It lasted for 7 days and was followed closely by Kalends (p. 156). Saturnalia was a wild festival of fire and light, held in honour of Saturn, the god of corn and harvest. It was a time of excess and anarchy. Masters and servants changed places or fed together. Food and drink were consumed in large quantities. Houses were decorated and greetings sent.

During December, Jews celebrate Channukah, an eight-day festival, when candles are lit as a reminder of their deliverance and the providence of God well over 2,000 years ago.

For Christians, this is the season of Advent, the preparation for Christmas. Advent begins on the Sunday nearest to St. Andrew's Day (30 November). Advent candles are lit in many churches. The collect (prayer) for this Sunday begins 'Stir-up, we beseech Thee, O Lord, the wills of Thy faithful people', so this became 'Stir-up Sunday' — the traditional day for making and stirring the Christmas pudding!

Christmas

Christmas is one of the main festivals of the year, celebrated in many lands in differing ways, common to all being that it is the festival at which the birth of Jesus Christ is celebrated. Most scholars agree that this was not the actual birthday, which was almost certainly much earlier in the year. To the early Christians this seemed to be a most convenient time, since it was already a major Roman holiday, the great festival of Saturnalia, and they could use this holiday to celebrate as they wished. It is not surprising that some aspects of Saturnalia became accepted as part of the normal Christmas festivities. Indeed, most of our cherished Christmas customs came originally from ancient pagan beliefs.

The name Christmas first appeared in Early English as *Cristes Maesse*, the Mass or celebration of the birth of Christ, in the 11th Century AD. The date of it varied from one country to another but eventually most agreed that it should be 25 December, though the Russian Orthodox and some other Churches decided to keep the festival in January.

It is customary, today, for Christians to celebrate the festival with special services in church — Midnight Mass or Holy Communion as Christmas Day dawns, family services on Christmas morning, services of lessons and carols, some by candlelight, just before Christmas and others that remind of the coming into the world of the one who said he was the 'Light of the World'. Many churches have a simple crib at this season as a reminder that the Son of God knew hardship from the beginning.

For most people, Christmas is a time of greeting and good wishes. In the weeks before Christmas, presents are bought for family and friends, whilst millions of Christmas Cards are written and posted. Christmas cards originated in 1843. Sir Henry Cole suggested the idea to an artist, John Callcott Horsley, and about 1,000 were printed. They cost one shilling each and one penny for postage. In 1870 the postage for unsealed envelopes was reduced to one halfpenny, putting the sending of cards within the reach of most people.

The giving of presents is sometimes thought to have come from the story of the Wise Men who brought gifts of gold, frankincense and myrrh to Jesus, but it is more likely that it came from the Roman custom of giving presents at Saturnalia.

The gifts given at Saturnalia and Kalends by the Romans were often charitable gifts to poorer neighbours. This spirit is reflected today in the helping of the poor and needy at Christmas and the growing sale of Christmas cards that are published by charitable organisations.

The bringer of gifts for children is Father Christmas or Santa Claus. The original Santa Claus was St. Nicholas, the benevolent Bishop of Myra in the 4th Century. He became a very popular saint in many lands. In Holland, as Sinter Klaas, he arrives by ship on the eve of his feast day, 6 December, and is met by the Queen before parading through the city with his servant, Black Peter. Dutch children hope he will leave a present in their shoes that evening.

Dutch settlers took Sinter Klaas to America, where he became Santa Claus, the jovial fellow in his red outfit, but there, as in most countries today, he arrives on Christmas Eve. His journey through the skies on a sledge pulled by reindeer owes its origin to the Norse tales of Odin who rode through the sky on his eight-legged horse Sleipnir, giving rewards to the good and punishments to the bad.

Before Christmas, people begin to decorate their homes for the festival. Most people like to have a Christmas tree. This was a German custom dating back to about the 8th Century. A few Christmas trees had been seen in Britain before 1841 but the fact that Prince Albert had one at Windsor in that year ensured its popularity. Trees were decorated with tinsel, brightly coloured baubles and, of course, candles, which Martin Luther had once said reminded him of the twinkling stars in the night sky at Bethlehem. Nowadays we use fairy lights instead.

Other greenery, once used for decoration, had its pagan associations. Holly was a symbol of everlasting life, fertility and good fortune. Ivy was a kindly, anti-witching plant with medical values. Rosemary was holy and magical. Bay was once sacred to Apollo and to Aescutapius, the god of medicine.

In the past, more so than today, mistletoe was hung in some suitable place so that young men could claim a kiss from any of the fairer sex who happened to stand beneath it. This custom probably arises from the former sex associations of this plant, which was once cut ceremonially by the Druids and has many associations with the folklore of pagan times.

119

For most people, Christmas is synonymous with feasting and parties, certainly reminiscent of Saturnalia with its excesses. The modern Christmas dinner may be a feast but very small compared with Tudor times when the feast would begin about midday and last for eight or nine hours. At one time, the main dish was a boar's head, inherited from the Norse Yule festivities. Other popular dishes were venison, swan, goose and, at the top of the list, peacock. Turkeys did not arrive on the scene until about 1518.

Christmas pudding was once plum porridge — a mixture of bread crumbs, raisins, fruit juices and spices. It was eaten with a spoon, gradually evolving into the pudding that we know today.

The Christmas pie eaten by Jack Horner in the nursery rhyme was probably a very large pie filled with meat. (An explanation of this rhyme is that the 'plum' Jack Horner pulled out was the deeds of a Manor in Somerset.) Smaller Christmas pies, or mince pies, were oval pastry pies, filled with minced meat and having a pastry 'baby' laid in the pie which represented the cradle. The baby was removed before eating. Some folk still believe that it is unlucky to refuse a mince pie and that to eat one on each of the twelve days of Christmas will ensure good fortune.

Drink has always been a part of the festivities — not the bottles and cans that are familiar today, but lambswool, a dish of ale with roasted apples, spices, cream, eggs, sugar and pieces of bread served in the wassail-bowl, or punch, or egg-hot, which was a mixture of heated cider with eggs and spices. There were other popular local drinks too, as well as ale and cider.

Mummers, performing their traditional plays, were a part of the old Christmas and are still found here and there. The pantomime possibly had its origin in Rome but was introduced about 1717 from Europe. Many of the home entertainments, party games, balloons, paper hats, forfeits and buffoonery came either from Yule or from Saturnalia.

1 December

A few milestones in history are recorded on 1 December.

In 1942, whilst Britain was at war, a report was published which had then to be set aside until peace had returned. Entitled 'Social Insurance and Allied Services', it had been prepared by Sir William Beveridge (later Lord Beveridge) at the invitation of the government. The Beveridge Report, as it is more commonly known, proposed a complete system of social security for all citizens of all ages — literally from the cradle to the grave. It was the blueprint for a new British Welfare State from which, amongst other things, were to emerge the National Health Service, National Insurance and new legislation for the old and the unemployed.

Another milestone in parliamentary history was 1 December 1919. As a result of a by-election at Sutton, Plymouth, a new Member of Parliament took her seat. She was Viscountess Nancy Astor, the first woman to sit in the British House of Commons. Thereafter she was re-elected at each general election until her retirement in 1945. Notable for her energy and wit, she was a champion of women's rights, improved public education and temperance.

Overseas, Iceland became independent on 1 December 1918, having lost its independence in 1264 to Norway and then to Denmark. In 1918 it retained the King of Denmark as sovereign but it became a republic in 1944.

In Germany, in 1933, dictatorship loomed with the signing of a decree identifying the Nazi Party with the state.

Pope Leo X died on 1 December 1521. Born Giovanni de Medici, son of Lorenzo the Magnificent, he became a cardinal at 16 and pope when 37. He is remembered for his lavish spending and patronage of the arts and culture. But he failed to reform the Church and his excommunication of Martin Luther was an important step in the Reformation.

On this day, in 1927, Robert Watson-Watt became Superintendent of the Radio Research Station at Slough. He researched radio waves, now extensively used, and developed RADAR.

2 December

The man who changed the shape of the world died on 2 December 1594. His name was Gerhardus Mercator, Latinised form of his Flemish name Gerhard Kremer. He changed the shape of the world by devising a means by which a round world could be drawn as a map on a flat sheet reasonably accurately. Mercator was an excellent cartographer and Mercator's Projection, which he produced in 1569, is still in use over 400 years later.

Napoleon Bonaparte planned to change the shape of Europe by bringing more and more of it under his control. He had already begun his campaigns when the First French Republic came into being in 1799 with himself as first consul. By 1804, he was already seeing himself as the head of an empire and so, on 2 December 1804, in Paris, he was crowned Emperor Napoleon of the First French Empire by Pope Pius VII.

For the next few years he had remarkable success and it was on the anniversary of his coronation, 2 December 1805, that he celebrated his greatest victory over the combined armies of Austria and Russia in the Battle of Austerlitz.

Hernándo Cortés set out to change the map of America by bringing more of it under Spanish control. As conquistador of Mexico he literaly burned his boats behind him so that there could be no retreat. He met with successes and disasters before the conquest was complete but he later suffered political intrigues and poor health. He died in Spain, disillusioned, this day in 1547.

John Brown, abolitionist (p. 60), was hanged on 2 December 1859, at Charlestown, Virginia, finally ending his hopes for freed slaves.

Enrico Fermi, an Italian physicist, helped change the pattern for the future as one of the chief architects of the nuclear age. In the 1930s he had discovered neutron-induced radioactivity for which, in 1938, he was awarded a Nobel Prize. In that year he went to the United States, where he worked on the development of an atomic bomb. It was on this day, 2 December 1942, in Chicago, that he achieved the first controlled fission, or nuclear chain reaction.

The spacecraft *Pioneer XI* passed Jupiter on 2 December 1974, sending back, as it did so, photographs and scientific data.

3 December

The world is so full of a number of things,
I'm sure we should all be as happy as kings.

Robert Louis Stevenson wrote these words in his *Child's Garden of Verses* — and they should be just as true for adults as they are for children. Some of those things to be enjoyed are books written by Stevenson himself — *Treasure Island, Kidnapped, The Strange Case of Dr. Jekyll and Mr. Hyde,* to mention but a few. Constantly ill, he went to live in Samoa and it was there, on his estate of Vailima, that he died on 3 December 1894.

Joseph Conrad was also a writer. Born this day in 1857, he spent the early part of his life at sea. It is hardly surprising that some of his novels and short stories are about the sea and the battle against relentless Nature.

Octavia Hill, who was born on 3 December 1838, loved the beauty of the wide open spaces. She became leader of the British open-space movement, which led to the foundation, in 1895, of The National Trust. She was also associated with housing reforms.

Another Hill, Sir Rowland, born this day in 1795, gave us the postage system we now enjoy. But Penny Postage, introduced in 1840, was only one outcome of the many interests of the man who studied educational methods, printing, astronomy, mathematics and transportation.

Other things and the people who gave them to us . . . .

Nicolo Amati, born this day in 1596, was a maker of the finest quality violins and teacher of the greatest of all, Stradivari.

Samuel Crompton, born on 3 December, invented the Spinning Mule which helped revolutionise the textile industry.

Carl Zeiss, the German industrialist who manufactured fine quality microscopes and other optical instruments, died in 1888.

Pierre Auguste Renoir, French Impressionist painter, died on this day in 1919. His paintings are full of colour and light.

Neon lighting, now common in display was first used on 3 December 1910 by Georges Claude at the Paris Motor Show.

St. Francis Xavier, Spanish missionary, went to 'spread the light' in the east, in India, Ceylon, Malaya and Japan. He died in 1552 and 3 December is kept as his feast day.

4 December

A spectacular ceremony took place on 4 December 1977, when the head of state of the Central African Republic, who, a year earlier, had declared his country to be an empire, crowned himself His Imperial Majesty Bokassa I in the sports stadium of his capital city, Bangui.

The ceremony, attended by 3,500 guests from more than 40 countries, is believed to have cost some £10,000,000 — and this is one of the poorest countries in the world.

His self-glorification was short-lived. His downfall came in 1979. In the January of that year there were demonstrations by students and school children. In May over 100 school children were massacred and it became known that the Emperor had participated personally. With the aid of French paratroops, his regime was brought to an end on 20 September, whilst Bokassa was in Libya. He was later granted asylum in the Ivory Coast.

This was the birthday, in 1865, of one who was more concerned with the well-being of others than of herself. Edith Cavell became a nurse in Brussels and it was there, during World War I, that she helped British soldiers to escape. She was caught, tried and executed by a German firing squad — an incident which shocked people in many lands.

Thomas Carlyle, the Scottish writer and historian, was also born on 4 December, in 1795.

I am about to take my last voyage, a great leap in the dark.

These were the last words of Thomas Hobbes, the writer and philosopher, who died on 4 December 1679.

Others who took their last voyage on this day. . . .
Luigi Galvani, the Italian pioneer in the study and use of electricity, in 1798.
John Fowler, the Wiltshire agricultural engineer who invented a steam-hauled plough, died on 4 December 1854, of tetanus after being thrown from his horse.
Benjamin Britten, one of the leading British composers of the 20th Century, died on this day in 1975. He was a versatile composer of opera, orchestral and choral music. He was awarded the Order of Merit in 1965.

Can anything be sadder than work left unfinished?
Yes; work never begun.

Words of Christina Georgina Rossetti, who was born in London on 5 December 1830 and is considered by many to be one of England's greatest poetesses. She was a devout Anglican and many of her poems are of a religious nature.

Today's people are those who saw opportunity in work of varying kinds and began a task in earnest.

Wolfgang Amadeus Mozart took up his vocation at a very early age. He began composing at 5 and, as a child, toured Europe with his father and sister, giving concerts. He was a prolific composer of music, which is as well, for he died on 5 December 1791, aged only 35.

Józef Pilsudski, born on 5 December 1867, was the son of a poor Polish nobleman. He had a vision of a free Poland, independent of Russian rule, and for that he was prepared to do battle, though he was twice arrested and banished to Siberia. Polish independence in 1918 saw Marshal Pilsudski as chief of state and twice, in later years, as prime minister.

Alexandre Dumas, author of *The Three Musketeers* and *The Count of Monte Cristo*, was one of the most prolific French writers of the 19th Century. Becoming extravagant in his tastes, he was compelled to write more and more. He died on this day in 1870.

Sir Henry Tate had an eye for business and his patent, the sugar cube, together with his refining industry, brought him great wealth, enabling him to build up a fine private art collection, which he donated to the nation shortly before his death on this day in 1899.

Walt Disney, born on 5 December 1901 in Chicago, became a pioneer of animated cartoon films. Mickey Mouse, his most famous creation, was 'born' in 1928, followed by many other lovable characters, full length films and the creation of a whole world of fantasy in Disneyland amusement park.

Tonight Sinter Klaas will arrive in Amsterdam and be welcomed by the sovereign. With Black Peter, his servant, he will parade through the streets as children hope for a present — for tomorrow is St. Nicholas's Day.

St. Nicholas, whose feast day this is, was bishop of Myra, Asia Minor, in the 4th Century. Various tales are told of his kindness and generosity. He is the patron saint of various groups of people including children, merchants and pawnbrokers. With the addition of customs and legend from elsewhere, St. Nicholas has become Santa Claus, or Father Christmas with his bright red cloak, his reindeer-hauled sleigh and his presents for children who eagerly await his arrival in some lands on this day, in others on Christmas Eve.

In the United States, in 1933, there was great celebration in the bars and cafés. It was not Christmas they were toasting but the end of Prohibition on the previous day and the chance again to buy openly the alcoholic drinks they wanted.

George Monk, who was born on 6 December 1608, lived through an age when such celebrations would have been frowned upon by the Puritans who controlled England under Cromwell. Monk, a successful military leader and royalist supporter, was captured and imprisoned in the Tower of London for two years. He then commanded armies sent to quell rebellions in Ireland and Scotland before being appointed one of the three generals at sea in the First Dutch War. At the end of the Commonwealth, Monk played an important role in the restoration of the Stuart monarchy. For his services to the king he was made Duke of Albemarle and received other recognitions.

Another parliamentary soldier was Thomas Pride. On this day, in 1648, he went to the House of Commons and expelled or arrested 140 Presbyterian (moderate) Members in what has become known as Pride's Purge.

Also on this day. . . .
In 1421 Birth of the prince who became Henry VI eight months later.
In 1492 Columbus discovered Haiti.
In 1732 Warren Hastings, colonial administrator in India, born.
In 1857 Battle of Kānpur (Cawnpore), Indian Mutiny.
In 1892 Ernst Wernher von Siemens, German inventor, died.
In 1917 The Halifax, Nova Scotia, explosion (ship collision).
In 1920 Jack Ashley, deaf MP, champion of disabled, born.
In 1921 Irish Free State (Saorstát Éireann) created.

7 December

Marshal Ney was shot today. Or was he? A Marshal of France, he fought bravely alongside Napoleon at Waterloo but, once that battle ended in defeat, Ney was placed on a charge of high treason by the Bourbon monarchy, found guilty and executed by firing squad on 7 December 1815.

A tale circulated, however, that soldiers faked the death of the popular Marshal and enabled him to escape to America where, some years later, a schoolmaster named Ney claimed he was the Marshal. Handwriting experts upheld this claim. But, according to history, Marshal Ney was executed on this day.

On Sunday morning, 7 December 1941, 190 aircraft, loaded with bombs and torpedoes suddenly appeared in the sky over Pearl Harbor, Hawaii, where many American warships were berthed or at anchor. They had come from six Japanese aircraft carriers. Caught off their guard, the Americans lost 8 battleships and eleven other warships sunk or badly damaged, and about 150 aircraft. Over two thousand servicemen were killed and half that number injured. It was the Japanese way of declaring war on the United States.

Exactly one year later, it was the Germans who were caught unawares. At 10 pm on 7 December 1942 a British submarine surfaced off Bordeaux, France. Soon five canoes, each with two Royal Marines were paddling toward Bordeaux with limpet mines to attach to the ships in port. On the night of 11 December, explosions rocked Bordeaux. The 'Cockleshell Heroes' had completed their mission.

This was a good day for the arts and the theatre. . . .
Gian Bernini, Baroque painter, sculptor, architect, born 1598.
Pietro Mascagni, composer (*Cavalleria Rusticana*), born 1863.
Rudolf Friml, operetta composer (*Rosemarie*) born 1879.
Covent Garden Theatre, London, first opened this day in 1732.

It was *not* a good day for. . . .
Marcus Tullius Cicero, Rome's greatest orator, murdered 43 BC.
Algernon Sidney, anti–royalist politician, beheaded 1683.
Comtesse du Barry, mistress of Louis XV, guillotined 1793.
Meindert Hobbema, Dutch artist, died a pauper in 1709.
Ferdinand de Lesseps, Suez Canal builder, died in 1894.

Once a word has been allowed to escape, it cannot be recalled.

Certainly many of the words of Horace, the Roman poet who rose to favour under Emperor Augustus are still remembered. Born on this day in 65 BC, he became Rome's most respected poet (see also p. 110), writing frequently on themes of love, friendship and philosophy.

No lot is in all respects happy.

When your neighbour's wall is on fire, it becomes your business.

Tomorrow we take our course once more over the mighty seas.

This last was what German admiral Graf von Spee was doing early in December 1914. Heading toward the Falkland Islands with his squadron of five cruisers, he intended destroying the radio station at Port Stanley. Strangely, a British squadron of two battle-cruisers and five cruisers had previously arrived at Port Stanley — their purpose to look for the German squadron.

On the morning of 8 December, von Spee saw the British ships and turned away, but too late. By that evening the Battle of the Falkland Islands was over. Admiral von Spee and four of his ships had gone to the bottom of the ocean.

Ironically, the German pocket battleship named after him met her fate not far from here in the Battle of the River Plate early in World War II (pp. 133 and 137).

This was the day, in 1660, when the first actress appeared on stage. Previously all female parts had been played by men or boys.

On stage in Vaudeville at the age of 3, Sammy Davis Jnr, who was born in New York on 8 December 1925, became a popular actor, singer and dancer, appearing in several Broadway shows.

It was in New York, on 8 December 1980, that John Lennon, formerly one of the very popular Beatles pop singing group, was shot dead.

Born on 8 December. . . .

In 1765 Eli Whitney, American engineer and inventor (p. 167).

In 1865 Jean Sibelius, Finnish symphonic composer.

'200 guineas reward to anyone who can pick this lock', was the challenge offered to those who looked in the shop window of Joseph Bramah. There were plenty to accept the challenge but the lock remained tightly closed for 67 years and then took a skilled mechanic 51 hours to open it.

The lock had been designed by Bramah and constructed by a young blacksmith, Henry Maudslay, who was a genius. Between them, they laid the foundations of the British machine-tool industry which was so important in making Britain the 'workshop of the world' in the 19th Century.

Joseph Bramah, who died on 9 December 1814, also invented a hydraulic press, a wood–planing machine, a machine for numbering bank notes and a lavatory flushing system.

Arthur Pearson was a man who unlocked the door to a whole new world for lots of people. He became a journalist and founded *Pearson's Weekly* in 1890. He raised funds to enable poor London children to 'escape' from the city and enjoy country outings. He never had good eyesight and became blind. Then, thinking of others with similar problems, he founded St. Dunstan's home for the blind and served as president of the National Institution for the Blind. He died on 9 December 1921.

This day was the birthday, in 1608, of another who was to suffer blindness in later life. John Milton is regarded as one of the greatest poets in the English language. His great epic poem *Paradise Lost* (1667) was the result of thoughts that had come over a long period.

A man with an eye for artistic accuracy and a flair for being able to show the character of those whom he painted was Sir Anthony Van Dyck, court painter to the Stuarts. He died on 9 December 1641.

Dame Edith Sitwell, English poet with a formidable personality but a deep concern for human problems, died this day in 1964.

In a much lighter vein we recall the humorous writings of Joel Chandler Harris, born on 9 December 1848, who gave us the stories of the wise genial old Uncle Remus . . .

Im def in one year, en I can't hear out'n de udder.

Today, in 1917, Jerusalem surrendered to the British.

10 December

The United Nations General Assembly, meeting in Paris on this day in 1948, approved the Universal Declaration of Human Rights, consisting of a preamble and thirty articles. It was overwhelmingly adopted with 48 nations in favour and none against, though 8 abstained and 2 were absent.

Today is the prize day for those who have worked for human rights or whose achievements have benefitted mankind. Nobel Prizes, worth considerable sums of money, are presented each year for peace, literature, physics and physiology or medicine. They have come to be the most highly regarded of international awards.

Nobel prizes are financed from the huge fortune left by Alfred Nobel, who died on 10 December 1896. He was a Swedish chemist, engineer and industrialist, who invented dynamite and other explosives. His fortune came from worldwide interests in explosives and holdings in the Russian Baku Oilfields. In spite of his work on explosives, he was pacifist in outlook and hoped that the knowledge of his explosives would deter nations from warfare. He was very generous in his lifetime to humanitarian and scientific causes.

For artists a great achievement is to have pictures hung in the Royal Academy and to be able to use the letters RA after their names. It was on 10 December 1768 that the Royal Academy was founded in London, with Sir Joshua Reynolds as its first president.

In libraries, one of the most famous names is Dewey, that which is given to the Decimal System of Classification. It takes its name from the American librarian Melvil Dewey, who was born on 10 December 1851.

Also on 10 December. . . .
In 1802 William Lloyd Garrison, American abolitionist, was born.
In 1822 César Franck, composer, was born in Belgium.
In 1845 Robert Thompson patented the first pneumatic tyres.
In 1891 Field-Marshal Lord Alexander of Tunis was born.
In 1902 the Aswan Dam, Egypt, was opened.
In 1936 King Edward VIII (later Duke of Windsor) abdicated.

The only Welshman to be officially recognised as Prince of Wales died on 11 December 1282. Since then the title has been given only to the eldest son of the reigning sovereign.

The Prince of Wales who died was Llywelyn ap Gruffydd, the prince of Gwynedd in North Wales and grandson of Llywelyn ap Iorworth, who had been accepted as the chief prince in Wales some years before. Now Llywelyn was determined to drive the English out of Wales. King Henry III of England was having problems with his barons and Llywelyn allied himself to Simon de Montfort, the king's chief opponent. After de Montfort had been killed, the Welsh prince signed an agreement by which he recognised the sovereignty of Henry III.

When Henry died and Edward I became king, Llywelyn again rebelled but was defeated. His last attempt to drive the English out came in 1282, when he and his brother led a rebellion. In a skirmish near Builth, Llywelyn was killed.

Who killed King Charles XII of Sweden on 11 December 1718? He was shot in the head whilst besieging a fortress in Norway. Was it an enemy shot? Or was it a traitor? It could have been someone anxious to help his sister Ulrica, who wore the crown after him. It remains a mystery.

Another mystery. . . . Why did the Mongols begin to retreat from Europe on this day in 1241? The fierce Mongols under Genghis Khan had swept through Asia, killing and destroying. When he died in 1227 he left instructions to his son Ögödei to conquer the world. Russia, Poland, Hungary and Silesia fell before them: Europe quaked and trembled. Suddenly they stopped and returned: Europe breathed again. There seems only one explanation: the Mongols had returned to elect a new leader. Ögödei had taken to drinking wine and had died of alcoholic poisoning.

On a sweeter note, it was on this day in 1803 that the French composer and conductor Hector Berlioz was born. Sent to Paris by his father, in 1822, to study medicine, he studied music instead. He spent many years touring through the countries of Europe. Berlioz is generally considered to be the greatest of the French Romantic composers.

Great rats, small rats, lean rats, brawny rats,
Brown rats, black rats, grey rats, tawny rats,
Grave old plodders, gay young friskers,
Fathers, mothers, uncles, cousins,
Cocking tails and pricking whiskers,
Families by tens and dozens,
Brothers, sisters, husbands, wives —
Followed the Piper for their lives.

So the rats followed the *Pied Piper of Hamelin* to the River Weser, where they drowned — and the story unfolds of the refusal of the Mayor and Corporation to pay their dues, in consequence of which the Pied Piper led away the children. It is a lesson on keeping promises, told in a racy style of verse by Robert Browning, who died on 12 December 1889.

Rats come in many shapes and sizes — and not all of them have four legs! Many people considered Judge Jeffreys as a first-class rat. He was a brutal judge who went to the West of England to try people after a rising against King James II. One old lady was sentenced to be burned, several hundred people were hanged and over eight hundred, including a party of school girls, were sent as slaves to the West Indies.

After James II fled, Judge Jeffreys went into hiding but was recognised and nearly lynched before taking refuge in the Tower of London on 12 December 1688. He died there a few months later.

Or what about Ferdinand Alvarez, the Duke of Alva? He was sent to the Netherlands, where he set up the 'Council of Blood' which condemned 18,000 to be executed and confiscated the property of many more. It was said of him that, during sixty years as a soldier, he never lost a battle and was never taken by surprise. He died on 12 December 1582.

Also on this day. . . .
Viscount Samuel Hood, British admiral, was born in 1724.
Erasmus Darwin, physicist and writer, was born in 1731.
Sir Marc Isambard Brunel, engineer, died in 1849.
Marconi sent the first transatlantic radio signal in 1901.
The Hovercraft was patented in 1955.

Today is St. Lucia's Day, celebrated especially in Sweden, where the eldest daughter of the family puts on her head a wreath with seven lighted candles, then takes coffee and ginger snaps to the rest of the family. Also known as Little Yule, it serves as a reminder of ancient festivals of light.

Today's firsts. . . .
In 1642 the Dutch navigator, Abel Tasman, became the first European to sight New Zealand.
In 1903 Italo Marcioni first patented the ice-cream cone in the United States.
In 1977 Jonathan Webb became the first man to wind-surf across the Channel, taking 4 hours to cross from Folkestone to Cap Gris Nez.

Also on 13 December. . . .
In 1939 the Battle of the River Plate began.
In 1962 the space probe *Mariner II* passed near Venus.

Three great men died on 13 December.
Moses Maimonides, greatest of all Jewish rabbis, wrote many books on astronomy, mathematics and medicine, but is remembered especially for codifying all Jewish law from the Bible and the Talmud in 14 volumes *(Mishneh Torah)* and for his *Guide to the Perplexed*. He died in 1204.
Conrad Gesner, a Swiss physician and naturalist, systematically compiled information on animals and plants in several languages. He also compiled a bibliography of writers and translated the Lord's Prayer into 22 languages. He died in 1565.
Samuel Johnson was one of the outstanding 18th-Century English men of letters with a reputation as poet, writer, critic and lexicographer. His friendship with James Boswell is one of the most famous in history and Boswell's *Life of Johnson* recalls many of his words including these:

It matters not how a man dies but how he lives. The act of dying is not of importance, it lasts so short a time.

Dr. Johnson died on 13 December 1784.

Will the world come to an end in the 1990s? Nostradamus must have thought so, for he wrote one verse for each year from 1555 to the end of the world. Born on 14 December 1503, Michel de Notredame practised as a doctor before beginning to make astrological predictions in 1547. These were published in *Centuries* with a rhyming quatrain for each year. However, to avoid prosecution, he changed the order of the verses so no one can be certain which verse applies to any particular year. Many of the verses do seem to have marked relevance to historical events in certain years. Nostradamus achieved widespread fame in his time, when astrology was at its peak, and his predictions have caused controversy ever since.

One would hardly have needed to be an astrologer to predict that George Washington would hold high office in America at the end of the War of Independence for he had led the colonists well. In fact he was unanimously chosen to be president of the Constitutional Convention and overwhelmingly voted first president of the republic in 1789, serving two terms in that office. After his death on 14 December 1799, he was described in Congress as '. . . a citizen, first in war, first in peace, first in the hearts of his countrymen.'

It was only after his death from typhoid fever on 14 December 1861, at the age of 42, that the British public began to realise the exceptional qualities of Prince Albert, consort of Queen Victoria. He had helpfully advised both the queen and her ministers; he had suggested and successfully organised the Great Exhibition of 1851; he had helped design Osborne House and proved accomplished in the arts and in music.

Also on this day. . . .
 In 1417 Sir John Oldcastle, Lollard supporter, was hanged and burned. (He was the model for Shakespeare's Falstaff.)
 In 1546 Tycho Brahe, Danish astronomer, was born.
 In 1624 Lord Howard of Effingham, admiral, died.
 In 1911 Roald Amundsen reached the South Pole.
 In 1918 women first voted in a British General Election.
 In 1947 Earl Baldwin, British Labour statesman, died.
 In 1959 Archbishop Makarios elected first president of Cyprus.

15 December

Please, Sir George, I wish to give notice. I was hired to drive, not to fly!

So spoke the terrified coachman, who had just landed after a flight across a Yorkshire valley. The year was 1853, fifty years before the first historic powered flight by the Wright brothers. The machine was a glider with a pram-like carriage beneath it. The designer was Sir George Caley, a wealthy Yorkshire landowner who took a great interest as a young man in science, mechanics and the possibilities of making flying machines that were heavier than air.

He made many sketches and models. His first full-size glider was built in 1809. He thought it should be possible to build a small engine capable of powering a heavier-than-air machine but his glider was as far as he was able to get with these experiments. Today he is recognised as one of the important pioneers of flight. But he was more than that. He was a keen astronomer. He was acutely interested in safety measures on the new railways. He urged the building of self-righting lifeboats. He designed an artificial hand with movable thumb and fingers. His humanitarian attitudes were widely recognised.

Most people acknowledge that Sir George Caley was a genius — a loss to the world when he died on 15 December 1857.

A quarter of a century earlier, on 15 December 1832, another was born, at Dijon, France, who, later in life, would be 'reaching for the sky' in a different sense. He was Alexandre Gustave Eiffel, the engineer who designed one of the best-known structures in the world, the Eiffel Tower, built in Paris for the 1889 World Fair. The Tower is 300 metres in height with lifts and stairways to the top, restaurants, a weather station, television transmitter and other facilities too. Eiffel designed many important buildings, bridges and the framework for the Statue of Liberty at New York.

Also on this day. . . .
Izaak Walton, writer (*The Compleat Angler*), died in 1683.
Dr. Ludwig Zamenhof, inventor of Esperanto, was born in 1832.
Chief Sitting Bull, American Indian, was killed in 1890.
World War I: the Battle of Verdun ended in 1916.
The British Broadcasting Company was incorporated in 1922.

One American who is known by sight to people in at least 48 countries is Colonel Sanders, for a picture of him with his white hair, goatee beard and white suit can be seen over every Kentucky Fried Chicken Shop. 'Colonel' is an honorary title for Harland Sanders, who opened his first restaurant in 1929. Ten years later he produced his recipe for 'finger-lickin' good chicken' using a secret blend of eleven spices and a pressure cooker to seal in the flavour and moisture. He died on 16 December 1980.

Also in America, on 16 December 1773, was the Boston Tea Party. This was nothing to do with eating food but a revolt by the American colonists against a tax on tea imposed by the British government. Under cover of darkness, some colonists dressed as Indians, threw overboard a cargo of tea from a ship in Boston harbour. It was one of the events which led up to the American War of Independence.

In South Africa, 16 December is Dingaan's Day, commemorating this day, in 1838, when the Boers defeated the Zulu King Dingaan after he had murdered the leader of the Boers who had taken part in the Great Trek into Natal. It was on this day in 1879, also in South Africa, that the Transvaal Republic was founded.

Some well-known people were born on 16 December. . . .
George Whitefield, evangelist, in 1714.
Gebhard Blucher, Prussian Field-Marshal at Waterloo, in 1742.
Ludwig van Beethoven, German composer, in 1770.
Jane Austen, novelist, in 1775.
Zoltán Kodály, Hungarian composer, in 1882.
Sir Jack Hobbs, English cricketer, in 1882.
Sir Noel Coward, playwright, composer and actor, in 1899.

And some who died. . . .
Wilhelm Grimm, collector of folk-tales and writer, in 1859.
Camille Saint-Saëns, French composer, in 1921.

Also on 16 December. . . .
Oliver Cromwell became Lord Protector in 1653.
Work began on the construction of the Mersey Tunnel in 1925.

Theophrastus Bombastus von Hohenheim was born on 17 December 1493. He gave himself the name of Paracelsus, which is much easier to remember. The son of a physician, he studied chemistry and alchemy, travelled widely and accumulated a vast knowledge of facts about medicines. He greatly influenced the medical scene by making new chemical compounds, improving pharmacy and encouraging research.

Thomas Guy's contribution in the world of medicine was in the provision of hospital accommodation in London. He was the son of a Thames lighterman but he set up in business as a bookseller, mainly concerned with importing, printing and selling Bibles. This and other business transactions made him a fortune with which he built and furnished three wards at St. Thomas's Hospital, founded Guy's Hospital in Southwark and built almshouses. He died on this day in 1724.

Another death on this day, in 1907, was that of William Thomson, 1st Baron Kelvin, the Scottish physicist and mathematician who researched, discovered and invented in various fields of electricity including submarine cables.

Some of today's birthdays. . . .
Sir Humphry Davy, the Cornish chemist (p. 63), in 1778.
John Greenleaf Whittier, American Quaker poet, hymn writer and abolitionist, in 1807.
Alison Uttley, writer of *Sam Pig* and other popular children's books, in 1884.

This was also the birthday of aircraft, for it was on 17 December 1903 that Orville Wright made history by becoming the first man to fly a machine that was heavier than air. The flight at Kitty Hawk, North Carolina, on a cold windy morning was only a few feet above the ground and lasted just a few seconds — but it was a beginning.

A naval drama ended on 17 December 1939. The German pocket battleship *Graf Spee*, which had been engaged in the Battle of the River Plate by the British cruisers *Ajax, Achilles* and *Exeter*, took refuge in Montevideo. On this day Captain Langsdorff sailed, scuttled his ship, then shot himself.

For any violinist, the name Stradivarius means perfection, for there is no better violin to be obtained than one made by the great master of violin-making, Antonio Stradivari, whose name is often written in the Latin form of Stradivarius. He was born in Cremona, Italy, about 1649 and was apprenticed to another well-known violin-maker, Nicolo Amati. About 1700, Stradivari went into business on his own. He then improved the shape of the violin in various ways to give an instrument which has never been bettered. He is thought to have made over 1,100 violins, violas and cellos before his death on 18 December 1737.

Another, regarded by many as the greatest of his kind, was Joseph Grimaldi, who was born in London on 18 December 1779. He came from a family of clowns and dancers, so it is hardly surprising that he began his theatrical career as a child. He was very talented as an actor, singer, dancer and clown but it was as a clown that he excelled. In fact his white faced 'Joey the Clown' was the forerunner of today's circus clowns. He continued to entertain in London and the provinces until 1828, a few years before his death on 31 May 1837.

An almost perfect hoax took place on 18 December 1912. It was announced that the prehistoric remains of a man had been found at Piltdown in Sussex which appeared to be a missing link in the evolution of man from apes. It was not until 1953 that the Piltdown skull was proved to be a clever fake.

Dr. William Moon was born on this day in 1818. He was the inventor of the Moon Alphabet for the blind.

This was also the birthday, in 1786, of Carl Maria von Weber, the German composer, conductor and pianist, whose works include the popular *Invitation to the Dance*. One of his operas, *Oberon*, was composed for the Covent Garden Theatre, London.

On 18 December 1969, both Houses of Parliament voted for the permanent abolition of the death penalty for crimes in Great Britain.

It was on this day in 1865 that slavery was finally abolished in the United States of America.

19 December

Sir William Edward Parry, who was born on 19 December 1790, spent much of his service in the Royal Navy sailing the icy waters of the Arctic. In 1810, his first voyage as a lieutenant was to protect the whale population and, in 1818, he served as commander in the Arctic under Sir John Ross.

Afterwards he made several expeditions on his own account to see whether he could discover a North-west Passage round the north of Canada from the Atlantic to the Pacific. His final voyage in the Arctic, in 1827, was an unsuccessful attempt to reach the North Pole. He wrote several books about his expeditions and held high offices before his death in 1855.

During the previous century, the Danish navigator, Vitus Bering (or Behring) had also been exploring the Arctic. Born in 1680 in Jutland, he served as captain in the navy of Peter the Great before being chosen to command a voyage of discovery in the Sea of Kamchatka. A few years later, in 1733, his Great Northern Expedition left Russia to sail round the north of Europe and Asia. It was eight years before he discovered Alaska and the waters that bear his name, the Bering Strait and Bering Sea. Then disaster struck. His ship was wrecked on an unknown desert island, where the men were forced to winter amid raging snowstorms. Bering, by now a very sick man, died there on 19 December 1741.

December 1981 brought Arctic conditions to Britain with heavy falls of snow and temperatures well below freezing. Gales battered the Cornish coast on 19 December and the freighter *Union Star* broke down near Land's End. In no time, the Penlee lifeboat, with its crew from the picturesque village of Mousehole, was on its way to the rescue, fighting its way through 70 — 80 knot winds and breakers up to 20 metres high. At 9.22 pm a radio message from the lifeboat said 'Four off' — they were going back for the others. That was the last message. Soon the freighter lay upside down on the rocks; the wreckage of the lifeboat was washed up in Lamorna Cove; and Mousehole mourned the loss of eight very brave lifeboatmen.

19 December saw the deaths, in 1848, of the novelist, Emily Brontë, and, in 1851, of Joseph Turner, the artist.

Yesterday's stories of arctic exploration serve as a reminder that, to many people, the northern sea routes are important for their necessary supplies. Today there are fleets of powerful icebreakers, which break a passage through the frozen waters in winter. History was made on 20 December 1959, when the Russian icebreaker *Lenin* came into operation. She was the first non-naval vessel to be driven by atomic power.

In much warmer waters, it was on 20 December 1952 that a different form of history was made — or rather uncovered. A fisherman off Anjouan, near Madagascar, found in his net a large ugly fish weighing about 45 kg. He killed it and slit it open. Fortunately it was seen before he could do more, by one who recognised it for what it was — a coelacanth, a prehistoric type of fish, of which the only previous living specimen had been caught in December 1938.

History was also made on 20 December 1879, when Thomas Edison, at his Menlo Park home, New Jersey, gave the first demonstration of a practical and effective electric lamp.

Born on 20 December 1868 was Harvey Firestone, the man who made tyres for the famous Ford Model T cars and whose name is still found on car tyres today.

James Hilton, the British novelist, died on 20 December 1954. His books include *Goodbye Mr. Chips* and *Lost Horizon,* a story set in a Tibetan monastery called Shangri-La.

One of the greatest pianists of the 20th Century died on 20 December 1982. Artur Rubinstein is especially remembered as the greatest player of the music of his fellow Pole, Chopin.

There must surely be more pleasant ways of doing so, but if any unmarried woman would like to dream of her future husband she could try this old form of divination tonight. As it is St. Thomas's Eve, she should take an onion, peel it, wrap it in a cloth, put it under her pillow and say the following words:

Good St. Thomas, do me right,
Let my true love come tonight,
That I may see him face to face
And in my arms his form embrace.

St. Thomas grey, St. Thomas grey,
Longest night and shortest day.

By St. Thomas's Day, Christmas is fast approaching and final preparations of food are under way. A reminder of Christmas is in the pealing of bells — an important aspect of the festival. It has been the practice, in some places, to begin ringing the bells on St. Thomas's Day and so 'ring in Christmas'.

It used to be the custom for people to go 'a-Thomassing' or 'a-corning' on this day to beg for the wheat they needed for making their Christmas bread and cakes. Sometimes the wheat was made into frumenty. The grains were soaked in a bowl of water in a warm oven until they swelled, burst open and formed a thick jelly, often eaten with hot milk.

There are various local customs. In Lichfield, for example, on St. Thomas's Day, a small loaf is provided by the Dean's Vicar for each household in the Cathedral Close.

At Old Bolingbroke, Lincolnshire, a candle auction is held on this day. A pin is stuck into a candle about an inch from the top and the candle lit. People then make bids for the use of a piece of land. When the flame of the candle reaches the pin, the pin drops out and no more bids are accepted. The last bidder becomes tenant for a year. Similar candle auctions are held elsewhere.

Born on 21 December 1803, was Sir Joseph Whitworth, the mechanical engineer. He invented a means of making perfectly flat metal surfaces and he made extremely accurate machine tools. The system of Whitworth threads for nuts and bolts is named after him.

Another 'man of steel' was born on this day in 1879. He was Joseph Dzhugashvili, who adopted for himself the name of Stalin ('Man of Steel'). He was the ruthless, dictatorial head of state of the USSR from 1929 until his death in 1953. Anyone opposing him was killed or sent to a labour camp.

Also on this day. . . .
In 1620 the Pilgrim Fathers landed on Plymouth Rock, USA.
In 1823 Jean Henry Fabre, French naturalist (insects), was born.
In 1958 Charles de Gaulle was elected President of France.

22 December

Some of the 'Magic of Christmas' is provided at children's parties by entertainers who use various forms of magic, conjuring and innumerable devices which prove that the hand is quicker than the eye. The development of magic in the 19th Century was largely due to John Nevil Maskelyne, who was born on this day in 1839. He invented many new tricks and went into partnership with George Cook. For eight years, until Cook's death, they went on tour with Maskelyne's trick box. Later he went into partnership with David Devant, England's most famous magician. Maskelyne's contribution to the world of magic was not only that of his inventions but his constant encouragement of other performers, the experienced and the novice.

For magic of a different kind, how about *Peter Rabbit*? Children are still pleased to read about the naughty little rabbit who first made his appearance in a letter to a sick child in 1893 and in a book seven years later. He, with *Jemima Puddle-Duck, Mrs. Tiggy-Winkle* and others, was the creation of Beatrix Potter, whose simple stories, with her true-to-life illustrations, have delighted generations of children.

Having married William Heelis, Beatrix spent the last thirty years of her life farming in the English Lake District. On her death, on 22 December 1943, her land passed into the care of The National Trust.

It was not magic that made a man of Mary Ann Evans. It was simply that women then were not expected to write books and so she wrote her famous novels, *Adam Bede, The Mill on the Floss* and others under the pen-name of George Eliot. She died on 22 December 1880.

It must have seemed like magic to Fyodor Dostoyevsky. There he was on the scaffold on 22 December 1849, about to be executed, when word came that his sentence was commuted to imprisonment in Siberia — from which he returned to give the world some masterpieces of literature.

Who has not thrilled to the magical tones of 'One Fine Day' from *Madame Butterfly*, or to the great arias of *La Boheme, Tosca* and *Turandot*? All are the works of Giacomo Puccini, who was born on 22 December 1858.

23 December

On 23 December 1952, a sick, weatherbeaten Frenchman stepped out of a 15 foot (4½ m) inflatable rubber life-raft on the island of Barbados in the Caribbean, having been at sea for 65 days. No, he had not been shipwrecked. He had just crossed the Atlantic to prove that it was possible to survive in such a craft without any supplies of food or water.

Alain Bombard was born into a wealthy Paris family and had enjoyed holidays by the sea. It was whilst in Boulogne that victims of a shipwreck were brought in, many having died of shock. He was sure that more could survive if only they were able to keep calm and use the sea's resources. He experimented with fish and fish juices. Then he tried out his theories with a friend on an 18-day voyage in the Mediterranean, eating and drinking nothing but fish, fish juice and sea water.

His solo voyage in his inflatable raft *Heretic* was to prove without doubt that a man on his own could survive. He succeeded, received a hero's welcome in France and then set about teaching the 'Bombard method' of survival, now adopted by most navies of the world. Bombard-type life-rafts, carried on ships of all kinds, have saved many lives.

It was much pleasanter to travel leisurely in 'the gondola of London'. That was the name given by Disraeli to the hansom cab, patented on 23 December 1834, by Joseph Hansom. It was a two-wheeled horse-drawn vehicle for two passengers with the driver behind, looking over the top.

Andrey Tupolev died on 23 December 1972. He was the man who created the world's first supersonic passenger aircraft, the Tu-144, as well as about a hundred other civil and military planes. He was recognised as one of the greatest aircraft designers of the Soviet Union.

T. R. Malthus also died on this day in 1834. He wrote of 'the perpetual struggle for room and food', believing that the population would always grow faster than food supplies.

Born on 23 December 1732, was Sir Richard Arkwright, who helped revolutionise the textile industry by inventing the water frame for spinning. He owned several cotton mills.

Yousuf Karsh, the outstanding portrait photographer, famous on both sides of the Atlantic, was born on this day in 1908.

On 24 December 1933, a precious package of parchment arrived in London to be placed in the care of the British Museum. It was the *Codex Sinaiticus*, an ancient manuscript of the Bible, probably written in the 4th Century AD, which has most of the Old Testament in Greek, the whole of the New Testament and other writings. It was found by Constantin Tischendorf, in 1844, in the monastery of St. Catherine on Mount Sinai. He persuaded the monks there to allow it to pass into the possession of the Tsar of Russia. In 1933 it was bought from the Soviet Government.

People born on 24 December include. . . .
John, King of England, in 1167.
St. Ignatius Loyola, founder of the Jesuits, in 1491.
Kit Carson, US frontiersman, trapper, soldier, Indian agent, in 1809.
Poets, George Crabbe in 1754 and Matthew Arnold in 1822.

Some who died on 24 December were. . . .
Vasco da Gama, Portuguese navigator and explorer, in 1524.
Novelist, William Makepeace Thackeray, in 1863.
Sister Dora, nursing heroine of Walsall, in 1878.
Frances Buss, pioneer of schools for girls, in 1894.

On Christmas Eve 1918, a new form of service was held in King's College, Cambridge. It was called the Festival of the Nine Lessons and Carols. It became very popular and has remained so ever since. It was first broadcast as long ago as 1930. Elsewhere people gather for other festivals of carols, or to sing around a Christmas tree, as in Trafalgar Square, London.

Over seven hundred years ago, on Christmas Eve, a church bell was tolled in Dewsbury, Yorkshire. It is a custom which continues to this day. Known as 'Tolling the Devil's Knell', the tolling begins at 11 pm with four sets of four bells, then one for every year since Christ was born — an event which heralded the end for the Devil!

As the bell is tolling in Dewsbury, people throughout the country will be making their way to church for the late night Mass, or Holy Communion, or service of praise to welcome Christmas and give thanks to God for Jesus Christ.

Christmas is Christ-mass (Old English *Cristes Maesse*), the festival on which the Christian Church celebrates the birth of its leader and founder, Jesus Christ. It is not that this day was his actual birthday. It was chosen because of its convenience, Christianising pagan festivals held at this time of year. Indeed most of our Christmas customs are those borrowed from others as has been noted on pages 118–20. So today is celebrated much as it has been for many years with family gatherings, feasting and festivities, Christmas cards and carols, with the wonder and worship of God incarnate, a baby in a stable.

It was on Christmas Day in the year 800 that Charlemagne was crowned Holy Roman Emperor. It was probably a moving rather than a spectacular occasion. Stories of Charlemagne, 'Charles the Great', may conjure up pictures of a mighty emperor with a colourful entourage and surrounded by splendour. In fact he was a chieftain of the Franks, son of Pepin the Short, used to fighting battles, occasionally barbarous, yet shrewd and with an imposing personality.

Charlemagne fought many campaigns to extend the influence of Christendom. In 754, when the Pope crowned Pepin, Charles had been given the title Patrician of the Romans, but he never saw himself as a Roman Emperor. After a visit to Rome in 774, when he had been struck by the splendours of the Church ceremonies, he did henceforth call himself 'King by the grace of God'. It was while at prayer on Christmas Day 800 that Pope Leo III placed the Imperial Crown on his head and people present shouted, 'Long life and victory to Charles Augustus, the crowned of God, the great powerful Emperor of the Romans.'

On Christmas Day 1497, the Portuguese explorer, Vasco da Gama, sighted the location of the present port of Durban, in South Africa. He called the land Natal in honour of the celebration of the birth of Christ.

It was on Christmas Day 1896 that John Philip Sousa wrote down a tune that had been on his mind for a month or so. He called it *The Stars and Stripes Forever*.

Sir Isaac Newton, scientist, was born on 25 December 1642.

Good King Wenceslas looked out
On the Feast of Stephen,
When the snow lay round about,
Deep, and crisp, and even:

No doubt many people have enjoyed singing this during the past few days as part of their Christmas festivities. Today, 26 December, is the Feast of Stephen, the day on which the Church recalls St. Stephen, the first Christian martyr.

And Good King Wenceslas? He was a Christian prince of Bohemia (Czechoslovakia) in the 10th Century, who became St. Wenceslas, the patron saint of Bohemia. He has no connection with this day: his feast day is 28 September. The story as told in the carol is, alas, fiction — just a pleasant story for a carol composed during the 19th Century.

Yet the thought behind the carol is one that has definite connections with today, the day on which, for many years, it has been customary to think about and help the poor and needy. It was on this day that church alms boxes were opened, hence the probable reason for this being known as Boxing Day. The custom grew of giving 'Christmas Boxes' — gifts of money to servants and others, on this day, in thanks for services rendered. Not so long ago people such as postmen and dustmen would call at houses on Boxing Day to receive their 'boxes'.

Today is a day for sports. In many places there are meets of fox-hunters as social occasions. Nowadays there is always a full programme of football fixtures and other popular sports to satisfy players and spectators alike. There are local traditional customs and events, such as sword dancing in Sheffield and mummers' plays, such as the play of the Paper Boys at Marshfield, Gloucestershire.

Born on 26 December were Thomas Gray, poet (1716), George Romney, painter (1734), Patrick Gilmore, bandmaster (1829), and Mao Tse–tung, Chinese leader (1893).

On 26 December 1898, Pierre and Marie Curie discovered how to obtain radium — a discovery they gave freely to the world.

St. John the Evangelist, of whom this is the feast day, was one of the original disciples of Jesus Christ, a Galilean fisherman and one of the closest to Jesus. He outlived the remainder of the twelve, was exiled to the island of Patmos and died in Ephesus, an old man about the year 100. In the fourth Gospel, and in his letters in the New Testament, his writings have earned him the reputation of the 'apostle of love'.

The command that Christ has given us is this: whoever loves God must love his brother also. (1 John 4; 21)

A well-loved writer of much later years was Charles Lamb. He wrote many essays under the name of 'Elia', the last of them appearing in the year before his death which occurred on 27 December 1834. These essays, which were almost wholly autobiographical, give a great insight to the writer, his profound thinking and his humour, his loyalty, tenderness and generosity. In one of the last essays he wrote:

The greatest pleasure I know is to do a good action by stealth, and to have it found out by accident.

Cardinal Jozef Mindszenty, Roman Catholic Primate of Hungary, made no secret of his opposition to the Communist government of his country. He became known worldwide when he was arrested, on this day in 1948, charged with treason and sentenced to life imprisonment. He was released in 1955 on grounds of ill health and, in the following year, was granted asylum in the American legation in Budapest.

Some other of today's people. . . .
Johannes Kepler, born this day in 1571, was the German astronomer who discovered the eliptical orbits of the planets and introduced the ray theory of light to explain vision.
Pierre de Ronsard, who died in 1585, was one of the greatest and most prolific French poets of his day.
Louis Pasteur, French chemist and microbiologist, born this day in 1822, originated 'pasteurisation' to kill bacteria.
Giovanni Pirelli, born 27 December 1848, Italian industrialist, pioneered the manufacture of electric cable and car tyres.
Marlene Dietrich, German actress, born this day in 1904, became a top Hollywood film star in the 1930s.

Although there were 120 chairs in the basement of a café in Paris, only 25 people came to see the films. The date was 28 December 1895 and those 25 people formed the audience for the first ever public film show, presented by the brothers Lumiére, who had invented a means of projecting pictures on to a screen. The idea caught on and public showings became very popular.

William Semple's idea became very popular too. On 28 December 1869, he took out a patent for 'the combination of rubber with other articles in any proportions adapted to the formation of an acceptable chewing gum'.

Earl 'Fatha' Hines also provided what many people wanted. Born on this day in 1905, he studied classical music but became a jazz pianist, then formed his own big band and had a great influence on the development of jazz music.

Maurice Ravel was also a bit of a rebel with his music, some of which was not well received, but his *Bolero* is popular with many. Ravel, a French Basque composer, died this day in 1937.

History was made this day in 1903, by Richard Cain of Bermondsey, London, issued with the first British driving licence.

History was made — or rather recorded — by Thomas B. Macaulay who wrote his *History of England* after serving as a Member of Parliament. As a boy he had been rather precocious — a trait which seems to have continued. Lord Melbourne said of him, 'I wish that I was as cocksure of anything as Tom Macaulay is of everything.' Macaulay died on 28 December 1937.

Two men born on 28 December became experts in their particular fields. Sir Archibald Geikie, born in Edinburgh in 1835, was one of the top geologists of his day, director-general of the Survey of the United Kingdom and head of the Geological Museum, London, honoured in many ways for his work. Sir John Bennet Lawes of Rothamsted, Hertfordshire, born in 1814, experimented with plants and crops, researched into various aspects of agriculture and developed artificial fertilisers.

Disaster this night in 1879. A violent storm caused part of the Tay railway bridge in Scotland to collapse. A train with its crew and 75 passengers disappeared below the waters. Thomas Bouch, designer of the bridge, opened only the previous year, never recovered from the shock.

29 December

Today, the feast day of St. Thomas of Canterbury, recalls the murder of the archbishop on the steps of the cathedral altar on 29 December 1170 — the result of hasty words spoken by Henry II, King of England: 'Will no one rid me of this turbulent priest?'

Three inventors were born today — Charles Macintosh, inventor of waterproofs, in 1766; Charles Goodyear, developer of vulcanised rubber, in 1800; and Alexander Parkes, chemist, inventor of celluloid, in 1813.

In the world of the arts, Pablo Casals, Spanish cellist, conductor and composer was born in 1876; Christina Rossetti, English poet, died in 1894; and Rainer Maria Rilke, Austrian lyric poet, died in 1926 — all on this day. Sarah Siddons, tragic actress, made her debut on the London stage on 29 December 1775.

This day, in 1930, saw the end of the longest ever swim. Fred P. Newton swam 1,826 miles (2,938 km, down the Mississippi from Fort Dam to New Orleans. He began the swim on 6 July and spent 742 hours in the water.

30 December

On 30 December 1865, Rudyard Kipling was born in Bombay. After being educated in England, he returned to India as a journalist. He became famous as a novelist, short-story writer and poet, with a passionate love for Britain and her Empire. He received a Nobel Prize for Literature in 1907.

Gregori Rasputin, the religious fanatic who had great influence over the Russian Czarina Alexandra, was murdered on 30 December (17 OS) 1916 — poisoned, shot and then drowned in the river Neva.

Social reformers Amelia Jenks Bloomer and Josephine Butler died on this day in 1894 and 1906 respectively.

This is Hogmanay, for people in Scotland and northern England a day that is celebrated with greater festivity than Christmas. The name probably comes from the French *aguillaneuf*, the Norman form of which, *hoguimané*, resembles the Scottish word.

It used to be a custom for children to go out on this morning to ask for their 'Hogmanay' or New Year gift. Sometimes this was done on New Year's Eve, sometimes New Year's Day. Children would blacken their faces and dress grotesquely ('guisers'), then go from house to house chanting such rhymes as

Get up, good wife and shake your feathers,
And dinna think that we are beggars;
For we are bairns come oot to play,
Get up and gie us oor hogmanay.

Hogmanay is party time, either at home or in public places. Scots who are 'in exile' may link up with their fellow-countrymen to enjoy an evening of Scottish dancing, singing and general festivity with the party spirit enhanced in many cases with a goodly supply of Scotch whisky.

It is not only the Scots who tend to celebrate this evening by drinking. There are many who drink too much and some, unfortunately, drive afterwards. The police are usually alert for drunken drivers and have their breathalysers handy. The first breathalyser tests, incidentally, were introduced on this day in 1938 by the police in Indianapolis, USA.

Many of the customs of this day date back to ancient Celtic times and include old superstitions and beliefs. Some of these are concerned with the winter fire rituals. At Comrie, Tayside, the Hogmanay celebrations include the Flambeaux Procession, in which townsfolk in fancy dress march to the main square, led by pipers and accompanied by torch-bearers. After the fancy-dress costumes have been judged, there is plenty of dancing, singing and good fun until the torches have burned out. At Stonehaven a celebration takes place on the stroke of midnight. Balls of rag in wire-netting, that have been soaked in paraffin, are set on fire and swung on wires until the marchers reach the High Street, where they release the balls in a skyward direction.

Further south, in Northumberland, there is a tar-burning ceremony at Allendale. Men in fancy dress, each carrying a tub of burning tar on his head, process through the parish to the place where the bonfire will be lit at midnight. Then there is dancing and merrymaking to herald the new year.

Apart from the participants, there are many who enjoy watching the fire celebrations. Fire-watching was not such a pleasant occupation during World War II. It was on this day in 1940 that fire-watching became compulsory in Britain, so that people would see any incendiary bombs dropped from enemy aircraft to set fire to buildings.

Other fires were caused by John Wycliffe, who died on 31 December 1384. They were lit by others to burn his writings, which included translations of part of the Bible into English. Wycliffe had spoken out against some of the teachings of the Roman Catholic Church and he had several influential people amongst his followers who were known as Lollards. Persecution followed and some Lollards were burned at the stake as heretics. Wycliffe himself escaped this — though in 1428 his remains were dug up, burned and the ashes cast into the river Swift.

Other happenings on this day. . . .
In 1491 Jacques Cartier, French explorer of Canada, was born.
In 1719 Jonathan Flamsted, first Astronomer Royal, died.
In 1720 Charles Edward, the Young Pretender, was born.
In 1738 Marquis Cornwallis, soldier and statesman, was born.
In 1923 the chimes of Big Ben were first broadcast.

Tonight the Mari Lwyd (Holy Mary) Mummers may visit certain houses in South Wales with their decorated horse's skull. They sing traditional songs and are normally refused entry at first. It is customary then to invite them in for food and drink.

In some churches Watchnight Services will be held to see in the new year. It is a custom begun by Methodists in the 18th Century and adopted later by others.

[See also page 156 — New Year]

Other December Events and Commemorations

(see also pp. 117–20)

Five Sundays before Christmas Newark, Nottinghamshire: Gopher Ringing. Bells are rung on each of these Sundays commemorating the guiding to safety by the church bells of a merchant named Gopher.

6th (St. Nicholas's Day) In various places: Election of a Boy Bishop. This is a thousand-year old custom, widespread until Tudor times when it was suppressed. The Boy Bishop held office until 28 December. In places the custom has been revived, the election of a choirboy to this office being common.

Second Sunday after 30 November Broughton, Northampton-shire: after midnight, Tin Can Band. Parades in the streets for about an hour making a din with all available kinds of can or bucket. An old medieval custom believed to scare away the gipsies.

18th Londonderry, Ulster: Closing the Gates Ceremony. It commemorates the beginning of the siege of the city in 1688, which lasted for 105 days.

Some time before Christmas Glastonbury, Somerset: Flowering of the Holy Thorn. Sprays are cut and sent to the Queen.

Christmas Eve Dunster, Somerset: Burning the Ashen Faggot. As each band round the bundle of faggots bursts in the flames, a round of cider is drunk.

25th and 26th In various places: Mummers' Plays.

Boxing Day Marshfield, Gloucestershire: Mummers' costumes are decorated with paper streamers. King William, the hero, is accompanied by Little Man John, Tenpenny Nit and Saucy Jack.

27th Melrose, Borders: Freemasons' Walk. Members of Masonic Lodge in full regalia process with banners and a silver band.

SOME DECEMBER FAIRS

About 10th Boston, Lincolnshire: The Beast Mart is declared open by a proclamation by the Town Clerk in the presence of the Mayor. The charter was granted in 1573.

Second Thursday Leicester: Sheep Fair.

SOME OTHER EVENTS

Early December Scottish Agricultural Winter Fair.
London: Royal Smithfield Show of prime animals.

JANUARY

January

January takes its name from the Latin Ianuarius, named after Janus, the Roman god of doorways. He it was who stood at the doorway of the year and is often shown as having two faces, enabling him to look forward and backward at the same time.

Janus was not only the god of the opening year but the god to whom the Romans prayed at the beginning of any important action, such as war, and the door to his temple was always left open during war. He was called upon at the beginning of every prayer.

The old calendar of the pagan Anglo-Saxons began on 25 December. The last month of the old year and the first month of the new were often linked together under the one name, Giuli, an old form of 'Yule', the actual meaning of which is uncertain. This first month was also known as Wulfmonath, the Wolf month, because wolves, which were common in England then, were hunting for food.

Other creatures are also hunting for food. January is one of the months when wild birds depend upon people who put out food for them, especially when snow covers the ground. A new fall of snow is soon patterned with tiny footmarks of birds and animals. Because it is winter we expect the cold. There is an old saying:

As the day lengthens, the cold strengthens.

Even the birds may give their warning:

If the birds begin to whistle in January,
there are frosts to come.

Even so, there are bright and sometimes warm days, but if the plants are encouraged to grow it is not good.

A January spring is worth nothing.

The grass that grows in Janiveer
Grows no more all the year

For the farmer, of course, the work on the land may well include sowing some of his crops.

Who in January sows oats, gets gold and groats

New Year

Since 1752, 1 January has been New Year's Day, celebrated by many people as a day for a fresh start and for New Year resolutions. It is welcomed in various ways but, on the whole, has a rather noisy reception, with the sound of bells, ships' sirens, bursts of cheering and noisy parties. One of the larger crowds is that which assembles in Trafalgar Square, London, where people are in a festive mood and some bathe in the fountains.

Bell-ringing has been a custom for many years. Church bells throughout the land have pealed their welcome.

> Ring out, wild bells, to the wild sky,
> The flying cloud, the frosty light:
> The year is dying in the night
> Ring out, wild bells, and let him die.
>
> Ring out the old, ring in the new,
> Ring, happy bells, across the snow;
> The year is going, let him go;
> Ring out the false, ring in the true.
>
> Alfred, Lord Tennyson

In the Royal Navy, where eight strokes on the ship's bell indicate the end of each watch, it is customary to sound sixteen bells at the end of the last watch of the year.

As the old year ends and the new begins, will there perhaps be those who give an eye to the wind? An old rhyme suggests an indication of weather to come.

> If New Year's Eve night wind blow south,
> It betokeneth warmth and growth.
> If west, much milk and fish in the sea;
> If north, much cold and storms there'll be;
> If east, the trees will bear much fruit;
> If north-east, flee it man and brute.

Some people will have given the new year a warm reception as they have lit their bonfires or engaged in their local fire cere-monies (p. 150) but they will need to be wrapped up well against the wintry wind, especially if they are then to go first-footing.

First-footing is common in Scotland, the north of England and some continental countries. When a knock comes at the door in the early hours of New Year's Day, householders hope that the person outside is dark-haired (though in some places he should be fair) and that he may have with him the symbolic gifts that are expected in that area. These may be a piece of coal, a little salt, a morsel of bread, a small coin or some other token to represent good fortune.

Local customs and superstitions may indicate even more fully what kind of man would be welcome. Cross-eyed or flat-footed men may be considered unlucky, so may ginger-headed men. Women first-footers are considered unlucky in most places.

It is customary for the First-foot to be invited in to receive the liberal hospitality of the house. A man of the right appearance can indulge himself well in food and drink by going from house to house. To ensure having the right First-foot, a householder may go out of his house with his gifts and then be let in again after the New Year has arrived.

Perhaps the custom of bringing small gifts to the household owes its origin to the Romans. At their three-day New Year celebration of Kalends, many gifts were given, especially to poorer neighbours. Often these were symbolic, such as sweets, money or precious metal gifts, to indicate a wish for a pleasant year full of good fortune. It is still customary for some people to give presents at New Year.

One interesting New Year gift is that presented to members of Queen's College, Oxford — a needle threaded with coloured silk, given with the command, 'Take this and be thrifty'. The French words for needle and thread are *aiguille et fil*, resembling the name of the founder, in 1341, Robert de Englesfield.

Local customs exist in many parts of the country and New Year's Day is observed as a public holiday. Most people make some form of resolution, if only to themselves. As Charles Lamb suggested: 'The man who does not at least propose to himself to be better this year than he was last, must be either very good or very bad indeed.'

A happy New Year!

Today is New Year's Day, the day for a fresh start, with good New Year resolutions and a desire to start with a clean sheet. It is only natural that this should also be the day for many new beginnings.

For many countries this day has proved to be a milestone in their history. Just a few are. . . .
1801 Act of Union between Great Britain and Ireland.
1887 Queen Victoria proclaimed Empress of India at Delhi.
1901 The Commonwealth of Australia formed.
1923 The Union of Soviet Socialist Republics formed.
1926 In China the Nationalist government was established.
1958 European Economic Community came into existence.
1973 Britain became a member of the EEC.

It is also the day on which some far-reaching British government decisions have come into force. A few are
1907 Old Age Pensions became payable in Britain to those over the age of 70 — a Welfare State landmark.
1910 The Act setting up Labour Exchanges in Britain came into operation.
1948 The nationalisation of independent railways to form British Rail came into effect.

This day marked a beginning for *The Times* newspaper in 1788, the Wolf Rock lighthouse in 1870 and the Manchester Ship Canal in 1894.
It was also the beginning for Lorenzo de Medici, 'Lorenzo the Magnificent', born on 1 January 1449, and for Baron Pierre de Coubertin, born this day in 1863. He was the founder of the modern Olympic Games in 1896.

But today marked the end for James Stuart, the Old Pretender, who died this day in 1766, and for Sir Edwin Lutyens, the architect, who died on 1 January 1944. He planned the city of New Delhi, designed the Cenotaph in London and left uncompleted plans for a Roman Catholic cathedral in Liverpool.

In pre-decimal coinage days, the smallest coin, the farthing, ceased to be legal tender on 1 January 1961.

At one time there were gates on all the main thoroughfares into the city of London. Within those boundaries, the citizens had a freedom of government of which they were proud. At Temple Bar, in the Strand, for example, there was an ancient barrier between the cities of London and Westminster. No English king could pass this bar into the city without the consent of the Lord Mayor. The king received the Lord Mayor's sword and then returned it, as is done to this day. The new Lord Mayor on the day of his Show, goes to the Temple Bar to present himself to the monarch's representative.

The original Temple Bar consisted of posts and a chain, to which a gatehouse was added in the reign of James I. After the Great Fire, a new one of Portland stone was designed by Sir Christopher Wren and erected in 1672.

But even in the 19th Century, such a gateway was a nuisance to London traffic and, on 2 January 1878, it was removed — but not lost for, after some years, it was re-erected at Theobald's Park, near Enfield. The old site is now marked by a monument topped with a dragon.

Lunik I (or *Luna I*) was launched on 2 January 1959 by the Russians. It was an unmanned space probe directed toward the moon, near which it passed before going into orbit round the sun. It was an important milestone in man's conquest of space.

There wasn't much space at the Ibrox Park Stadium, Glasgow, on 2 January 1971. At the end of the football match the crowds surged from the stadium but a barrier collapsed, some spectators fell and were trampled upon by the crowds that followed. In Britain's worst sports disaster, 66 were killed and 145 injured.

So to some 'soldiers' connected with 2 January. . . .

General James Wolfe was born this day in 1727. He served with distinction in Europe and North America and it was there, in the battle of Quebec, that he was mortally wounded (p. 18).

Onward Christian soldiers has long been a popular hymn. The original 'soldiers' were children marching in procession at Horbury Brig, Yorkshire, where the hymn was written for them by the curate, the Rev. Sabine Baring-Gould. He later went to a living in Devon, where he wrote many books, about 150 being published. He died on 2 January 1924.

Marcus Tullius Cicero, orator, writer and statesman of ancient Rome, was born on 3 January 106 BC. He made a name for himself for his oratory in the courts and he held important offices of state. It was one of his most famous speeches, delivered against Mark Antony after the death of Julius Caesar, that was to cost him his life. Learning that his name was on the list of 'enemies', Cicero fled but was overtaken by soldiers of Antony and murdered.

It was on this day that Martin Luther also reaped the reward of speaking his mind. For his criticisms of the Roman Catholic Church he had been called before the Diet of Worms at the end of which, on 3 January 1521, he was excommunicated.

Some words of Father Damien, born on 3 January 1840, were, in effect, a sentence of death. He asked to be allowed to go as priest to the lepers who lived on the island of Molokai. In those days there was no cure for leprosy and it was only a matter of time before Father Damien caught the disease, from which he died, but only after he had given great comfort to those sufferers to whom he had gone.

Three of today's birthdays. . . .
In 1823 Robert Whitehead, English engineer, who invented the first self-propelling torpedo.
In 1883 Clement Attlee, English Labour Party statesman, who served as prime minister from 1945 to 1951.
In 1892 J. R. R. Tolkien was born at Bloemfontein, South Africa, later becoming professor of Anglo-Saxon at Oxford from 1925 to 1945, then professor of English language and literature. His interests in language, saga and folklore led to his writing *The Hobbit* and later the three-volume *The Lord of the Rings*, now holding an honoured place in English literature.

To most people, Wedgwood means one thing — fine pottery as created by the master potter Josiah Wedgwood, who died on this day in 1795.

This was the day, in 1911, of the Sidney Street siege in London led by the anarchist 'Peter the Painter'.

Many blind people have been thankful for the Braille alphabet, the system of raised dots on paper by which they can read with their fingers. It was the invention of a Frenchman, Louis Braille, who was blinded at the age of three and spent his life helping other blind people. This was his birthday in 1809.

This was the birthday, four years later, of another man, who was to invent a different kind of writing. Sir Isaac Pitman was a clerk and then a schoolmaster before developing the system of shorthand which bears his name and working on spelling reform. He founded his own publishing house and was knighted in 1894.

On 4 January 1785, Jakob Grimm was born at Hanau, Germany. He became interested in folklore and collected stories from many sources, both written and oral. These tales were published by Jakob and his brother Wilhelm as *Grimm's Fairy Tales*. Less known is Jakob's study of linguistics and his contribution to the basis of modern German grammar.

Augustus John, the Welsh artist, was born on 4 January 1878. He gained an early reputation for his etchings and later for his paintings of gipsies, fishing folk, lovely women and character portraits. He was elected to the Royal Academy in 1928.

General Tom Thumb was the name under which Charles Sherwood Stratton travelled on tour with showman Phineas T. Barnum. He was a dwarf, though perfectly proportioned. As a youth he was only 25 inches (64 cm) tall but grew to 40 inches (100 cm). He married Lavinia Warren, another of Barnum's midgets. This was his birthday in 1838.

The first pop music chart was published this day in 1936 in the New York magazine *Billboard*.

Civil War in England came one step nearer on this day in 1642, when King Charles I attempted to arrest five Members of Parliament. Delaying tactics allowed the five to escape and led to the institution of the custom of the Gentleman Usher of the Black Rod now going to the Commons to summon Members to meet the sovereign in the Lords — and having the door slammed in his face to allow time for Members to escape!

On 4 January 1967, Donald Campbell sped across the surface of Coniston Water, Cumbria, in his turbo-jet engined *Bluebird K7*, determined to raise the water speed record. When travelling at 328 mph (527.8 km/h), *Bluebird* hit some floating debris, hurtled into the air, somersaulted and disappeared into the depths of the lake, taking Donald Campbell with it.

Son of Sir Malcolm Campbell, also a speed king, Donald had set out to achieve both land and water records.

The interests of Cornelius Vanderbilt were also in the water and the land, not for speed but for business. Born on Staten Island, New York, he bought a ferry boat when sixteen. Later he owned steamships running up the Hudson and to Boston, then transported people to California for the gold rush. He financed railways and roads so that his many ventures made him a multi-millionaire — one million dollars of which he gave to found the Vanderbilt University at Nashville. After his death, on 4 January 1877, his son William extended the business.

This day, in 1958, saw the death of Sir Alliott Verdon Roe. His interests were in the air and he became the first Englishman to design, build and fly an aircraft. In 1910, he founded A. V. Roe and Co., one of the world's largest aircraft firms and builders of many kinds of 'plane bearing the name 'Avro'.

The creative genius of T. S. Eliot was in the field of literature. Born in America, the British poet, critic and dramatist gained a high reputation, which resulted in his being awarded, in 1948, both the Order of Merit and the Nobel Prize for Literature. Many of his plays were of a religious nature and reflected his own religious convictions. He died on 4 January 1965.

The religious convictions of Swami Vivekananda, who also died on this day, in 1902, were somewhat different. A Hindu philosopher, he became a disciple of Ramakrishna and an ardent worker for the reform of some ancient Indian social customs.

On this day, in 1885, the first operation to remove an appendix was performed. The operation was popularised after it was performed on King Edward VII.

In the small raised chapel behind the High Altar of Westminster Abbey is the tomb in which King Edward the Confessor lies buried. He it was who had this great abbey church built and died on 5 January 1066 only shortly after the church had been consecrated.

Edward the Confessor, son of Ethelred the Unready, was the last of the old line of Anglo-Saxon kings, not a particularly strong king but one whose piety and virtues earned his canonisation.

This is the feast day of St. Simeon the Stylite, who spent the last 36 years of his life on top of a pillar 20 metres high and one metre in diameter from which he preached and prayed. He died in 459.

This day marked the end of the road for several who had lived lives packed with adventure.

Sir William Hillary died on 5 January 1847. After service in the army and travelling, he settled at Douglas, Isle of Man, where he was a regular member of the lifeboat crew. He is especially remembered for his work in founding what is now the Royal National Lifeboat Institution.

Sir Ernest Shackleton served as a junior officer on the *Discovery* on Captain Scott's antarctic expedition of 1901–3. This whetted his appetite for further antarctic exploration. In 1909 he came within 97 miles of the South Pole. In 1915 his ship was crushed in the ice and Shackleton made a perilous voyage with five others in an open boat to South Georgia, 800 miles away. It was at South Georgia, on his fourth expedition, that he died on 5 January 1922.

Amy Mollison was drowned in the Thames estuary on this day in 1941 after baling out of an aircraft. Better known by her maiden name, Amy Johnson, she was one of the women pioneers in the new sport of flying. She made an adventurous solo flight to Australia in 1930 and followed this by others to Japan via Siberia and to Cape Town, creating records in each case. In 1932, she married her male rival Jim Mollison.

Born on this day, in 1779, was Zebulun Pike, who gave his name to Pike's Peak, in Colorado, USA. An American general and explorer, Pike explored the upper Mississippi River and other areas in the south-west of the USA.

George Washington Carver was born of slave parents in Missouri. As he grew, he became interested in plants and their growth habits, earning himself the title of 'the plant doctor'. This was to become his life's work, winning him international fame for agricultural research.

He was particularly concerned with the introduction of new crops to the southern states as a replacement for cotton, encouraging the farmers to grow peanuts, sweet potatoes and pecans. From the peanut alone, Carver made more than 300 products.

By the time he died, on 5 January 1943, he had many honours bestowed upon him and, two years later, Congress designated 5 January as George Washington Carver Day. Six years later, part of the farm on which he was born became the George Washington Carver National Monument.

Another American with new ideas was born on 5 January 1855. King Camp Gillette was the inventor of the safety razor and, in 1901, founded the company which would manufacture his disposable razor blades and other products.

Still in America, it was this day, in 1933, that the 30th president of the USA (1923–9), Calvin Coolidge, died.

These also died on 5 January. . . .
In 1589 Catherine de Medici, consort of Henry II of France.
In 1762 Elizabeth I, empress of Russia.
In 1858 Austrian Field-Marshal, Count Josef Radetzky.

King Louis XV of France might have died on this evening in 1757. As he was entering his coach at the Palace of Versailles, Robert Damiens rushed forward from the shadows and stabbed the king with a long knife. But it was a cold evening and the king had put on extra thick clothing, so the knife inflicted only a superficial injury.

On 5 January 1919, the German Labour party was formed at Munich. It later became the National Socialist (Nazi) Party with one of its earliest members, Adolf Hitler, as leader.

This day was the birthday, in 1876, of the man who was to lead Germany after the defeat of Hitler, Konrad Adenauer. He had been twice imprisoned by the Nazis.

163

In the Christian Church, 6 January is celebrated as the Feast of Epiphany, recalling how the Wise Men from the East found the young child, Jesus, and offered him the symbolic gifts of gold, frankincense and myrrh.

This is commemorated today, as it has been for seven centuries, in the Chapel Royal, St. James's Palace, London, where, at the Royal Epiphany Service, three purses, representing the gifts of the Wise Men, are presented by Gentlemen Ushers of the Royal Household on behalf of the sovereign.

Today is also known as Twelfth Day or Twelfth Night, the last day of Christmas. In one sense that is not quite correct, because the Christmas season in the Christian Church calendar continues until Candlemas, 2 February, when the Easter season begins. But, for people of the past, this was the end of the Christmas holiday. Most people take down their Christmas decorations today, believing that it is unlucky to leave them up any longer, but this old superstition used to be concerned with Candlemas rather than today.

At one time it was the custom to have a Twelfth-tide feast with a large cake. Concealed in the cake was a bean and the lucky man who got it became King of the Bean or Epiphany King, presiding over all the festivities. In some cakes a pea was also hidden, the girl who found it in her slice becoming the Queen. Twelfth-tide cakes had almost disappeared by the middle of last century as people made Christmas cakes instead.

One place in which a cake is still seen is in the Green Room of the Drury Lane Theatre, London. When Robert Baddeley died in 1794, he left £100 in his will to provide each year, on 6 January, some wine and a cake to be shared by the company then acting at the theatre. Baddeley had once been a chef but became an actor. By providing the Baddeley Cake, he ensured that he would be remembered.

The ancient custom of wassailing the apple trees on this day continues here and there. Cider is poured on the roots and toast soaked in cider placed in the branches. Shots are then fired through the branches and songs sung to encourage the tree.

There used to be many strange customs observed on this day in farming communities. In some places, bonfires were lit on the bare fields, one to represent Our Lord and one each for his eleven apostles. If a thirteenth were lit, representing Judas Iscariot, it was stamped out shortly after being lit. It was quite common for this to be followed by a feast in the farmhouse. In some areas, such as Herefordshire, Worcestershire and Gloucestershire, a toast in warm cider was drunk to the next harvest. Plum cake was eaten as a sign of plenty.

In some places a plum cake with a hole in the centre was taken to the cattleshed and placed on the horns of the best ox. The ox was encouraged to toss its head and throw off the cake. It was considered good for the farm if it fell in front of the animal. If, however, it fell behind, it was not a good omen.

In the Isle of Axholme, Lincolnshire, the Hood Game is played at Haxey on 6 January. It is probably an ancient game related to the rituals of the mid-winter festival but there is a legend that it was first played in the thirteenth century after twelve local labourers rushed to retrieve the scarlet hood of Lady Mowbray, blown away by strong winds.

The game is played by twelve Boggans of whom the chief is King Boggan. As each of twelve hoods is thrown into the air there is a scramble to catch it. Anyone doing so and carrying it to the nearest inn without being touched by a Boggan is rewarded.

It was on much more serious a note that President Franklin Delano Roosevelt addressed the United States Congress on 6 January 1941. The world was at war and people were giving thought to the rights of any person. He said:

We look forward to a world founded on four essential human freedoms. The first is freedom of speech and expression — everywhere in the world. The second is freedom of every person to worship God in his own way — everywhere in the world. The third is freedom from want — everywhere in the world. The fourth is freedom from fear — anywhere in the world.

Today, in 1919, President Theodore Roosevelt, USA, died.

On St. Distaff's Day
Neither work nor play

This was the day, long ago in England, when women began to spin again after the Christmas festivities, but it was a light-hearted day on which men might amuse themselves by trying to set light to the flax or wool and, for their trouble, be drenched by the spinners with pails of water. The men may have started back on the land but this was usually done in earnest after Plough Monday, the first Monday after Epiphany (6 January) with its ceremony of Blessing the Plough and dancing.

There were celebrations of a different kind on 7 January 1785, when the English Channel was crossed for the first time by air. Jean Pierre Blanchard, a Frenchman, had previously planned an 'air-ship' powered by oars — but it did not work. For this flight from England to France, with his American patron, Dr. John Jeffries, he attached his 'ship' to a Montgolfier balloon.

Another pioneer to find that his invention was not practical was Henry Mill. He was granted a patent on 7 January 1714 for the first typewriter but 160 years were to pass before a practical machine was produced by Philo Remington (USA).

One innovation on this day that did work was the new transatlantic telephone service between London and New York in 1927.

André Maginot planned a defensive line of fortifications between France and Germany and it bore his name. He died on 7 January 1932 so did not live to see that his Maginot Line failed in its purpose in 1940.

Another French occasion: in 1558, Calais, the last English possession in France, was recovered by that country.

Two other pioneers. . . .
Sophia Jex-Blake campaigned for medical schools for women and succeeded in 1876 when examinations for women medical students were permitted. She died on this day in 1912.
Born on 7 January 1925 was Gerald Durrell, founder of the Jersey Wildlife Preservation Trust and author of zoo books.

Galileo Galilei was born in Pisa, Italy, in 1564, studied medicine and mathematics and became a professor of mathematics, first at Pisa then at Padua. From watching a suspended lamp, he deduced how to use a pendulum for the exact measurement of time. He also perfected the refracting telescope, which was a Dutch invention.

Galileo was a great thinker who disagreed with accepted theories of his day and he earned the displeasure of many. But it was in his study of the universe with his telescope that he brought great trouble upon himself. Amongst other things, he insisted that the theories of Copernicus were right: the earth moved round the sun and not the sun round the earth. After a long trial by the inquisition and period of imprisonment, he was forced to say he was wrong but it is said that immediately after doing so he was heard to remark, 'Yet it *does* move.'

Though his sight and hearing began to fail, he continued his researches, making yet more discoveries. He became totally blind in 1637 and died on 8 January 1642.

Some others who died on this day. . . .

In 1775 John Baskerville, printer and inventor of the style of print lettering that bears his name.

In 1825 Eli Whitney, American mechanical engineer, inventor of the cotton gin and manufacturer of firearms. He introduced the idea of mass production of interchangeable parts for firearms and other machinery.

In 1941 Lord Baden-Powell, soldier hero of the Boer War and founder of the Boy Scout movement.

In 1976 Chou En-lai, Chinese revolutionary leader, who became prime minister of The People's Republic of China in 1949 and was re-elected to that office when the new Constitution was introduced in 1955.

Maximilian Kolbe was born on this day in 1894 but he is remembered for his death in Auschwitz concentration camp in 1941. He was then a Franciscan priest and he offered to take the place of a married man who had been condemned to die, with nine others, following an escape from the camp.

On 8 January 1956, five missionaries to the Auca Indians in Equador were happy to radio that ten of the warlike Aucas were coming to meet them. The Aucas did — and killed all five.

When times are difficult, it is sometimes good to have someone to laugh with or laugh at. During World War II, Tommy Handley provided that outlet. His weekly radio programme ITMA ('It's That Man Again'), with its humour, slapstick, satire and parody, was very popular. Tommy, a Liverpudlian, had previously worked in variety and concert parties. He died on 9 January 1949.

Also very popular was 'Our Gracie' — Gracie Fields, music hall comedienne with comedy songs

> We're going to string old Hitler
> From the very highest bough
> Of the biggest aspidistra in the world.

Born in Rochdale, Lancashire, on 9 January 1898, she appeared in eight royal command performances and, through records, radio, television and films, became internationally known.

Another internationally known entertainer to be born on this day, in 1941, is Joan Baez. A folk musician and pacifist, she has been associated with many peace marches and rallies.

Theatre-goers of past years also enjoyed the sophisticated comedy performances of Beatrice Lillie. Born in Toronto, she made her debut in London. Her first appearance in New York was in a revue on 9 January 1924.

Nowadays we are used to robots of many kinds. They were invented in 1920 for a play *Rossum's Universal Robots (RUR)* by Karel Čapek, internationally renowned Czechoslovakian author, short-story writer and playwright, who was born on 9 January 1890.

Robots are far removed from William Hedley's colliery steam locomotive *Puffing Billy* (1813) but that must have caused excitement. Hedley died on this day in 1843. Not long after *Puffing Billy* appeared, the Davy Safety Lamp was first used — on 9 January 1816.

A modern engineering achievement has been the building of the Aswan High Dam. Work began on this day in 1960.

Today's birthdays include Admiral Earl St. Vincent (1735), French novelist and advocate of equality of sexes, Simone de Beauvoir (1908) and US President Richard Nixon (1913).

Income Tax was first levied in Britain on 9 January 1799 to pay for the Napoleonic War. It was just a temporary measure!

10 January

Today is a very important day in communications.

On 10 January 1840, people were able, for the first time, to buy a postage stamp for one penny, stick it on a letter, post it and be assured that it would be delivered to the person to whom it was addressed. It was the brain-child of Sir Rowland Hill and was to be of the greatest value in helping people to communicate with each other. 'Penny Postage' was the beginning of a system that came to be adopted throughout the world, used every day by millions of people.

Each day thousands of people travel into London or across London in the course of their business. Many of them use the underground railway, or 'tube'. The first part of the underground system, the section of the Metropolitan Railway from Paddington to Farringdon Street, opened on 10 January 1863. There was great excitement on that day as crowds of people sampled this novel form of transport — taken for granted today by all those who use it as a part of their daily travel.

As the first World War was drawing to an end, leaders of nations were wondering how to prevent a similar war in the future. The answer seemed to be an organisation in which the leaders or representatives could talk to each other, to discuss any problems which arose and to see whether such matters could be settled peacefully. On this day, in 1920, the League of Nations came into being. It failed in that some important nations did not join and others disregarded it. In 1939 the world was again at war: the League had collapsed.

At the end of World War II a new body, known as the United Nations Organisation, was set up as a forum at which nations could communicate and through which help could be offered. The first meeting of the General Assembly was held in London on 10 January 1946.

Communications failed in England during the Civil War and in the Commonwealth, under Cromwell, it could be dangerous to say what one believed. William Laud, Archbishop of Canterbury, openly supported Charles I against the Puritans. He was executed on 10 January 1645.

Sir Hans Sloane was a well-travelled man. Born in Ulster, he studied in London and France before settling in London as a physician. He was also a naturalist and spent over a year in Jamaica, where he collected a herbarium of 800 species. A Fellow of the Royal Society, he served it variously as secretary and president. He was also royal physician and physician-general to the army.

After his death, on 11 January 1753, his library of 5,000 volumes and 3,560 manuscripts, together with his large collection of curiosities, formed the basis of the British Museum.

The British Museum today houses many priceless items and has exhibits of differing kinds. Among them is a statue of Shakespeare by the French sculptor Louis François Roubillac, who had settled in London. Some of his other famous works are the statues of Handel in Westminster Abbey and of Newton at Cambridge. Roubillac died on 11 January 1762.

Selfridge's, the well-known store in London's Oxford Street, was founded by the American Harry Gordon Selfridge, born on this day in 1864.

And so to America. Ezra Cornell was born on 11 January 1807. He founded the Western Union Telegraph Company and made a fortune, much of which he used for founding Cornell University and for other philanthropic projects.

Francis Scott Key was an American lawyer and writer. Seeing the American flag still flying after the British attack on Baltimore in 1814, he was inspired to write 'The Star-Spangled Banner', which was to become the US national anthem. Key died on this day in 1843.

Today also saw the death, in 1928, of Thomas Hardy, who trained as an architect but achieved fame as a novelist and poet, with works inspired by his Wessex upbringing.

Also from the West Country was Fred Archer, born in Cheltenham, Gloucestershire, on 11 January 1857. He became one of the most successful English jockeys riding many winners in the Derby, the Oaks, the St. Leger and other classic races. At a time of mental instability, at the age of 39, he shot himself.

There is but one law for all, namely that law which governs all law, the law of our Creator, the law of humanity, justice, equity — the law of nature and of nations.

This is just one of the many sayings and writings of Edmund Burke, who was born in Dublin on 12 January 1729, studied law, turned to writing and came to be one of the greatest political thinkers in British history. He had a vast knowledge of affairs and an ability to convey his beliefs powerfully and expressively. A couple more of his thoughts:

Example is the school of mankind, and they will learn at no other.

Good order is the foundation of all things.

Both of these might apply to Johann Pestalozzi, the Swiss educationalist, who was born on 12 January 1746. In one sense his work seemed a failure, for venture after venture in running schools failed through faulty organisation. Yet his work with orphan children and his educational ideas became widely known, spreading to many countries and starting an educational revolution.

The idea of Sir Isaac Pitman was also new — a system of shorthand which became widely accepted. He died in 1897.

This day also saw the passing of Dame Agatha Christie, in 1976. She gained a wide reputation as author of 70 detective novels and several stage productions (p. 108), noted for their clever plots.

Born on 12 January 1856, John Stringer Sargent could be called an international artist. He was once described as 'An American born in Italy, educated in France, who looks like a German, speaks like an Englishman, and paints like a Spaniard.' He is best known as a painter of portraits but he also painted landscapes and decorative paintings for buildings.

Some other 12 January birthdays. . . .
In 1862 Swami Vivekananda, Hindu reformer.
In 1876 Jack London, American novelist of adventure stories.
In 1893 Hermann Goering, German Nazi leader under Hitler.
In 1948 Supermarkets in Britain: the first was opened in Manor Park, London.

In 1978 gales and rough seas battered the east coast.

Maybe 13 January is not a good day on which to be born. Those who are, numerology suggests, are likely to suffer from melancholia, mental disorders, pains in the head, back, kidneys or bladder, or from anaemia. Perhaps that is why most people seem to have avoided being born today! But a search will reveal some who have managed to make their contribution to the world.

Charles Perrault, for example, was born in Paris on this day in 1628. He had trained as a lawyer and worked as an official responsible for royal buildings. Then he took to writing, becoming a poet, writer and story-teller as well as a prominent member of the Académie Français. He is especially remembered for his fairy stories, written to amuse his children but which are still very popular today — 'The Sleeping Beauty', 'Puss in Boots', 'Red Riding Hood' and others, which were modernised versions of old folk tales, retold in a simple way.

Another born today, in 1864, was Wilhelm Wien, later professor of physics and a Nobel Prize winner in 1911 for his study of radiation from a black body. He also studied cathode rays, X-rays and other atomically charged beams.

Launched on 13 January 1870, was one of the most famous of the clipper ships, the *Cutty Sark*. Her name, meaning 'short shirt', came from Burns's poem 'Tam o'Shanter'. In the 1870s she sailed in the China Tea trade, then carried Australian wool before becoming a training ship. Now, fully restored and in a permanent drydock at Greenwich, she is a tourist attraction popular with London's visitors.

Also launched on this day, in 1921, was a new idea for motorists — windscreen wipers, patented by Mills Munitions of Birmingham.

Today witnessed the passing, in 1691, of George Fox, who, seeking a religion that met his needs, founded the Society of Friends, or Quakers. His life became a catalogue of insults, imprisonments and persecutions, yet he had within him nothing but love for his fellows and a Christian desire for social improvement.

James Joyce, 20th-Century Irish writer of literary masterpieces, died on 13 January 1941.

On this day, in 1752, Parliament passed an Act changing New Year's Day from 25 March to 1 January.

Today, or some say yesterday, is traditionally the coldest day of the year. Perhaps the tradition stems from the great frost which blanketed England in 1205. According to Stowe, the antiquary, 'On this day, in 1205, began a frost which continued until the two and twentieth day of March, so that the ground could not be tilled.' There is record that food prices rocketed.

It was also on 14 January that the River Thames froze between London Bridge on two different occasions, in 1716 and in 1814. Londoners took the opportunity of such times to hold a Frost Fair on the frozen waters. There are records, in 1814, of sheep-roasting on the thick ice, roundabouts, swings, gambling booths and lots more fun of the fair. On this occasion they were let down. The fair had only been going for four days when a thaw set in and some lost their possessions and their lives through leaving it too late to get safely to the bank.

So to somewhere a little warmer. Dr. Albert Schweitzer, who was born on this day in 1875, believed that his mission in life was to serve the people of Central Africa and startled many people when he announced his decision. His talents, which had allowed him to qualify four times over as a doctor, were henceforth to be used to help people around Lambarene in what was then the Gabon province of French Equatorial Africa (see also p .10).

Also born on this day, in 1847, was Rev. Wilson Carlile (p. 31), who wanted to make things hot for the Devil and his disciples! He founded the Church Army, an Anglican organisation for lay evangelists concerned very much with social work of many kinds.

Three who died on 14 January. . . .
Edmund Halley, astronomer and mathematician, who calculated the orbit and appearances of Halley's Comet, died in 1742.
Charles Lutwidge Dodgson, better known as Lewis Carroll, author of the 'Alice' books, died in 1898.
The Earl of Avon, formerly Sir Anthony Eden, British politician and prime minister, died in 1977.

This is Mallard Night at All Souls' College, Oxford, when fellows hunt the great Mallard, supposed to have been found when the foundations were laid in 1437. Once held every year, the custom is now every hundredth year. Next time – 2001.

15 January

A mini-tour of London might begin on 15 January 1559 at the Tower of London. Those were the days before television and newspapers and so the young Queen Elizabeth wanted as many people as possible to be able to see her on her coronation day. Her 'royal coach' was a chariot beside which four knights walked holding a canopy.

On the way, she stopped to speak to her subjects and receive gifts — simple ones such as a sprig of rosemary which she still held when reaching Westminster. Westminster Abbey was suitably decorated for the imposing ceremony, after which a banquet for 800 people was held in Westminster Hall. It lasted for ten hours.

Two hundred years later, the British Museum was opened on this day in 1759, in Bloomsbury. It contains a huge library as well as exhibits that are unique, priceless and very interesting.

A very strange object was seen in London in 1797. It was 'a tall structure having a shining lustre, calculated to alarm timid people.' No. It wasn't a UFO: it was the first silk top hat and the wearer, London haberdasher John Hetherington, was summoned on this day for wearing it.

Not far from the British Museum is Covent Garden, where a theatre had been founded a few years earlier. In the 1820s, its manager Charles Kemble was facing bankruptcy and his eldest daughter made her debut there to help him. Fanny Kemble was an immediate success and brought prosperity to Covent Garden for three years. After acting in England and America, she died in her native London on 15 January 1893.

That was the same day on which Ivor Novello was born in Cardiff. London theatre-goers loved his romantic musicals, such as 'The Dancing Years', in the 1930s and 1940s.

London parks are popular in summer and winter. In the hard frost on 15 January 1826, some 100,000 were skating or spectating on the Serpentine in Hyde Park. On this same day in 1867, many died in an ice tragedy in Regent's Park.

The London Telephone Company published the United Kingdom's first telephone directory today in 1880. It contained 255 names.

And elsewhere in the world on 15 January. . . .
Martin Luther King, American civil rights leader, born 1929.
Sir Abubakar Tafawa Balewa, first federal prime minister of Nigeria, was killed in an army coup in 1966.

16 January

Some people are renowned for their massive works which took years of effort and patience, some never being completed.

Edmund Spenser began writing his great poem *The Faerie Queene* in 1588. The first three volumes of twelve were published in 1590 and the next three in 1596. Only part of the seventh was written when he died on 16 January 1599.

Edward Gibbon took twelve years to write his *Decline and Fall of the Roman Empire*. He died this day in 1794.

Also on this day. . . .
In 1547 Ivan the Terrible, first Tsar of Russia, was crowned.
In 1891 Leo Delibes, French opera and ballet composer, died.
In 1909 two of Shackleton's expedition reached the Magnetic South Pole.
In 1920 Prohibition came into force in the USA.

Born on 16 January 1832 was Dorothy Pattison, who joined the Order of Good Samaritans and took charge of a hospital in Walsall. Her compassionate and dedicated work after a colliery disaster and a boiler factory explosion, as well as during an epidemic of smallpox, led to the erection, in gratitude, of a statue in Walsall to 'Sister Dora', as she was known.

17 January

Today's mystery. . . . On 17 January 1949, the 'plane *Star Ariel* took off from Bermuda with a crew of seven and thirteen passengers. An hour later, the captain reported: 'Fair weather. Expected time of arrival as planned.'

Star Ariel was never seen nor heard of again. It was one of the mysteries of the Bermuda Triangle.

Today's birthdays. . . .
In 1706 Benjamin Franklin, American statesman.
In 1863 David Lloyd George, British prime minister.
In 1942 Cassius Clay, who adopted the name Muhammad Ali, became world heavyweight boxing champion and many think he lived up to his boast, 'I am the greatest!'

18 January

Words! Words! Words!

How many people have turned the pages of *Roget's Thesaurus* for information about words and help in solving puzzles? Peter Mark Roget, born on 18 January 1779, became a great scholar and physician. He was a Fellow and secretary of the Royal Society and an original member of the senate of London University. His *Thesaurus of English Words and Phrases* saw 28 editions in his lifetime alone.

The words of A. A. Milne were designed to please children. His poems, written for his son Christopher Robin, together with his children's classics, such as *Winnie-the-Pooh*, have given pleasure to millions of children — and adults too. This was his birthday, in 1882, two years before that of Arthur Ransome, who also made a name for himself as a writer of books for young readers, including the classic *Swallows and Amazons*.

Rudyard Kipling died on 18 January 1936. He, too, was a man of words — stories for children, poems and great literature for which he was awarded a Nobel Prize in 1907 — and words which are widely known.

> *If you can fill the unforgiving minute*
> *With sixty seconds' worth of distance run,*
> *Yours is the Earth and everything that's in it,*
> *And — which is more — you'll be a Man, my son!*

'For God's sake look after our people' were the final words in the diary of Captain R. F. Scott as his life was ending in March 1912. On 18 January he had reached the South Pole, disappointed to discover that Amundsen had been there first.

It was on this day, in 1778, that another sailor-explorer, Captain Cook, first discovered the Pacific island of Hawaii.

Words were of minor importance to Oliver Hardy. His actions and expressions spoke for themselves in the Laurel and Hardy films. This was his birthday in 1892. Cary Grant, born Alexander Archibald Leach on this day in 1904, became one of the great film actors. This was also the birthday, in 1841, of the French composer of operas and *España*, A. E. Chabrier.

The Week of Prayer for Christian Unity begins this day each year.

Music hath charms to soothe a savage breast,
To soften rocks, or bend a knotted oak.

This is one of the well-known quotations from the writings of William Congreve, the English poet and dramatist, who died on 19 January 1729 and was interred in Westminster Abbey. His brilliant comic dialogue and satirical portrayal of fashionable society had shaped English comedy during the Restoration period.

Born on 19 January 1809, was Edgar Allan Poe, the American poet and story writer. For a time he worked as an editor but his great imagination found an outlet in his writings. He is sometimes said to be the inventor of the detective story.

Some other of today's birthdays. . . .

In 1736 James Watt was born at Greenock, Scotland. After learning the trade of a mathematical-instrument maker, he was employed as a surveyor and engineer of canals and harbours. He is remembered for his work with steam, improving engines and pumps and later working in partnership with Matthew Boulton.

Still on the industrial scene, Sir Henry Bessemer was born this day in 1813. His great invention was the Bessemer Converter, by which steel could be produced cheaply.

General Robert E. Lee, Confederate General during the American Civil War, was born in 1807.

Paul Cézanne, the French artist, was born in 1839. He was one of the greatest post-impressionist painters, whose ideas and styles could be said to be the forerunner of 20th-Century movements in art, especially Cubism.

William Keen, born on 19 January 1837, was the first brain surgeon in the USA. The operation, in 1888, to remove a brain tumour, was performed in secrecy on board a yacht.

Auguste Mariette, French Egyptologist, became conservator of monuments for the Egyptian government and founded the Egyptian Museum. He died in Cairo this day in 1881.

There was a meeting on 19 January 1958, at the South Pole, of two transantarctic explorers, Sir Vivian Fuchs having come from the Weddell Sea and Sir Edmund Hillary from the Ross Sea.

One very important date in the history of Parliament in Britain is 20 January 1265, the date on which a Parliament that had been called by Simon de Montfort met in Westminster. For the first time, not only barons and bishops were called but two knights from each county and two citizens from each borough. It was another thirty years before a Parliament of this nature, known as the Model Parliament, met regularly, but Simon de Montfort is sometimes referred to as the 'founder of the House of Commons'.

Across the Atlantic, in the United States of America, 20 January is Inauguration Day. The President of the United States holds office for a term of four years, towards the end of which elections are held to choose the next President, who takes up his office on Inauguration Day.

In his inaugural address, the President may state his own policies and ideals and, perhaps, encourage his fellow citizens to act themselves. At his inauguration on 20 January 1961, John F. Kennedy spoke thus: 'My fellow Americans: ask not what your country can do for you, ask what you can do for your country.'

Doing something for one's country or for one's fellows in need is, of course, a good attitude to life and is of particular importance in times of national or personal need or disaster. It was on this day in 1953 that many people along the East Coast of England faced a natural disaster. Unusually high tides backed up by strong winds broke through the sea defences in many places, destroying homes and flooding farmland, thus causing great damage and personal loss. There were many teams of people who went to the help of people and animals and there was much work done afterwards to strengthen sea defences, so reducing the chances of similar flooding in the future.

Some people who died on 20 January, are remembered for their particular contribution to the world. . . .
David Garrick, actor, in 1779.
John Ruskin, art critic and writer, in 1900.
R. D. Blackmore, novelist (*Lorna Doone*), in 1900.

John Howard died on 20 January 1790. He will always be remembered for the work he did to improve conditions for prisoners. He discovered that many prisons were cold, dark and damp, that food was bad and that many gaolers were bullies. He travelled from town to town gathering information which was used to persuade Parliament to pass laws relating to prisoners. A statue to John Howard in St. Paul's Cathedral, London, stands as a memorial to his work.

One who helped prisoners many years earlier was a soldier named Sebastian under the Emperor Diocletian late in the 3rd Century. He helped Christian prisoners, as a result of which he was himself sentenced to death, tied to a tree and shot with arrows. Today is St. Sebastian's Day. He is the patron saint of soldiers, archers, arrowsmiths and pinmakers — as well as those suddenly struck with sharp pains. Because he was tied to a tree, there are those who have refused to eat fruit on this day.

Tomorrow, 21 January, is St. Agnes' Day. She was another of the Christian martyrs under Diocletian. She came to be regarded as the patron saint of virgins and consequently young women would seek her aid, on the eve of her feast, finding a partner by carrying out certain routines.

> *They told her how, upon St. Agnes' Eve,*
> *Young virgins might have visions of delight,*
> *And soft adornings from their loves receive*
> *Upon the honeyed middle of the night,*
> *If ceremonies due they did aright;*
> *As supperless to bed they must retire,*
> *And couch supine their beauties, lily white;*
> *Nor look behind, nor sideways, but require*
> *Of heaven with upward eyes for all that they desire.*

'The Eve of St. Agnes', Keats.

One of the routines was to make a 'Dumb Cake'. This was made from flour, water, eggs and salt and had to be prepared in complete silence. If eaten just before going to sleep, it was believed that the eater would have a vision of her husband-to-be. Why not try it?

21 January

Many people like to escape from cities and towns to enjoy the scenic beauties of parts of Britain — mountains and moorland, lakes, forests and rugged coasts. Some of these areas have been formed into National Parks to preserve their character and to encourage their use. The first of these, the Snowdonia National Park, in North Wales, was formed on 21 January 1935.

The open spaces enjoyed by Umberto Nobile were the sky and the North Polar regions. Born on this day in 1885, he became an aeronautical engineer and built the airships *Norge* and *Italia*. He was wrecked in the latter on Spitzbergen in 1928 on his third Arctic flight. Although rescued with 7 others, 17 lives were lost and Nobile was judged to be responsible.

Thirty years later, the US submarine *Nautilus* sailed under the North Pole. She was the first nuclear submarine to be built, having been launched on 21 January 1954.

Born on 21 January. . . .
In 1824 Stonewall Jackson, Confederate General in the American Civil War and a skilful military tactician.
In 1840 Sophia Jex-Blake, physician and pioneer for equal rights for women in the medical sphere.
In 1905 Christian Dior, French fashion designer, who led the fashion world in the years following World War II.
In 1940 Jack Nicklaus, American professional golfer, who became one of the leading figures in world golf from the mid 1960s.

Life ended on this day for these. . . .
King Louis XVI of France, imprisoned by the Revolutionaries, went to the guillotine in Paris in 1793.
Lenin (born Vladimir Ilich Ulyanov), Russian revolutionary leader, founder of the Russian Communist Party (Bolsheviks) and first head of the Soviet state, died in 1924.
George Orwell, novelist, essayist and critic, author of *Nineteen Eighty-four*, died in 1950.
Cecil B. de Mille, film producer and director, died in 1959. He was one of the leading figures in Hollywood in the heyday of films, renowned for spectaculars such as *The Greatest Show on Earth* and *The Ten Commandments*.

An era of British history came to a close on this day in 1901 with the death of Queen Victoria. She had come to the throne in 1837 at the age of 18 and reigned for 64 years, so becoming Britain's longest reigning monarch. She married Prince Albert of Saxe-Coburg-Gotha, to whom she was devoted and never recovered from his untimely death in 1861. She remained in mourning for her last 40 years, spending much of her time at Osborne House, Isle of Wight, where she died.

Victoria's reign marked a time of the expansion of British influence overseas and of British industry. Amongst the leading industrialists was Sir Joseph Whitworth, who was recognised internationally for his precision toolmaking. He produced a measuring machine and master gauges to go with it. In 1841 the Whitworth standard screw threads were adopted by the Woolwich Arsenal and they are still in use today.

His tools were renowned for their accuracy and he produced machines for cutting, drilling, planing and slotting. He improved guns. He helped found a chair of engineering at Manchester and financed Whitworth Scholarships. He was created a baronet in 1869 and died on 22 January 1887.

Those were days of social change. Beatrice Webb, born on 22 January 1858, with her husband Sidney, did much to foster the Labour movement, trade unionism and education.

It was on 22 January 1924 that the first Labour Government was formed under Ramsay MacDonald. King George V wrote in his diary: 'Today twenty-three years ago dear Grandmama *(Queen Victoria)* died. I wonder what she would have thought of a Labour Government.'

Born on this day. . . .
In 1561 Francis Bacon, lawyer, courtier and statesman.
In 1788 Lord Byron, English romantic poet.

Today's firsts. . . .
In 1822 First mail steamer between Calais and Dover.
In 1927 First broadcast of a Football League Match (Arsenal v Sheffield United from Highbury)
In 1952 First jet airliner; *Comet I* test flight.

23 January

This day has witnessed the passing of a number of great people in the world of entertainment.

In 1931 Anna Pavlova, the great Russian ballerina (p. 189), died.

Five years later, on 23 January 1936, Dame Clara Butt died. She was well-known for her singing of ballads and oratorios.

Paul Robeson, who died this day in 1976, was a fine singer of negro spirituals, an actor and film star.

Born in Hungary, Sir Alexander Korda became a British film director, making lavish films and contributing greatly to the British film industry, for which he became the first film maker to receive a knighthood. He died this day in 1956.

The entertainment of Thomas Love Peacock, who died on 23 January 1866, was of a different kind, through his satirical writings of a conversational nature.

Born in Paris on 23 January 1832 was Édouard Manet, who was one of the forerunners of the Impressionist school.

A forerunner in a different sphere was Elizabeth Blackwell, who, on 23 January 1849, in the USA, became the first woman to qualify as a doctor.

It was on this day in 1571 that Queen Elizabeth I opened the Royal Exchange in London.

One of the able political leaders in British history was William Pitt the Younger, prime minister during the French Revolutionary and Napoleonic Wars. He died on 23 January 1806. He once said: 'England has saved herself by her exertions; and will, as I trust, save Europe by her example.'

In England there were those who looked for changes that would improve the lot of many who were repressed. One was Charles Kingsley, who died on 23 January 1875. Clergyman, teacher, novelist and writer for children, he spent his life urging social reforms. To Thomas Hughes he wrote:

> *Do the work that's nearest,*
> *Though it's dull at whiles,*
> *Helping, when we meet them,*
> *Lame dogs over stiles.*

Crossing England from the Solway Firth to the River Tyne is Hadrian's Wall, built by order of the Roman emperor Hadrian to keep out the Scots. It was one of the many works of this emperor, who paid much attention to the internal affairs of his empire. Born on 24 January 76, Publius Aelius Hadrianus was Emperor from 117 to 138.

This was also the birthday, in 1712, of Frederick the Great, King of Prussia. His domain was much smaller than that of Hadrian but he made of it a great military state capable of leading the united Germany of later years. He was also anxious to improve the lot of his people, encouraging farmers, building roads and canals, and relaxing controls. He was a gifted musician and writer.

I have nothing to offer but blood, toil, tears and sweat.

These were not the words of a military conqueror but of one who was about to lead his people in the struggle to remain free. Winston Churchill spoke thus when he became prime minister in 1940. His speeches and his own courageous example put heart into people in the darkest hours of World War II. Sir Winston Churchill died on 24 January 1965, the 70th anniversary of the death, in 1895, of his father, also a prominent politician, Lord Randolph Churchill.

Events of the day. . . .
In 1616 the first rounding of Cape Horn began by the Dutch navigator Willem Schouten. It took a week.
In 1684 there was a Frost Fair on the frozen Thames.
In 1848 gold was discovered in California.
In 1908 the first Boy Scout troop was formed in England.
In 1915 the naval Battle of the Dogger Bank was fought.

Today we remember St. Timothy, travelling companion of St. Paul. Tomorrow is St. Paul's Day. There was an old Cornish custom on St. Paul's Eve, known also as 'Paul's Pitcher Day'. Stones were thrown at a pitcher until it shattered, supposedly commemorating Paul's part in the stoning of Stephen. It was an evening for jollification and drinking.

Today is the day on which the Christian Church remembers one of its greatest leaders and teachers — St. Paul. Brought up as a Jewish Pharisee, he was determined to destroy the followers of Jesus Christ, until one day, on the way to Damascus, he had a remarkable experience which changed the whole course of his life. Afterwards, with various companions, he travelled to many lands to teach Christianity, until he was taken as a prisoner to Rome, where he was eventually put to death.

We can read of his adventures in *The Acts of the Apostles,* and his teachings in the letters he wrote, which are to be found in the New Testament of *The Bible.*

St. Paul's Day used to be a holiday, and the weather on that day was believed to be an indication of the weather that could be expected for the rest of the year. An old saying from the Isle of Man, one of many such sayings, runs:

> *St. Paul's Day stormy and windy,*
> *Famine in the world and great dearth of mankind;*
> *St. Paul's Day fair and clear,*
> *Plenty of corn and meal in the world.*

The *Shepherd's Almanack* of 1676 predicts, '. . . if the sun shines it betokens a good year; if it rain or snow, indifferent; if misty it predicts a good dearth; if it thunder, great winds and death of people that year.'

Some people read ominous signs into the sighting of the Aurora Borealis, the Northern Lights, from Britain. These were seen clearly on this day in 1938.

And who could have predicted what would happen to Ruth Pierce on 25 January 1753? She was one of three women in Devizes market who agreed to buy a sack of wheat and share the cost. Ruth was accused of not paying her share. She insisted that she had and wished she might drop dead if that was not the truth. To the amazement of the crowd she did drop dead . . . with the money still in her hand. A statue in Devizes market place stands as a reminder of Ruth Pierce, and of the advisability to be honest in one's dealings.

Few people would have predicted the result of an event which took place in Uganda on 25 January 1971. It was on that day that Idi Amin overthrew President Milton Obote and began a long period of terror and torture, massacre and murder, with disastrous consequences for that country.

One does not need to be a prophet to predict that tonight will be a night of merrymaking and enjoyment for people in many parts of the world as Scots gather together for their Burns' Night festivities to celebrate the birth, in 1759, of their great national poet, Robert Burns. Burns' Night suppers are sumptuous meals, with pride of place being given to the haggis, carried in to the sound of the pipes and addressed in the immortal words of Burns:

> *Fair fa' your honest, sonsie face,*
> *Great chieftain o' the puddin-race!*
> *Aboon them a' ye tak your place,*
> *Painch, tripe, or thairm;*
> *Weel are ye wordy of a grace*
> *As lang's my arm.*

> *Ye Pow'rs, who mak mankind your care,*
> *And dish them out their bill o' fare,*
> *Auld Scotland wants nae skinking ware,*
> *That jaups in luggies;*
> *But, if ye wish her gratefu' prayer,*
> *Gie her a Haggis!*

There are toasts to the Queen, to the immortal memory of Burns and to 'the lassies'. Naturally there is a plentiful supply of Scotch whisky to wash down the meal and loosen the tongues to sing and to recite the poems of Burns. The evening of singing and dancing ends with *Auld Lang Syne*, the old poem that Burns rewrote.

Also born on this day were. . . .
Robert Boyle, physicist, in 1627.
Lord Lonsdale, sportsman, in 1857.
W. Somerset Maugham, writer, in 1874.
Wilhelm Furtwängler, conductor, in 1886.

On 26 January 1788, the First Fleet anchored in Sydney Cove, Australia. On board the ships were 1,030 men, women and children, 7 horses, 7 cows and bulls, 29 sheep, 74 pigs, 4 goats and 5 rabbits. They were there to set up a new colony in a land which had been claimed for Britain by Captain Cook a few years earlier. Of the people, 750 were prisoners and others the soldiers who had been sent to guard them. From that early beginning Australia developed into the great country it is today and 26 January became Australia Day. Nowadays the Monday following that date is the national holiday.

Also on this day. . . .
Edward Jenner, discoverer of vaccination, died in 1823.
General Gordon was killed at Khartoum in 1885.
Arthur Cayley, mathematician, died in 1895.
The Rugby Football Union was founded in 1871.
First test photograph at Mount Palomar Observatory in 1949.

27 January

On 27 January 1814, Londoners flocked to the River Thames between London Bridge and Blackfriars Bridge. During the night ice had drifted down the river, jammed against London Bridge and frozen solid, remaining so for four days. Soon there were, on the ice, stalls, booths, tents, skaters, sports, ox-roasting and even printing presses to print mementos of the greatest, and last of all the Frost Fairs. When the thaw came, some left it too late. Merry-go-rounds, booths and equipment were last seen drifting toward the sea; three men were drowned; and many others had a very cold bath!

Born on this day were Wolfgang Amadeus Mozart, composer (1756); Lewis Carroll (Charles Lutwidge Dodgson), writer (1832); Jerome Kern, composer (1885). John James Audubon, naturalist and artist, died in 1851 and Giuseppi Verdi, composer, in 1901.
On this day, in 1880, Edison patented the electric light bulb; in 1926 Baird gave the first public demonstration of television; and 1973 saw the ceasefire ending war in Vietnam.

28 January

Walter Arnold had the distinction of being the first driver in Britain to be found guilty of speeding. At Tonbridge, Kent, on 28 January 1896, he was fined one shilling for driving at over 2 mph.

Another for the road. . . . It was on this day, in 1807, that the first street lighting appeared. Pall Mall, London, was lit by gas.

Some of today's birthdays. . . .
In 1457 King Henry VII of England, first Tudor monarch.
In 1706 John Baskerville, printer and inventor of the printing type that bears his name.
In 1833 General Gordon, hero of China and Khartoum.
In 1841 Sir Henry Morton Stanley, explorer of Africa.
In 1855 William Burroughs, inventor of the adding machine.

And some who died. . . .
In 814 Charlemagne (Charles the Great), Holy Roman Emperor.
In 1547 King Henry VIII of England.
In 1596 Sir Francis Drake, adventurer and circumnavigator.

The Diet of Worms began this day in 1521.

29 January

The Victoria Cross was instituted on 29 January 1856. The bronze Maltese Cross, inscribed 'For Valour' is the highest award for conspicuous bravery in the face of the enemy.

The summer soldier and the sunshine patriot will, in this crisis, shrink from the service of their country

— an observation by Thomas Paine, political journalist and pamphleteer, writing in America in 1776. He was born in Thetford, Norfolk, on this day in 1737.

Earl Haig never shrank from serving his country as British Commander-in-Chief during World War I, nor from helping the disabled afterwards. He died on 29 January 1928.

Born on this day were Anton Chekhov, Russian playwright and short-story writer (1860), and Frederick Delius, composer (1862).

And therefore I tell you (and I pray God it be not laid to your charge) that I am the Martyr of the People.

With these words King Charles I faced the executioner with dignity on the scaffold in Whitehall on 30 January 1649, having been condemned as tyrant, traitor and murderer by his parliamentary opponents. It was one of a number of very sad events associated with this day.

On 30 January 1948, one of the greatest Indian leaders of this century, Mahatma Gandhi, climbed some steps to begin an open-air prayer meeting, when he was shot dead by a Hindu assassin. A man of peace, he had done much to help his people toward independence. Gandhi, regarded by Hindus as a national hero and a saint, offered these words of advice:

I shall not fear anyone on earth, I shall fear only God,
I shall not bear ill-will toward anyone. . . .

The state funeral of Sir Winston Churchill took place on this day in 1965. Full honours were paid to the great national leader in London before his burial in the Oxfordshire village of Bladon.

This was 'Bloody Sunday' in 1972 in Londonderry, when thirteen civilians were killed in disturbances in the city.

On 30 January 1933, Adolf Hitler was appointed Chancellor of Germany, paving the way for over a decade of dictatorship, persecution and war.

On this day, in 1982, Stanley Holloway died at the age of 91. The cockney entertainer had given pleasure to many for 77 years with monologues such as *The Lion and Albert* and performances in revues, plays, films and on television.

Also on this day. . . .
In 1882 Franklin Delano Roosevelt, president of the USA from 1932 to 1945, was born.
In 1948 Orville Wright, pioneer aviator, died.
In 1858 the Hallé Orchestra gave its first regular public performance.

31 January

Today has witnessed a number of interesting launchings.

In 1790, the first lifeboat, *The Original*, was launched at South Shields. It was the forerunner of many which have been used to save life from shipwreck and difficulty at sea.

In 1858, the *Great Eastern* was launched at Blackwall on the Thames and many people breathed a sigh of relief. There had been several attempts to launch her since the previous November but the great ship, larger than any built previously, had no wish to enter the water. A failure as a passenger ship, she later laid the transatlantic cable.

In 1958, *Explorer* was launched, not into the water but into space. This was the first American artificial satellite, which had been produced under the direction of Wernher von Braun the former German rocket scientist.

Some lions were launched today into public view at the unveiling, in 1867, of the lions in London's Trafalgar Square, the work of Sir Edwin Landseer.

Franz Schubert also made his first appearance on this day, his birthday, in 1797. Born in Vienna, he learned both the violin and piano before entering choir school at the age of eleven. He tried his hand at almost every kind of composition and left a great heritage of music including some well-loved symphonies and songs.

This was also the birthday, in 1885, of Anna Pavlova, the great Russian ballerina. She played with several companies before forming her own, with which she toured the world. Her most famous part was in *The Dying Swan*, a solo ballet written especially for her.

This day saw the final curtains for Guy Fawkes, Gunpowder Plot conspirator, who was hanged on 31 January 1606.

In 1888, John Bosco passed to his reward in Turin after years of service to poor and needy young men in the city. He is remembered on this day as St. John Bosco.

The end came on 31 January 1956 for A. A. Milne, the author of children's books and poems (p. 176).

Today also saw the death, in 1982, of Lord Ritchie-Calder, a scientist and journalist who became the first chairman of Britain's Metrication Board.

Other January Events and Commemorations
(See also pp. 155–6,164–5)

New Year's Day   In various places: Dole distributions.
6th (Epiphany)   Haxey, Lincolnshire: Hood Game (p. 165).
Sunday after 6th   Chichester, Sussex; Exeter, Devon; and elsewhere: Blessing of the Plough services.
12th   Burghead, Scotland: Burning the Clavie. A barrel is cut in two, the larger part filled with wood chips and tar then fastened to a pole. The tar is set alight and the clavie is paraded around the town before being used to light a bonfire.
17th   Carhampton, Somerset: Wassailing the Apple Trees. An old pagan ceremony to drive away evil spirits and encourage the trees to produce good cider apples. Guns are fired through the branches of the largest tree, cider is thrown over the trunk and toast soaked in cider is placed on the branches. An old wassail song is sung and a toast drunk in cider.
Last Thursday   Lerwick, Shetland: Up-Helly-A'. A festival reminiscent of Viking times. A 30 foot (9 m) model of a Viking longboat is drawn through the town accompanied by about 300 guisers in a torchlight procession. It ends by the sea, where bands play, maroons are fired, 'The Norseman's Home' is sung and torches are flung into the ship, which goes up in flames. The fun and enjoyment continues.
Sometime in the month   Margate, Kent: Blessing the Sea. It is conducted by the Greek Orthodox Archbishop. As part of the ceremony, a decorated crucifix is thrown into the water . . . and recovered by a swimmer who does not mind cold water.

FEBRUARY

February

February was the Roman Februarius. The name comes from the Latin verb *februare* (to purify) for it was on 15 February that a Roman festival of purification (Februa) was held. The Christian Church also has its festival of purification during this month — Candlemas, the Feast of the Purification of the Blessed Virgin Mary — which marks the end of the Christmas and beginning of Easter periods in the Church Calendar (p. 198).

At one time the Roman calendar ended with February. March began the new year. That is why the months September to December are the seventh to the tenth months according to their names.

February is the shortest month of the year, having only 28 days, except in Leap Years, when it has 29. At one time it was of the same length as other months but one day was taken from it to add to July, which had been renamed in honour of Julius Caesar. Then, when Augustus Caesar named the next month after himself, he also took a day off February so that he would be equal with his uncle. So February became the shortest month but, as some have remarked, 'With the kind of weather experienced in February, who wants more than 28 days?'

For the ancient Celts, 1 February was an important festival called Imbolc. This was lambing time and the festival celebrated the fact that the ewes were producing milk. Milk offerings were made to the goddess Brigid. February is still lambing time and many lambs are born during this month of bad weather, sometimes during blizzards.

The Anglo-Saxons also made offerings to the gods during this second month. They called it Solmonath, which Bede translates as 'month of cakes' (though 'sol' does not mean 'cake'), because of the cakes that were offered.

If February should be dry, farmers can make good use of their fine days but no doubt many will have thoughts about the future. An old saying is,

All the months in the year curse a fair February.

Another says.

> *If in February there be no rain,*
> *Tis neither good for hay nor grain.*

No doubt this thought lies behind the words of Thomas Tusser, the Suffolk farmer of Elizabethan days (1524?–80):

> *February, fill the dyke*
> *With what thou does like.*

And 'February fill-dyke' often does that and more, with flooding especially after heavy falls of snow. Another old saying is:

> *February fill the dyke*
> *Be it black or be it white;*
> *But if it be white its better to like.*

'Winter's back breaks about the middle of February', we are told, and an old Scottish saying from Aberdeen would confirm this:

> *The fair of Auld Deer* (3rd Thursday in February)
> *Is the worst day of the year.*

Certainly before the end of the month there are flowers to be seen; catkins hang on some of the trees; and many creatures are emerging from their winter sleep.

> *The frozen ground is broken*
> *Where snowdrops raise their heads,*
> *And nod their tiny greeting*
> *In glades and garden beds.*
>
> *The frozen stream is melted,*
> *The white brook turns to brown,*
> *And flaming through the coppice*
> *Flows helter skelter down.*
>
> *The frozen air is golden*
> *With February sun,*
> *The winter days are over,*
> *Oh, has the Spring begun?*

P. A. Ropes

Shrovetide

Shrovetide nearly always falls during the month of February but very occasionally in March. The few days of Shrovetide end with Shrove Tuesday, the eve of lent, the forty-day period leading up to Easter. Since Easter is a movable feast, it determines when Lent will begin. Shrove Tuesday can therefore be as early as 3 February or as late as 9 March.

Lent used to be observed as a very strict period of fasting. The first day, Ash Wednesday, was the day on which people went to church to be shriven, or shrove — that is to confess their sins and receive absolution from the priest. The previous few days were boisterous ones in which people let off steam before Lent, eating up those foods which were forbidden during Lent and engaging in all kinds of practical joking and merrymaking.

In the Roman Catholic countries of Europe, Shrovetide fell at the end of the even gayer time of Carnival, culminating with Mardi Gras, or Fat Tuesday, with its colourful processions.

The first day of Shrovetide is Egg Saturday and this is followed by Quinquagesima Sunday but the main activities take place on the following two days.

The Monday may be referred to as Shrove Monday but more often as Collop Monday, from the practice of eating up bacon, eggs and collops of meat before the fast began.

During Shrovetide there were always those who begged for food:

> *A-shrovin', a-shrovin',*
> *I be come a-shrovin';*
> *A piece of bread, a piece of cheese,*
> *A bit of your fat bacon,*
> *Or a dish of dough-nuts,*
> *All of your own makin'!*
>
> *A-shrovin', a-shrovin',*
> *Nice meat in a pie,*
> *My mouth is very dry.*

In time it was mainly the children who begged for food — or the money to buy food on Collop Monday in readiness for their feast on Shrove Tuesday. Usually they went in groups, chanting outside the doors rhymes such as this one commonly used in Devonshire.

> I see by the latch
> There is something to catch;
> I see by the string
> The good dame's within;
> Give a cake, for I've none;
> At the door goes a stone,
> Come give, and I've gone.

The end of the rhyme gives a clue to what happened if the children received nothing. They were usually well-armed with missiles to hurl at the door, often broken earthenware crocks. Hence the evening of Collop Monday was Lent-sherd Night — and is still observed as such in parts of the West Country.

In Cornwall this evening was Nickanan Night, when many practical jokes were played such as the removal of gates, knockers or anything else that had not been locked away. In some parts it was Dappy-door Night when children knocked at doors then ran away, maybe having previously tied string to the handle so that the door could be jerked out of the hand of the householder.

On Shrove Tuesday, until the 19th and early 20th Centuries, it used to be the custom to ring the Pancake Bell in most parishes. It may have gone by other names too. At Daventry it was the Pan-burn; at Maidstone it was the Fritter-bell; and in Cheshire it was the Guttit bell. It called people to church but it also indicated that it was time to down-tools for a holiday. It was a happy-go-lucky day on which, in some places, villagers rang the bell themselves and maybe had the 'run of the church' for the day.

> When Pancake bell begins to ring,
> All Halifax lads begin to sing.

And they didn't sing hymns!

The reason for making pancakes was that eggs and fats were foods forbidden during Lent. So Shrove Tuesday was Pancake Day.

Today, Pancake Races are held in several places, the most famous being that at Olney, Buckinghamshire. There is a story that, long ago, in 1445, an Olney woman heard the shriving bell whilst making her pancakes and dashed to church still wearing her apron and carrying her frying-pan. It is celebrated today with a race for women who must be wearing an apron and a hat or scarf, each carrying a frying-pan with a partially-cooked pancake which must be tossed three times during the 415 yard race from the market square to the church.

A similar race is run in Liberal, Kansas, and, in recent years, there has been friendly rivalry between Olney and Liberal to see which records the best time for that year.

Westminster School has its own ceremony — the Pancake Greaze, in which a pancake is tossed over a high iron bar and a prize awarded to the boy who gets it, or the largest part of it.

Shrove Tuesday is also a day for boisterous games, notably football or other ball games. One of the most famous is at Ashbourne, Derbyshire. Played between the Up'ards, who were born north of the river, and the Down'ards, who were born south of the river. The goals are mill-wheels three miles apart and anyone scoring a goal is entitled to keep the ball, which is then replaced.

Shrove Tuesday football has many variations. At Atherstone, Warwickshire, the ball is filled with water and decorated with red, white and blue ribbons. Women and children can join in too.

In St. Columb Major, Cornwall, the ancient game of Hurling the Silver Ball takes place. The silver ball can be thrown or tossed but not kicked.

At Scarborough, Yorkshire, there is skipping on the fore-shore, a relic of the old Shrovetide fair.

Children's activities include Egg-shackling at Stoke St. Gregory, Somerset. Children take to school eggs with their names on them. The eggs are shaken gently in a sieve, each being removed as it cracks. There is a prize for the owner of the last egg to remain uncracked. Cracked eggs go to the local hospital.

1 February

On this day, in 1811, the light first shone from the Bell Rock Lighthouse, built by Robert Stevenson to warn ships of the treacherous Inchcape or Bell Rock off Scotland's east coast. It was Bell Rock because, years before, a bell had been placed there as a warning to sailors. Robert Southey's poem *The Inchcape Rock* tells how Sir Ralph the Rover decided to have fun.

> *He felt the cheering power of spring,*
> *It made him whistle, it made him sing;*
> *His heart was mirthful to excess,*
> *But the Rover's mirth was wickedness.*

He cut away the bell which sank beneath the sea. But the joke turned sour. After a long voyage Sir Ralph returned, to be wrecked on the selfsame rock and drowned. Fun that can harm is not really fun at all.

How much better the good clean fun of the entertainer who is able to keep people spellbound with his escapades, or splitting their sides with laughter at his antics, perhaps without his having to say a word. Such an actor died on 1 February 1966. He was Buster Keaton, one of the most famous slap-stick comedy actors of the days of the silent films.

There was nothing silent about Dame Clara Butt. Born on 1 February 1873, she became one of the most popular concert singers of her time, her fine contralto voice arousing the emotions of many. Also born on this day, in 1859, was the Irish composer, Victor Herbert.

For many people, there is no better fun or entertainment on a Saturday afternoon than a game of football played well and cleanly by a couple of good teams. And if there should be a wizard with the ball in one of the teams, so much the better. One of the most famous English footballers was born on this day in 1915. He was Sir Stanley Matthews, who played for Blackpool and Stoke, took part in eighty-six international matches and was the first footballer to be knighted.

On a more serious note, on this day, in 1910, the first British state labour exchanges were established.

Keep an eye on the weather today! It has long been the custom for people to look at the weather on this day with an eye to the future. Weather lore associated with Candlemas may be found in most parts of the country.

If Candlemas Day be fair and bright,
Winter will have another flight:
But if it be dark with clouds and rain,
Winter is gone and won't come again.

If the wind's in the east on Candlemas Day
It's sure to stay to the Second of May.

If Candlemas Day be fine and clear,
Corn and fruit will then be dear.

For country folk who could not read and had no calendars, saints' days and religious festivals became a kind of almanack, and were used as a guide to the right time for the planting of crops. Candlemas was the time for bean planting.

Candlemas Day, put beans in the clay;
Put candles and candlesticks all away.

Candlemas was also the time for a clean sweep, both in the home and in the church. In the Christian calendar it marks the official break between the seasons — the end of Christmas and the beginning of Easter. It was important, therefore, that all Christmas decorations should be removed by this date. In past days, when homes had been decorated with greenery, every twig and leaf had to be removed, for superstitious folk believed that the goblins would cause trouble for any lazy housewife who had not done so.

Churches, too, had to be thoroughly cleaned before this day, also known as the Feast of the Purification of the Blessed Virgin Mary. It celebrates the presentation of Jesus Christ at the Temple forty days after his birth. The candles were lit because, on that occasion, the old man, Simeon, in the Temple, referred to Jesus as the Light that God had sent to the gentiles. The candles are symbolic of the 'Light of the World'.

There are some interesting local customs observed on Candlemas Day. In Blidworth, Nottinghamshire, on this day or the nearest Sunday, the last boy child to have been baptised before Candlemas is placed in an old wooden cradle and rocked by the priest. After a rededication service, the baby is returned to his parents whilst the ancient hymn from the Bible, the *Nunc dimittis* is sung. It serves as a reminder of the story in the Bible of the Presentation of Christ and also of the old Mystery Plays of the Middle Ages, in which this ceremony used to take place.

The mention of an ancient hymn is a reminder that Giovanni da Palestrina died on 2 February 1594. An Italian composer, he spent most of his life writing music for the Church, producing hundreds of works, large and small, religious and secular.

Two world-famous violinists were born on this day, Fritz Kreisler in 1875 and Jasha Heifetz in 1901. Kreisler was born in Austria and studied in Vienna and Paris. A talented musician, he made his debut in New York at the age of thirteen. He was a fine player and composer of violin music. Heifetz was born in Russia, making his debut at the age of six. He, too, gained an international reputation and commissioned new violin works, including Walton's Violin Concerto.

James Joyce was born on 2 February 1882. He was an Irish writer, who is considered by many people to be one of the greatest authors of the present century. His books include *A Protrait of the Artist as a Young Man, Ulysses* and *Finnegan's Wake*.

On 2 February 1976, the Queen opened the new National Exhibition Centre on the outskirts of Birmingham. It is used, amongst other purposes, to house some of the great trade fairs and shows, such as the Motor Show, previously held at Earls' Court or Olympia in London. This site was chosen as being near the centre of the country, without city parking problems, easily reached from the M6 motorway and on a main railway line, having a new station especially built.

Today is one of the Scottish Quarter Days.

St. Blaise is not one of the important names in the history of the Christian Church, nor is he one of the better-known martyrs, yet the circumstances surrounding his death led to the celebration of his day in various ways in Britain.

Blaise was Bishop of Sebaste in Armenia and was martyred there about 316. Legend tells how he was forced to flee and took refuge in a cave, where he was visited by many animals which came to him for his blessing or to be cured. However, he was taken captive and beheaded but, before death, he was tortured by having his flesh torn by sharp iron combs.

These combs were similar to the combs that were used by the woolcombers and so he came to be adopted as their patron saint. At one time, his day was kept in nearly all the wool towns in Britain. Many had processions and pageants, usually with an effigy of St. Blaise on horseback. Naturally there was feasting in honour of their patron saint.

Perhaps it was a part of the festivity that huge bonfires were also lit on the hilltops, or perhaps it was the association of his name with the blaze of the bonfire but certainly the size of the fires rivalled those on other 'bonfire' nights.

The story also tells how St. Blaise, on his way to imprisonment and death, saw a child with a fishbone stuck in the throat. The saint touched it and the bone was dislodged. This, and the animal legend above, led to his aid being invoked for children and cattle who were sick. It also led to the custom of Blessing the Throats on this day.

One church in which this is done is St. Etheldreda's Church, London, when people suffering from throat complaints gather for a special service. Two candles are tied together with ribbon in the form of a St. Andrew's Cross and then blessed by the priest. As the sufferers kneel before the altar, the priest holds the lighted candles under their chins, touches the throat with the ribbon and offers a prayer. Then it is up to St. Blaise!

In Japan people celebrate the festival of Setsubun on 3 February. Setsubun ('Change of Season') separates winter from spring. It is customary to throw beans to drive off imaginary devils and to scatter them in the home to discourage evil spirits.

This day is also the feast day of St. Ansgar (or Anskar), who died on 3 February 865. He was one of the important Christian missionaries of medieval Europe, known as the Apostle of the North. A native of Picardy, he went, in 826, to carry Christianity to the northmen of what is now Denmark and north Germany. Later he went to Sweden and, in 832, was appointed archbishop and papal legate to the Scandinavians and Slavs. Much of his work was centred upon Hamburg, where he founded a monastery and a school. He died in Bremen and was canonised soon afterwards.

From those northern European lands came the Vikings, who struck terror into the hearts of many. A leading Viking warrior was Sweyn Forkbeard, Sweyn I of Denmark. By conquest he added Norway and England to his domains. He died on 3 February 1014, shortly after his conquest of England.

A leading figure in medieval England was John of Gaunt, Duke of Lancaster. Born at Ghent, now in Belgium, he more-or-less ruled England during the latter part of the reign of his father, Edward III, and the early part of the reign of Richard II. Edward had become senile and Richard was only a boy. After a very eventful life, John of Gaunt died on 3 February 1399.

Richard 'Beau' Nash 'reigned' in Bath during the 18th Century as master of the ceremonies, leader of fashion, promoter of building schemes and entertainment, all of which transformed Bath into a fashionable holiday centre. A gambler himself, he tried to dissuade others. On one occasion he won from a young earl everything he possessed in money and lands, then gave it all back provided the earl promised never to gamble again. 'Beau' Nash died on 3 February 1792.

Born today. . . .
Felix Mendelssohn-Bartholdy, composer, in 1809.
Elizabeth Blackwell, first woman doctor (USA), in 1821.
Gertrude Stein, American writer, in 1874.

Today's firsts. . . .
In 1919 First meeting of the League of Nations.
In 1966 First soft moon landing (by Russian *Luna IX*).

4 February

Let me have my own way exactly in everything, and a sunnier and pleasanter creature does not exist.

This was Thomas Carlyle's assessment of himself, and it was probably near the truth, for he was known for his irritability and intolerance, even toward those close to him. Yet his nature was not one that was insincere or vindictive. Born in Dumfrieshire in 1795, he became a historian and man of letters, moving in the highest literary circles, where he gained a reputation as a literary genius. He died on 4 February 1881, having influenced not only literature but religious and political beliefs of his day.

Born on 4 February 1906 was a man who was to influence religious thinking in the 20th Century. Dietrich Bonhoeffer was a pastor in the German Lutheran Church with the courage to speak out against Hitler, which cost him his life in 1945. His *Letters from Prison* and other writings had a wide readership and influence.

Also born on this day, in 1902, was Charles Lindbergh, the aviator who flew the Atlantic. And on this day in the Atlantic, and elsewhere, German submarine warfare began in 1915.

5 February

On 5 February 1810, Ole Bull, the great Norwegian violinist, was born. One day he was asked why he was sitting by the sea. He replied: 'Listening to the surge and fall of the breakers, that I may catch the music of the sea.' His interpretation of the sounds of nature and his playing of Norwegian folk music earned him a high reputation in much of Europe and America.

Others who were born on 5 February. . . .
In 1788 Sir Robert Peel, statesman and police founder.
In 1837 Dwight L. Moody, American evangelist.
In 1840 John Boyd Dunlop, inventor of pneumatic tyres.
In 1840 Hiram Maxim, inventor of the automatic machine-gun.
In 1900 Adlai Stevenson, American politician.
In 1920 The Royal Air Force College at Cranwell, Lincolnshire.

New Zealanders celebrate 6 February as National Day, or Waitangi Day, commemorating the signing at Waitangi, on 6 February 1840, of the treaty which brought New Zealand under the sovereignty of the British crown.

On the previous day, the British consul and lieutenant-governor, William Hobson, met many of the Maori chiefs and worked out the agreement which also protected Maori rights and possessions as well as making the Maori signatories full British subjects.

When they met again on 6 February, forty-five Maori chiefs signed the Treaty of Waitangi.

Some of todays birthdays. . . .

In 1665 the future Queen Anne of Great Britain was born. She was the second daughter of King James II and she became queen after the death of William, her sister Mary's husband, in 1702. She had no surviving children and so she was the last of the Stuart monarchs.

A 20th-Century leader, Ronald Reagan, who became president of the United States in 1981, was born on 6 February 1911. He was a film star before entering politics.

Sir Charles Wheatstone was born on this day in 1802. He was a physicist who experimented with electricity. He developed such things as the stereoscope and, with Sir William Fothergill Cooke, the first electric telegraph. He also invented the concertina.

Sir Henry Irving, the famous actor, was born on this day in 1838. He once wrote

It is the fate of actors to be judged by echoes which are altogether delusive — when they have passed out of immediate ken, and some fifty years hence some old fool will be saying — there never was an actor like Irving.

There must be a good many old fools — for he is certainly regarded as the best of his day, the first actor to be knighted and one laid to rest in Westminster Abbey.

'Capability' Brown, landscape gardener, died this day in 1783, and Joseph Priestley, discoverer of oxygen, in 1804. Most of the Manchester United football team died on 6 February 1958, when their 'plane crashed at Munich.

What is it that causes someone to destroy an article that is of great value?

On 7 February 1845, attendants and visitors in the British Museum, London, were startled to hear the sound of breaking glass, followed by a loud sound as an object smashed to the ground. They were horrified to discover that it was the Portland Vase, the most valuable glass object in the world. A man named William Lloyd admitted having broken the glass in the exhibition case and hurling the vase to the floor.

The beautiful Portland Vase had been made in Italy, about the 1st Century BC or 1st Century AD. The Duchess of Portland bought it in 1792 from the Berberini family, in whose possession it had been for at least a century and a half. It had been placed in the British Museum in company with other priceless treasures.

The many pieces of broken glass were carefully gathered up then painstakingly sorted out and stuck together so that the Portland Vase is still there to be seen and admired. It is only on close examination that the damage can be seen . . . but, of course, such damage can never be undone.

From the world's most valuable to the world's largest. . . . It was on 7 February 1976, that the world's largest telescope began operating. It is on Mount Semirodriki in the Caucasus Mountains, USSR. It is a 6 m (236.2 inch) telescope with a reflecting mirror weighing 7 tonnes. It can pick up the light of stars millions and millions of miles away. In fact it could detect the light of a candle if it were 15,000 miles (24,000 km) away.

This is the birthday of two men whose names were to become widely known and respected. Sir Thomas More was born in 1477. At one time he was Chancellor of England but, after he had refused to acknowledge Henry VIII as head of the English Church, he was sentenced to death and beheaded.

Charles Dickens, born on 7 February 1812 into a very poor home, first became popular as an author, in 1837, with the serialisation of *The Pickwick Papers*. He wrote many other books and is considered to be one of the greatest English novelists.

Adolphe Sax, who invented the saxophone (p. 88), saxhorn, saxtuba and other instruments, died on 7 February 1894.

8 February

When we build, let us think that we build for ever.

So wrote John Ruskin, the writer and artist, who was born on 8 February 1819. He wrote books on art and architecture and greatly influenced art in Victorian England. Ruskin was strongly in favour of the Gothic Revival Movement in English Architecture.

The Gothic style was adopted for the design of the new Anglican Cathedral in Liverpool on which the building work, in red sandstone, began in 1904. The architect, who also designed other famous buildings in London, Cambridge, Oxford and elsewhere, was Sir Giles Gilbert Scott, who died on 8 February 1960.

William Tecumseh Sherman, born on 8 February 1820, was an architect of a different kind. As a soldier he made a name for himself in the American Civil War, destroying the Confederate army as he marched through Georgia. General Sherman has been described as 'a major architect of modern warfare'.

Similarly, Jules Verne might be described as the architect of modern science fiction. Certainly he wrote in his books about things that were then impossible — journeys under the sea, to the moon and *Around the World in Eighty Days*. Jules Verne was born at Nantes, France, on 8 February 1828.

Mary, Queen of Scots, was executed on 8 February 1587, guilty of plotting against Queen Elizabeth I. Was she the architect of many plots including the murder of her husband. . . .

9 February

. . . Lord Darnley? On 9 February 1567, his house in Edinburgh was blown up — possibly after he had been strangled. It was thought to be the work of the Earl of Bothwell, whom Mary married three months later.

On this day: Charles Sturt, the Australian explorer, discovered the source of the Murray River in 1830; Brendan Behan, Irish author and dramatist, was born in 1923.

10 February

A new word was coined, and a new phase in naval warfare introduced at Portsmouth on 10 February 1906, when HMS *Dreadnought* was launched. She was the forerunner of the battleship which dominated the naval scene for nearly half a century and which was often described as a 'dreadnought.'

Samuel Plimsoll, who was born on 10 February 1824, became very interested in ships and seamen. He was particularly concerned that some ships, referred to as 'coffin ships', were sent to sea overloaded or unseaworthy, many of them being lost and the crews drowned. He was instrumental in passing in Parliament the Merchant Shipping Act in 1876, by which all ships were to have a load line painted on their hulls to indicate the limit to which they could be laden. It became known as the Plimsoll line.

It so happened that in the same year a Phillip Lace hit upon the idea of a strip of rubber round canvas shoes to protect from the dampness of grass or sand. They became known as 'plimsolls' — though Samuel had no part in their invention.

So to sport — and two great sportsmen born on 10 February. In 1893, the great tennis player of the 1920s, Bill Tilden, was born in Philadelphia. He was one of the greatest all-rounders.

Mark Spitz, born this day in 1950, achieved fame in the 1972 Munich Olympics, when he won a record 7 gold medals for swimming, a climax to his many swimming achievements.

Harold Macmillan, born on 10 February 1894, was British prime minister from 1957 to 1963. He is remembered for his 'winds of change' speech acknowledging the emergence of new African nations, and for reminding people in Britain that they had 'never had it so good'.

Two great Russian writers are remembered, each of whom upset the authorities of his day, Alexandr Pushkin, acknowledged to be Russia's greatest poet, died this day in 1837. Boris Pasternak, writer of *Dr. Zhivago*, was born on 10 February 1890.

Also on 10 February. . . .
Charles Lamb, English essayist (p. 147), was born in 1775.
Lord Lister, surgeon, introducer of antiseptics, died in 1912.

Genius is one per cent inspiration and ninety-nine per cent perspiration.

So said Thomas Alva Edison in a newspaper interview, and he should know, for he was a genius in electrical and other matters, taking out patents for hundreds of inventions including some in telegraphy, and others for such as electric lighting, phonograph, megaphone, kinetoscope and metallurgic methods.

Edison, who began life as a railway newsboy, used the baggage car as a laboratory for his early experiments but much of his experimenting was at his laboratory in Menlo Park, New Jersey, USA, where he was known as 'The Wizard of Menlo Park'. This was his birthday in 1847.

Traffic lights were not included amongst Edison's inventions: they came later. The first traffic lights in Britain were given a one day trial in Wolverhampton on this day in 1928.

Henry Willis was a genius with organs and is considered the finest organ builder of the 19th Century. He built a large organ for the Crystal Palace and later built or restored about a thousand church and concert hall instruments. He died on 11 February 1901.

William Henry Fox Talbot, who was born on this day in 1800, was a physicist who set his creative mind to the improvement of photographic processes. He first used the negative and found new means of obtaining prints. He was also interested in archaeology and was one of the first to translate the cuneiform writing from Nineveh in Assyria.

Auguste Mariette, the French archaeologist (p. 177) who excavated temples in Egypt and elsewhere, and who directed the uncovering of the great Sphinx, was also born on this day, in 1821.

Also on this day. . . .
    In 1858 Bernadette Soubirous saw her first vision of a lady near a small cave at Lourdes.
    In 1929 the Vatican city became an independent state.
    In 1940 John Buchan, 1st Baron Tweedsmuir, statesman, writer *(The Thirty-Nine Steps* and others) and biographer, died.

12 February

On 12 February 1976, some workmen in Romsey Abbey, Hampshire, discovered a rose, perfectly preserved, that had been hidden in the wall in 1120. It is believed to be the oldest botanical specimen found in Europe. The oldest in the world is a posy that lay in Tutankhamun's tomb in Egypt.

Alexander Selkirk was also 'discovered' but on a desert island in the Juan Fernandez group about 400 miles (643 km) west of Valparaiso, Chile. In September 1704, after a quarrel with his captain, he was put ashore, where he remained alone until February 1709 when, on this day, he was taken aboard an English ship. His story provided inspiration for Defoe when writing *Robinson Crusoe*.

Born on this day, in 1809, was one of the best–known men in American history, its 16th president, Abraham Lincoln. From a poor family background, he educated himself in law and entered politics. He had a passionate desire for equality and for freedom for the slaves — and for that he fought.

I intend no modification of my oft-expressed personal wish that all men everywhere could be free.

Tadeusz Kościuszko, born in 1746, wanted freedom for his country, Poland. After fighting for the colonists in the American War of Independence, he returned to Poland, where he fought against the Russian invaders. But the armies of Russia and Prussia were too powerful. He was imprisoned and then exiled, eventually settling in Switzerland, where he was killed when his horse plunged over a precipice.

Sharing the same birthday as Abraham Lincoln was Charles Darwin, English naturalist, who startled many with his ideas of evolution as published in *On the Origin of Species*.
  This was also the birthday, in 1870, of Marie Lloyd, foremost cockney music-hall artist of her day, remembered for her songs such as 'Oh, Mr. Porter' and 'A little of what you fancy does you good'.

On this day, in 1554, Lady Jane Grey, queen of England for 9 days, was beheaded in the Tower of London, aged 16.

13 February

Today's dirty deed took place on 13 February 1692, in the beautiful valley of Glencoe, Scotland. All Highlanders had been ordered to swear an oath of allegiance to King William III but the leader of the Macdonalds of Glencoe had delayed. The Campbells took this opportunity to settle old scores. Early in February, 120 of their soldiers arrived in Glencoe and received hospitality for 12 days. Then, on this day, at 5 am, they rose from their beds, slew the chief and about 40 others, then drove about 300 more into the snow, where many of them perished. The Massacre of Glencoe is a blot on the pages of history.

In today's world people in many lands are suppressed, especially if they are in disagreement with those in authority. For many years it has been customary in the USSR for such people to be sent to labour camps in Siberia. Alexander Solzhenitsyn was one. After service in the Red Army in World War II, he dared to criticise Stalin and was sentenced for so doing. His writings of his experiences, and his attack on Stalin's purges in *Gulag Archipelago* earned him a Nobel Prize in 1970 and the further wrath of the authorities, who finally lost patience and expelled him from the Soviet Union on 13 February 1975.

A fighter for the rights of women was Christabel Pankhurst, a daughter of Emmeline Pankhurst and, with her mother, one of the leaders of the Suffragettes, suffering imprisonment for her actions. She died on 13 February 1958.

Lord Randolph Churchill, father of the future prime minister, Sir Winston, was born on 13 February 1849. A prominent Conservative, he became leader of the House of Commons when 37 but a miscalculation as to the effect of offering his resignation ended his promising political career.

Also on this day. . . .
  In 1571 Benvenuto Cellini, Italian goldsmith and engraver, died.
  In 1883 Wilhelm Richard Wagner, German composer, died.
  In 1903 the Belgian author Georges Simenon was born. From being a reporter he turned to writing thrillers then detective stories, notably those about Maigret. He wrote over 500 books, using 19 different names.

Hail to thy returning festival, old Bishop Valentine! Like unto thee, assuredly, there is no other mitred father in the calendar.
Charles Lamb

St. Valentine is one of the most popular of saints because of the special associations of his day. But was it Bishop Valentine? Or was it a priest named Valentine? Both were martyred on this same day but in different years. So which was the lovers' saint? Perhaps neither had anything to do with lovers.

Was it perhaps because both Greeks and Romans observed a special day at this time for their goddesses, Hera and Juno, who represented women and marriage and that St. Valentine's Day was a Christianisation of this? Or was it because this was the day on which birds were believed to mate?

You'll be mine and I'll be thine,
And so, good morrow, Valentine.
As I sat in my garden chair,
I saw two birds fly in the air,
And two by two and pair by pair,
Which made me think of you, my dear.

There used to be many superstitions regarding this day. To see a cock and hen together was a sign that a girl would be married during the year. The number of animals seen would indicate the number of months before this happened. The kind of bird seen would indicate the kind of husband: a sparrow indicated a countryman, a blackbird a clergyman, a robin a sailor, a goldfinch a rich man. To see a yellow bird was a sign of good luck and it was also considered lucky to wear a yellow crocus, which was St. Valentine's flower.

There was also a belief that the first man a woman saw on this day would automatically be her Valentine. Samuel Pepys records in his diary for 1662 that Mrs. Pepys was compelled to go about the house with her eyes covered because there were painters there and she was afraid to see one of them before her true Valentine arrived.

It was not unusual for married women then to be sent Valentines which were sometimes expensive presents. So Valentine also came to mean a gift and children used to go out begging for their Valentines — money, sweets or cakes.

Gloves were once a popular gift, probably with a rhyme such as

If from this glove you take the G
Then glove becomes love, — which I send thee.

Later, the gift was replaced by a Valentine card. By the end of the 19th Century, about a million and a half were being sent each year. In 1935 Valentine telegrams were introduced. Nowadays Valentine messages may be published in daily papers.

One who should know about the mating habits of birds was Sir Julian Huxley, who died on 14 February 1975. He was a biologist who studied the behaviour of birds and animals. He was Secretary of the Zoological Society of London from 1935 to 1948 and Director General of UNESCO from 1946 to 1948.

There wasn't much love shown on this day in 1779 by the natives of Hawaii toward Captain Cook and his crew. There was a fight in which Cook was stabbed with knives and killed.
Neither was there much love between the English and the French and Spaniards at the end of the 18th Century. On 14 February 1797, the English fleet met the Spanish fleet off Cape St. Vincent. It was the first battle in which Nelson showed his greatness as a naval officer. Serving under Admiral Sir John Jervis, he was responsible for capturing two of the four Spanish ships taken, having fought all four. He was promoted and honoured with a knighthood.

Two popular characters from books are Bertie Wooster and his 'Gentleman's gentleman' Jeeves. They were the creation of Pelham Grenville Wodehouse, who wrote over 60 novels and 20 musical comedies. He was knighted in 1975 and died a few weeks later, on 14 February of that year, at the age of 93.

Thomas Robert Malthus, who died on 14 February 1834, was concerned, even in those days, that food supplies would not be enough for the world's population (p. 143).

Tonight, just before midnight, at Norham-on-Tweed, is the annual Blessing of the Salmon-net Fisheries, so opening the fishing season — which should provide just a little of the world's food.

15 February

New things are highlighted today — inventions, discoveries, ideas. Most revolutionary were those of Galileo, born on 15 February 1564, in Pisa, Italy. His scientific thoughts and observations offended many in his day but he is now recognised as the first modern scientist and one of the greatest experimental philosophers.

Jan Swammerdam, the Dutch naturalist, found many new things with his microscope. He was the first to describe red blood cells and accurately recorded many observations regarding insects and tadpoles that were of great scientific value. He died this day in 1680.

Born this day in 1809, Cyrus Hall McCormick, American inventor and industrialist, patented, in 1834, the first mechanical reaper.

On this day in 1882, the *Dunedin* arrived in England carrying the first ever cargo of frozen meat from New Zealand.

Sir Ernest Shackleton, born this day in 1874, went on four expeditions which shed new light on Antarctica.

British people had to get used to new coins on 15 February 1971. New metric coins replaced the old shillings and pence.

The official excavation of the cave at Qumran, where the Dead Sea Scrolls were found, began on 15 February 1949. The Scrolls themselves were not new but they shed new light on Biblical scholarship.

During World War II, the island of Singapore fell to the Japanese on 15 February 1942.

Graham Hill, British car racing driver, who twice won the world championship (1962 and 1968), was born this day in 1929.

16 February

Most important people and events appear to have avoided 16 February. Richard Mead was one exception. He was a leading 18th-Century physician in London who studied poisons and preventive medicine. He died on this day in 1754.

G. M. Trevelyan, English historian, was born in 1876.

Fidel Castro became premier of Cuba on 16 February 1959.

The patent for a new synthetic fibre, Nylon, was taken out in Seaford, Delaware, USA, on this day in 1937.

17 February

'Cough, please!' Most people, at some time or other, have visited a doctor because of illness and been asked to cough whilst a cold stethoscope is pressed against the chest or back. With it the doctor is able to listen to what is happening inside the body and make a diagnosis. This day was the birthday, in 1781, of the French physician René Laënnec, who invented the stethoscope and is generally regarded to be the father of chest medicine. His first stethoscope was a wooden cylinder through which he listened to the sounds and then, after a person had died, recalled in connection with the autopsy, which sounds he had recorded.

Horace de Saussure, who was born on 17 February 1740, was a Swiss physicist and geologist who, in fact, introduced the word geology into science. A professor of physics at the Academy of Geneva, he was an early Alpine explorer, and developer of such instruments as the hygrometer.

On to Germany, where a new machine was patented on 17 February 1818. It was called a 'draisine', being named after its inventor, Karl de Drais de Sauerbrun, a baron who needed some transport over rough country around Mannheim. The machine, which was pushed along by the feet was a development of the hobby-horse and had iron wheels, the front one being steerable. It was one forerunner of the bicycle.

Three other creators in their respective fields. . . .

Molière was the stage name of Jean Baptiste Poquelin, the French dramatist who came to be accepted as one of the greatest of French writers. During an early performance of a new play in Paris (*The Imaginary Invalid*), he collapsed on stage, dying on that same night, 17 February 1673.

Sir Edward German was born on 17 February 1862 and became a composer of various kinds of music including the popular *Merrie England* with its folk melodies and dance forms.

Graham Sutherland, painter of portraits and landscapes, designer of Coventry Cathedral tapestry, died on this day in 1980.

Geronimo, one of the most famous of the North American Indians and the last of the Indian guerilla fighters, died a prisoner at Fort Sill, Oklahoma, on 17 February 1909. His lightning raids on white settlers had ended when he finally surrendered in 1886.

'You see many stars at night in the sky but find them not when the sun rises, can you say there are no stars in the heaven by day? So, O man! Because you behold not God in the days of your ignorance, say not there is no God. As one and the same material, water, is called by different names by different peoples, one calling it water, another calling it eau, a third aqua, and another pani, so the one Sat-chit-ananda, the everlasting intelligent-bliss, is invoked by some as God, by some as Allah, by some as Jehovah, by some as Hari, and by others as Brahman. As one can ascend to the top of a house by means of a ladder or a bamboo or a staircase or a rope, so divers are the ways and means to approach God, and every religion in the world shows one of these ways. Different creeds are but different paths to reach the Almighty.'

These are the words of Sri Ramakrishna, who was born on 18 February 1836. Brought up a Hindu, he later followed the way of Islam, then studied Christianity. He concluded that each religion could help people to find God who, by whatever name he was known, was at the centre of everything.

It was on this day in 1546 that Martin Luther died. He, too, was a man who had definite views about religion and was not afraid to say what he thought. He disagreed with some of the teachings of the Roman Catholic Church, of which he was a member. He made a list of his ninety-five objections and nailed them to the door of the cathedral at Wittenburg in his homeland, Germany.

Luther was called to appear before a council, known as the Diet of Worms, and was told that, if he did not withdraw his statements, he would be excommunicated (turned out of the Church) and regarded as a heretic, which could result in his being put to death. He stood fast by what he had written and said so in his famous words, 'Here I stand, I cannot do otherwise.'

Martin Luther was excommunicated and was forced to go into hiding, during which time he translated part of the Bible into German and wrote hymns about his faith. Many people in Germany and elsewhere were greatly helped by his teachings.

Nowadays, the Lutheran Church, which follows the teachings of Martin Luther, is very strong in northern Europe and in other parts of the world to which Lutheran missionaries have gone.

Which was the true Christian religion — the Roman Catholic or the way of the reformers such as Luther? Some people thought one thing; others thought the opposite; and there were many years of bitterness and cruelty. Roman Catholics were persecuted in the reigns of Protestant kings or queens. Protestants were imprisoned and put to death in the reigns of Roman Catholics, none more so in England than during the reign of Queen Mary I, whose birthday was 18 February 1516 and who became known as 'Bloody Mary'.

This day also marked another date in the story of man's seeking after God. It was on 18 February 1678, that *The Pilgrim's Progress* was first published. It was to become one of the most famous books in the world. Its author, John Bunyan, was a man who suffered for his beliefs, having twice been imprisoned because he refused to stop preaching. Many people have been greatly helped by this story of Christian, who makes his way toward the celestial city through difficulties and distractions of many kinds but succeeds. 'So he passed over, and all the trumpets sounded for him on the other side.'

Others have pointed a way to God through works of art, few of which can be greater than that painted by Michelangelo on the ceiling of the Sistine Chapel of the Vatican in Rome. It is about 930 square metres in size and some 30 metres above the chapel floor. It took Michelangelo four years to paint it whilst lying on his back on scaffolding. He left many treasures of art and sculpture when he died, aged nearly ninety, on 18 February 1564.

Still in Italy, 18 February was also the birthday, in 1745, of Count Alessandro Volta, the physicist whose name is familiar in connection with electricity, including the invention of an electric battery. The unit of electric pressure, the volt, is named after him.

George, Duke of Clarence, younger brother of Edward IV, was executed in the Tower of London on 18 February 1478, convicted of treason for changing sides in the Wars of the Roses. It is said that he asked to be drowned in a butt of his favourite malmsey wine and that he was — but there is no evidence of this.

David Garrick was born in Hereford on 19 February 1719. A pupil of Dr. Samuel Johnson at Lichfield, he travelled with his master to London, proposing to study law. The stage, however, was to be his life's work. His first London appearance, at Goodman's Fields, was as Richard III in Shakespeare's play of that name. He eventually settled at Drury Lane where, as actor manager, he drew large crowds. He also did much to reform the theatre, including more realistic approaches to costume and the removal of all members of the audience, however important, from the stage. Considered the most versatile of British actors, for he was equally at home in tragedy, comedy or farce, he was honoured with burial in Westminster Abbey after his death in 1779.

Still in the world of entertainment, this was the birthday, in 1843, of Adelina Patti, daughter of a Sicilian tenor. She sang in New York at the age of 7 and never looked back. She developed a high, rich soprano voice, greatly enjoyed wherever she appeared.

Many people like some of their entertainment at home and listen to recordings. This was the day when such pleasures began. Thomas Alva Edison patented his phonograph on 19 February 1877. The recording was on a cylinder turned by a handle.

Sven Hedin, who was born in Stockholm on 19 February 1865, became an explorer and geographer. He is remembered for his journeyings across Asia, in Tibet, across the Gobi desert and in the interior of China, travelling where no European had previously been and making important maps and observations.

The expeditions of Charles Clermont-Ganneau, born in Paris on 19 February 1846, were archaeological ones in the Middle East. He was expert in the translation of ancient languages.

Also on this day. . . .
In 1622 Sir Henry Savile, scholar and mathematician, died.
In 1718 Baron George Rodney, British admiral, was born.
In 1789 Sir William Fairbairn, Scottish engineer, was born.
In 1915 British and French ships attacked The Dardanelles.
In 1963 the USSR agreed to withdraw troops from Cuba, so ending a confrontation with the USA.

National Savings Certificates were first issued in 1916.

Katherine ('Kate') Douglas is one of the heroines of Scottish history. She was a lady-in-waiting to the queen of James I of Scotland. One night, as the king and his family were at dinner in Perth, the king's enemies, led by Sir Robert Graham, arrived to assassinate the king. To ensure entry they had previously removed the bolts from the doors but, at the sign of trouble, Katherine thrust her arm through the bolt rings to keep the door barred. It was a heroic act but unsuccessful. Katherine's arm was broken and the king stabbed to death.

Katherine recovered and was given the name 'Barlass'. Her descendants, the Barlass family, adopted a broken arm symbol on their crest.

A hero of a different kind was John Glenn. In the early days of space travel, he was the first American to orbit the earth. On 20 February 1962, he orbited the earth three times in the *Mercury* space capsule *Friendship 7*. He had previously made a record-breaking supersonic flight in 1947 between Los Angeles and New York.

An American whose adventures were at ground level was Robert Peary. An admiral and explorer, he made a number of Arctic voyages and expeditions, travelling extensively in Greenland. His greatest achievement was to be the first to reach the North Pole, in 1909. He died on this day in 1920.

Another American achievement, on this day in 1969 in New York, was the transplanting of the heart, kidneys and liver of a man who had died, one of the early examples of modern organ transplant surgery.

The achievements of Sir Leonard Woolley were also spectacular, though spread over a lengthy period of time. Born in London, he became an archaeologist, responsible for some of the greatest excavations in the Middle East. After working at Carchemish and Sinai, he directed the excavations at the Chaldean city of Ur, the birthplace of Abraham. Among the many artifacts revealed between 1922 and 1930 was the great Ziggurat. Sir Leonard, who also wrote on archaeological matters, died on 20 February 1960.

21 February

Ils ne passeront pas! 'They shall not pass!' were the words of the famous battle call of General Pétain on this day in 1916 as powerful German attacks were launched on the French frontier fortress of Verdun. In the long struggle that followed, over one-third of a million Frenchmen died and nearly as many Germans. The battle is regarded as one of the vital battles of World War I.

During World War II, the defenders of Stalingrad were equally determined and held out against the German armies. To commemorate their success, King George VI announced on this day in 1943 that a sword of honour would be presented to the city.

To more peaceful matters. . . .

Leo Delibes, the French composer of light operas and ballet music, was born on 21 February 1836. His most popular work is the ballet *Coppelia*.

Wystan Hugh Auden was born at York on 21 February 1907. His early poems, reflecting the social problems of the thirties, earned him the title of 'Poet of the Thirties'. In 1939 he emigrated to New York and became a naturalised American citizen. His many poems reflect his conversion from humanism to Anglicanism.

Richard Trevithick was a pioneer of railway locomotives. His first locomotive puffed its way along ten miles of track in Glamorgan with a load of ten tonnes on this day in 1804.

Jethro Tull's chief claim to fame is his invention of the seed drill which planted seeds regularly in rows. He died on 21 February 1741.

On 21 February 1861, the spire of Chichester cathedral suddenly collapsed into the centre of the cathedral. Fortunately the building was empty and no one was hurt. It was rebuilt within six years.

On a more serene religious theme, Cardinal John Henry Newman was born this day in 1801. He led the Oxford Movement in the Church of England and later became a cardinal-deacon in the Roman Catholic Church. This great scholar and preacher wrote this, and many other words of wisdom:

> *The thought of God, and nothing short of it, is the happiness of man.*

Olave St. Clair Soames, the daughter of a Chesterfield businessman, was always on the move with her family. By the time she was 22 she had lived in almost as many homes. In that year, 1912, she went on a cruise to Jamaica, on which she was overjoyed to meet one of her heroes, General Sir Robert Baden-Powell. They struck up a friendship and discovered that they shared the same birthday, 22 February — Olave in 1889 and Robert in 1857.

Within a year they were married and, ere long, Olave was as committed to Girl Guiding as B.P. was to Boy Scouting. As Lord and Lady Baden-Powell, they each led their respective movements for the rest of their lives, inspiring many as leaders and giving pleasure to millions of boys and girls in many parts of the world.

If, among all the pedestals supplied by history for public characters of extraordinary nobility and purity, I saw one higher than all the rest, and if I were required, at a moment's notice, to name the fittest occupant for it, I think my choice, at any time during the last forty-five years, would have lighted, and would now light upon Washington.

This fine tribute by a great British prime minister, W. E. Gladstone, indicates his respect for the man held in the highest esteem in America, its first President, George Washington. This was the birthday, in 1732, in Virginia, of the man who led the American colonists to independence. His skills of strategy and tactics, coupled with his high reputation, made him the natural choice as Commander-in-chief and later as President.

On 22 February 1797, the last invasion of Britain took place when French troops landed at Fishguard but were frightened off by local Welsh people.

Also on this day. . . .
   In 1677 Benedict Spinoza, Jewish philosopher, died.
   In 1797 Baron Munchausen, German storyteller, died.
   In 1810 Frédéric Chopin, Polish composer, was born.
   In 1949 'Niki' Lauda, Finnish racing driver, was born.

Eric Gill, sculptor, engraver, typographical designer and writer, was born in 1882. Jean Corot, French artist, died in 1875.

A thing of beauty is a joy for ever: its loveliness increases:
it will never pass into nothingness.

With these words, John Keats began his 4,000 line poem *Endymion*, the story of a shepherd who loved and won the moon goddess. Like so many of his poems, it reflects on the beauty of the world and the seeking after eternal truth. He became ill with tuberculosis and went to Italy but it was too late to benefit from the warmer climate. He died in Rome on 23 February 1821 at the age of 25.

Sir Joshua Reynolds also died on 23 February, in 1792. He, too, had an eye for beauty as seen through the eyes of an artist. One of the greatest English portrait painters, he became the first president of the Royal Academy and 'painter to the king'. He associated, too, with literary men and wrote himself on matters concerning art. Some of his words of wisdom and advice:

A mere copier of nature can never produce anything great.

No-one could ever accuse L. S. Lowry of copying nature but his factory scenes and match-stalk men have led to his wide recognition as an artist of distinction. He died on this day, too, 23 February 1976.

For many people a thing of beauty is a delicious Peach Melba — a peach in syrup with ice-cream and crushed raspberries. It was first made by the chef of the Savoy Hotel, London, and presented to Dame Nellie Melba, in whose honour it was named. The great Australian singer, who took her stage name from Melbourne, and who captured the hearts of the world, died on 23 February 1931.

Also on this day. . . .
Johannes Gutenberg, printing pioneer, died in 1468.
Samuel Pepys, diarist, was born in 1633.
George Frederik Handel, composer, was born in 1685.
Erich Kästner, German writer and poet, was born in 1899.
Sir Edward Elgar, composer, died in 1934.
Stan Laurel, slapstick film comedian, died in 1965.
The Cato Street Conspiracy, a plot to murder members of the British government on this day in 1820, failed.

24 February

Abū 'Abd Allāh Muhammad Ibn 'Abd Allāh Al-Lawāti, At-Tanji Ibn Battūtah was born in Tangier on 24 February 1304. Better known simply as Ibn Battūtah, he was the greatest Arab traveller of the Middle Ages and author of the *Rihlah*, one of the most famous travel books in history. To visit nearly all the Muslim countries, he travelled about 75,000 miles (120,000 km) in Europe, Asia and Africa.

Best known by his nickname 'Bluebeard', Henri Désiré Landru went to the guillotine in Versailles on 24 February 1922. He won the hearts of many women from whom he extorted money and then disposed of them, piece by piece, it is said, in his stove. He was eventually charged with the murder of 10 women and a boy but no bodies were ever produced and he was convicted on circumstantial evidence.

On a pleasanter note, in France, this was the birthday, in 1858, at Le Mans, of Arnold Dolmetsch whose name and work are greatly respected in the world of music. He learned piano- and organ-building from his father, played stringed instruments, then studied old instruments and the sounds they produced. In 1914 he settled in England where, on his 70th birthday, 24 February 1928, the Dolmetsch Foundation was established to support him and spread his ideas.

Robert Fulton was a man with ideas, too. An American painter of miniature portraits, he became interested in mechanical engineering. He invented a mill for sawing and polishing marble. He drew plans for a machine for spinning flax, for bridges, a dredging machine and a submarine torpedo boat. But he is probably best remembered as the first successful builder of steam boats. He died on 24 February 1815.

It was on this day, in 1946, that Juan Peron became President of Argentina, setting up a corrupt dictatorship. This day in 1966 saw the end of the corrupt dictatorial presidency of Kwame Nkrumah of Ghana, overthrown by a military coup.

Wilhelm Grimm, German folklorist, was born in 1786.
Henry Cavendish, physicist and chemist, died on 24 February 1910.

25 February

Baron Paul von Reuter died on 25 February 1899. He was born Israel Beer Josaphat of Jewish parentage but adopted the name of Reuter when he became Christian. It was an acquaintance with Carl Gauss, who was working on the electric telegraph, that gave Reuter some ideas. From Paris he began collecting items of news, which he sent to Germany. Then, in 1850, he set up a carrier pigeon news service between Aachen and Brussels, where the respective telegraph systems terminated.

In the following year, Reuter moved to London and set up a telegraph office near the stock exchange. Before long, Reuter had developed the news agency, Reuters Ltd., which bears his name and transmits news across the world.

So what is the news for 25 February?

'Earl of Essex executed.' The Elizabethan courtier and soldier was a one-time favourite of Queen Elizabeth I but fell from favour and there were bitter disagreements over appointments and strategy. In 1601, he tried to rouse Londoners in rebellion but unsuccessfully. He was found guilty of treason and beheaded in the Tower of London on this day in 1601.

'Wallenstein murdered.' Albrecht von Wallenstein, generalissimo to Holy Roman Emperor Ferdinand II during the Thirty Years' War, was a great military leader of his time. But the Emperor became convinced that Wallenstein was a traitor and relieved him of his office. He was murdered soon afterwards on this day in 1634.

'New invention.' The electric motor was patented today 1837 by Thomas Davenport of Rutland, Vermont, USA.

'Clay gets knockout in 7th round.' On this day in 1964, Cassius Clay, later to become Muhammad Ali, won his first world heavyweight championship, by defeating Sonny Liston.

Obituary for 25 February. . . .
Frederick I, first king of Prussia, died in 1713.
Sir Christopher Wren, architect, died in 1723.
Sir John Tenniel, illustrator (*Alice* books), died 1914.

And some destined to make news. . . .
Pierre Auguste Renoir, French artist, born this day in 1841.
Enrico Caruso, Italian operatic tenor, was born in 1873.
Dame Myra Hess, British pianist, was born in 1890.

26 February

Every day, and in every way, I am becoming better and better.

These are the well-known words of Émile Coué, who was born on 26 February 1857. He was a French pharmacist who opened a clinic at Nancy in which he practised psychotherapy. He maintained that, if people repeated these words and believed what they were saying, they would, in fact, become better. Coué claimed that a number of his patients had been healed by auto-suggestion.

There is a stage at which it is difficult for anything to become better. We hear people say that something is 'as safe as the Bank of England' by which they mean that it is thoroughly reliable. At the end of the 18th Century, the Bank of England had its problems in meeting the demand for gold. So, on 26 February 1797, it issued the first £1 notes. Some people did not like this idea: they wanted real money! If you look at a £1 note you will see a piece of paper, some coloured ink and a thin metal strip, all of which are worth very little. But you will also see a written promise: 'Bank of England, I promise to pay the bearer on demand the sum of one pound.' It is this promise that makes the note worth its value in coins; and it is this promise that has been found fully reliable since 1797.

William Frederick Cody, 'Buffalo Bill' to most people, was born on 26 February 1846. His life was packed with adventure. He was a Pony Express rider, professional buffalo hunter, horse wrangler, Indian fighter, plainsman, scout and marksman, a man of courage and endurance. His exploits were widely reported which led to his becoming a showman and touring with his famous 'Wild West Show'.

This was also the birthday, in 1802, of the French novelist Victor Hugo, remembered for his *Hunchback of Notre Dame* and other books as well as for his fine poetry.

A sad event this day in 1852 was the wrecking, off South Africa, of the troopship *Birkenhead*, with great loss of life but exemplary discipline, courage, bravery and self-sacrifice.

On 27 February 1939, an oil lamp fell over in Borley Rectory, Essex, setting fire to the house. Soon it was a blazing inferno and completely destroyed. Several people who watched the blaze said they saw a nun at an upstairs window and that two strange figures left the house.

Who were they? Nobody can tell and it will probably remain a mystery, for Borley Rectory had the reputation for being the most haunted house in England, in which all sorts of strange things had happened.

The story is believed to have begun in the 17th Century, when a nun left her convent to be married but was murdered instead by the man she was to marry. She was probably buried on the site where the rectory was built in 1843.

From the outset the hauntings began. A ghostly coach was seen to drive right through the house and the ghost of a nun often appeared. There were whispering voices, ringing bells and footsteps at night. The hauntings became worse during the time the house was occupied by the Reverend and Mrs. Foyster, between 1930 and 1935. Vases were broken; objects were thrown across rooms; strange messages appeared on the walls; and, in 1935, the Foysters moved out. In 1937, a group of forty people went to stay in the house to see for themselves whether it really was haunted. They soon discovered that it was. Several were hit by flying objects; others heard strange noises.

Was it the ghost of the nun who was so often seen? When the rectory was burned down, people thought that the story had come to an end. But, though the bones of a young woman found on the site were buried in the local churchyard, there are still tales told of some of the rubble moving of its own accord . . . and of a nun wandering nearby.

Six years earlier to the day, on 27 February 1933, there was another fire which gutted a building, but the building was an important one — the German Reichstag or lower house of parliament. A Dutchman, Marinus van der Lubbe, was found guilty of starting the fire. But was there much more to it than that? It was only a month previously that Hitler had become Chancellor. The fire gave him an excuse to set up a one-party state, to eliminate Communists and purge all rivals. Very convenient!

Still on the subject of fire, we dip into John Evelyn's diary for an interesting snippet of information. Evelyn was an English writer who lived in the 17th Century. Born in Surrey on 31 October 1620, he died there on this day, 27 February 1706. He published many books but by far the most important are his memoirs, diary and letters. In his *Diary* he records many facets of the times in which he lived. This is his description of a professional fire-eater.

'He devoured brimstone on glowing coals before us, chewing and swallowing them; he melted a beer-glass and eat it quite up; then taking a live coal on his tongue, he put on it a raw oyster; the coal was blown with bellows till it flamed and sparkled in his mouth, and so remained till the oyster gaped and was quite boiled. Then he melted pitch and wax with sulphur, which he drank down, as it flamed; I saw't flaming in his mouth a good while; with divers other prodigious feats.'

An entertainer of a different kind was born on 27 February 1848. She was Dame Ellen Terry, who was a sensational actress, excelling in Shakespearian roles such as Portia and Ophelia. As such, for many years, she worked alongside Sir Henry Irving. She has been described as 'one of the most remarkable figures in the history of the stage'. Born on the same day as Ellen Terry was the English composer, Sir Charles Hubert Parry. His tune *Jerusalem* for Blake's poem is very well-known.

Also born on this day in 1807 was the American poet, Henry Wadsworth Longfellow. He wrote many narrative and shorter poems, including *Hiawatha* and *The Wreck of the Hesperus*. Here is one of his verses that may be appropriate for today.

> *Out of the bosom of the Air,*
> *Out of the cloud-folds of her garments shaken,*
> *Over the woodlands brown and bare,*
> *Over the harvest fields forsaken,*
> *Silent, and soft, and slow*
> *Decends the snow.*

28 February

It is not what you have that matters. It is what you do with what you have.

These words of Sir Wilfred Grenfell were certainly true of the man who used all his abilities to the full in his work amongst the Eskimos of Labrador, where he will always be remembered with affection for his work as Christian missionary, founder of a children's home and a hospital. This was his birthday in 1865.

So to some others who used what they had to give pleasure to many. . . .

Vaslav Nijinsky was born in Kiev on 28 February 1890. He is generally regarded as the greatest ever male ballet dancer, whose leaps have become legendary.

Sir John Tenniel was born in London on this day in 1820. He made a name for himself as a cartoonist and caricaturist but is especially remembered for his illustrations for *Alice's Adventures in Wonderland* and *Through the Looking Glass.*

Arnold Dolmetsch, the French reviver of interest in old musical instruments (p. 221), died on 28 February 1940.

When Columbus first sailed to America in 1492, he had with him two brothers, Martin and Vicente Pinzon. Martin was part owner of the *Pinta* and *Nina*: Vicente commanded the *Nina*. Vicente became an important explorer in his own right and later crossed further south where, on 28 February 1500, he discovered the Amazon.

On 28 February 1888, John Boyd Dunlop put new wheels on his son Johnnie's tricycle and the boy went out to test them. That was the first vehicle to be fitted with his new invention — the pneumatic tyre.

There was great rejoicing in Britain on 28 February 1900, when news was received of the relief of Ladysmith, in Natal, which had been beseiged by the Boers for four months.

On this day in 1975 there was disaster on the underground at Moorgate, London. A train crashed, killing 41 people.

Give me a laundry list and I'll set it to music.

Perhaps that was not too wild a claim, for Rossini was a versatile composer, able to write just the right words to set to his catchy, lively melodies. Born on 29 February 1792, Gioacchino Antonio Rossini, was trained at Bologna, then embarked upon a career as a leading Italian composer of opera, both comic and tragic, including a masterpiece *The Barber of Seville* but many others too — as many as three or four in a year.

In 1824, Rossini moved to Paris, where he wrote, amongst other works, *William Tell* with its well-known overture. Within five years, he had given up opera writing and wrote various kinds of religious, vocal and instrumental music. By this time he was not always in good health but a famous host to Parisian society, who enjoyed his company for his intelligence and his humour.

Louis Joseph de Montcalm-Gozon was born near Nimes on 29 February 1712. He joined the French army at the age of 12 and was a captain at 17. He acquitted himself well and, by 1756, as Marquis de Montcalm, commanded the French troops in America. Those were the days of battle between English and French settlers in North America. It seemed that a decisive battle could be fought at Quebec and there Montcalm massed his troops. In the battle there, on 13 September 1759, the English won but their General, Wolfe, was slain and, on the following day, Montcalm died from injuries received.

The St. Gotthard railway tunnel through the Alps was completed on this day in 1880.

One of the greatest churchmen of Anglo-Saxon England was Oswald, Bishop of Worcester and later Archbishop of York. St. Oswald, who established several religious houses, died on 29 February 992.

There are various customs and traditions associated with this day, which exists only in leap years. People have been advised to lose no time in starting something important since it is assured of success. It is also the day when women, in the days before 'women's lib', were allowed to propose to the young men of their fancy who were too shy or reluctant to do so themselves.

Other February Events and Commemorations

(See also pp. 194–6)

2nd Woodbridge, Suffolk: Carlow Bread Distribution under a bequest of a local tanner, George Carlow. About 20 loaves are distributed at his tomb in the grounds of the Bull Hotel.

Monday of Candlemas Week St. Ives, Cornwall: Hurling the Silver Ball. The ball is thrown by the Mayor at 10.30 am and is passed from one person to another. Whoever is holding the ball at noon receives a prize from the Mayor in return for the ball.

After Candlemas Jedburgh, Borders: Fastern E'en Ba'. Unusual football game between Uppies and Downies. The ball is said to represent an Englishman's head and the game may have originated long ago in the days of border warfare, when the victorious Scots, after a battle, cut off the heads of the English and kicked them around.

Shrove Tuesday Some events other than those on p. 196:
Sedgefield, Durham: Football. The goals are a stream and a pond. The first goal ends the game.

Alnwick, Northumberland: Football. The ball is piped on to the field to be played by teams which may consist of over 150 players. After three goals the game ends.

Corfe, Dorset: Court of the Purbeck Marblers. Election of officers and initiation of apprentices. Then a football is kicked along an old road to preserve the ancient right of way to Ower Quay.

Gittisham, Devon: Tip-toeing by children asking for money.

20th London: Memorial service in St. Botolph's Church, Aldgate for Sir John Cass, who died in 1718. He died of a haemorrhage and the students of Sir John Cass School wear red quills as a token of remembrance.

SOME FEBRUARY FAIRS

2nd Dorchester, Dorset: Candlemas Fair.

About 9th Stamford, Lincolnshire. Horse, cattle and sheep fair.

14th Wymondham, Norfolk: Charter fair held in Kings Head Meadow since the reign of Henry I.

14th and next two days Kings Lynn, Norfolk: Charter granted for fair by Henry VIII but it began before that. Opened by the Mayor.

Index of related themes

Entries are listed under main headings. For other themes, check in the General Index where an indication will be found of the main heading in this index (e.g. Balloons is a sub-heading of AIR TRAVEL).

232

Wheatstone, Sir Charles (P), 63
Wien, Wilhelm (P), 172
see also ASTRONOMERS
MATHEMATICIANS

SEAFARERS

Admirals
 Collingwood, Lord, 31
 Hawke, Sir Edward, 102
 Hood, Samuel, Viscount, 132
 Howard of Effingham, Lord, 134
 Jellicoe, John, Earl, 102
 Jervis, Sir John, 211
 Nelson, Horatio, Lord, 35, 65,
 Peary, Robert (US), 217
 Rodney, George, 216
 St. Vincent, Earl, 168
 Shovell, Sir Cloudesley, 66
 Spee, Graf von (German), 128
 Vernon, Edward, 94
 Villeneuve, de (French), 65
Circumnavigators
 Chichester, Sir Francis, 22
 Del Cano, Juan, 12
 Drake, Sir Francis, 31, 187
Navigators and navigation
 Henry the Navigator, 95
Various seafarers
 Bligh, Capt. William, 15
 Conrad, Joseph, 123
 Cook, Capt. James, 70, 211
 Frobisher, Sir Martin, 105
 Gama, Vasco da, 105, 144, 145
 Gilbert, Sir Humphrey, 15
 Grenville, Sir Richard, 15
 Lawrence, James, 45
 Magellan, Ferdinand, 12
 Raleigh, Sir Walter, 72
 Royal Navy, 155
 Schouten, Willem, 183
 Spanish Armada, 94, 105
 Tasman, Abel, 133
 Wallis, Capt. Samuel, 95
See also EXPLORERS, TRANSPORT — Ships

SETTLERS AND FRONTIERSMEN

Boone, Daniel, 83
Carson, Kit, 144
Penn, William, 58
Pilgrim Fathers, 12, 141

SLAVERY

Abolition in USA, 138
Abolitionists, 60, 122, 130, 137

Hawkins, Sir John, 94
Lincoln, Abraham, 208
Slave Trade ended (Britain), 18

SOLDIERS

Alexander, Field-Marshal, 130
Alvarez, Ferdinand, 132
Baden-Powell, Lord, 10, 167, 219
Bernadotte, Folke, 22
Blucher, Gebhard von, 17, 186
Burnside, General, 18
Chandos, Sir John, 24
Chiang Kai-shek, 75
Clive, Robert, 35
Cornwallis, Marquis, 49, 151
Eisenhower, Dwight D., 58
Essex, Earl of, 222
Foch, Marshal, 46
Gaulle, Charles de, 90, 105, 141
Gordon, General, 186, 187
Haig, Earl, 187
Hillary, Sir William, 162
Hindenburg, Paul von, 46
Jackson, 'Stonewall', 180
Kitchener, Lord, 8
Lafayette, Marquis de, 12
Lee, Robert E., 56, 177
Monk, George, 126
Montcalm, Louis, 18, 227
Montgomery, Sir Bernard, 67, 99
Ney, Marshal, 127
Pershing, John J., 18
Pike, Zebulun, 162
Pride, Thomas, 126
Radetzky, Joseph, 205
Roberts, Earl, 36
Rommel, Erwin, 97
Rupert, Prince, 112
Sherman, W. T., 205
Sidney, Sir Philip, 27, 61, 113
Smuts, Jan Christiaan, 16
Standish, Myles, 47
Wallenstein, Albrecht von, 232
Washington, George, 134
Wellington, Duke of, 19
Wolfe, James, 18, 158, 227

SPACE

Astronauts
 Glenn, John, 217
Spacecraft
 Explorer, 189
 First soft moon landing, 201
 Friendship 7, 217
 Lunik I, 158

244

245

ZOOLOGY

General Index

Entries marked with an asterisk * in this index are indexed more fully in the Index of Related Themes (pp. 229–46) under the heading that is indicated beside the asterisk if different.

McPherson, Aimee Semple, 32, 53
Magellan, Ferdinand, 12, 25
Magic *MYSTERY
Magic Flute, 36
Maginot, André, 166
Mahdi, The, 8
Maimonides, Moses, 133
Makarios, Archbishop, 134
Malcolm III ('Canmore') of Scotland, 95, 99
Malta, 11, 26
Malthus, Thomas Robert, 143, 211
Manchester Ship Canal, 157
Manchester United F.C., 203
Manet, Édouard, 182
Man in the Iron Mask, 101
Mao Tse-tung, 15, 146
Marathon, Battle of *WARFARE
Marathon race, 35 *SPORTS
Marconi, Guglielmo, 132
Mardi Gras, 194
Margaret, child Queen of Scotland, 31
Margaret, St., Queen of Scotland, 99
Marie Antoinette, 60, 83
Marie de Medici, 49
Mariette, Auguste, 177, 207
Mari Lwyd mummers, 151
Mariner space probes *SPACE
Mars, 95
Martin of Tours, St., 92
Martinmas, 79, 91, 92, 114
Martyrs of Equador, 167
Mary I, Queen, 60, 99, 214
Mary II, Queen, 87
Mary Celeste, 87, 108
Mary, Queen of Scots, 205
Mary Rose, 55
Mascagni, Pietro, 127
Maskelyne, John Nevil, 142
Mass, 144, 145
Mata Hari, 59
Mathematicians *
Matisse, Henri, 84
Matthews, Sir Stanley, 197
Maugham, W. Somerset, 185
Maxim, Hiram, 202
Mayflower, 12
Mayors, — election of, 34
Mead, Richard, 212
Medical scientists *MEDICINE AND SURGERY
Medici, Lorenzo de ('the Magnificent'), 157
Meikle, Andrew, 110
Melba, Dame Nellie, 220
Mendelssohn-Bartholdy, Felix, 85, 201

Mercator, Gerhardus, 122
Merrie England, 93
Mersey Tunnel, 136 *ENGINEERING
Methodists *CHRISTIAN CHURCH
Metropolitan Opera House, 66
Metropolitan Railway, 169
Mexico, 122
Michael, St., 34, 35
Michaelmas, 5–6, 34–5, 42
Michaelmas fairs *FAIRS
Michelangelo Buonarotti, 215
Mickey Mouse, 100, 125
Midwinter 117 *FESTIVALS
Mill, Henry, 166
Miller, Arthur, 61
Milne, A. A., 176, 189
Milton, John, 90, 129
Mindszenty, Cardinal, 147
Mischief night, 85
Mississippi, 149
Mistletoe, 117, 119
Mitchell, Margaret, 90
Model Parliament *PARLIAMENT
Modjeska, Helena, 56
Molière, 213
Mollison, Amy, 162
Mompesson, Rev. William, 13
Monaco, 19
Monet, Claude, 96
Mongols, 131
Monk, George, 126
Mont-Saint-Michel, 16
Montcalm, General, 18, 227
Montfort, Simon de, 45, 98, 131, 178
Montfort Parliament *178
Montgolfier balloon, 103
Montgomery, Field Marshal, 67, 99
Moody, Dwight L., 202
Moon, 51, 201
Moon, Dr. William, 54, 138
Moorgate Underground disaster, 226
Moors, 73
Mop fairs *FAIRS
More, St. Thomas, 204
Morris, William, 47
Moscow, 19
Moses, 'Grandma', 13
Moss, Stirling, 22
Motor cycling *SPORTS AND PASTIMES
Motorway, 83
Mount Palomar Observatory, 186
Mount Semirodriki Observatory, 204
Mousetrap, The, 108
Mozart, Wolfgang Amadeus, 36, 125,' 186
Muhammad Ali, 175, 222